Microsoft Dynamics AX Implementation Guide

Your all-in-one guide to exploring and implementing Microsoft Dynamics AX

Yogesh Kasat

JJ Yadav

BIRMINGHAM - MUMBAI

Microsoft Dynamics AX Implementation Guide

First published: September 2015

Production reference: 1140915

Published by Packt Publishing Ltd.
Livery Place
35 Livery Street
Birmingham B3 2PB, UK.

ISBN 978-1-78528-896-8

www.packtpub.com

Credits

Authors
Yogesh Kasat
JJ Yadav

Reviewers
Palle Agermark
Fatih Demirci
Stephanie Kroese
Ravi Shankar Kumar

Commissioning Editor
Priya Singh

Acquisition Editors
Kevin Colaco
Neha Nagwekar

Content Development Editor
Anand Singh

Technical Editor
Parag Topre

Copy Editors
Sarang Chari
Sonia Mathur

Project Coordinator
Vijay Kushlani

Proofreader
Safis Editing

Indexer
Mariammal Chettiyar

Graphics
Sheetal Aute
Disha Haria
Abhinash Sahu

Production Coordinator
Nilesh R. Mohite

Cover Work
Nilesh R. Mohite

About the Author

Yogesh Kasat is a cofounder of Real Dynamics, which is one of the first Microsoft Dynamics AX IV&Vs (Independent Verification and Validation services provider). The goal of Real Dynamics is to help businesses and their internal IT teams to take their Dynamics AX implementation to the next level with independent and unbiased recommendations.

Yogesh has led a number of large Dynamics AX implementations and turned them into success stories. He has a unique blend of knowledge of financial and supply chain modules, technical architecture, and business process optimization, and he has held project management, leadership, and solution architect roles. Yogesh is one of the founding partners of Real Dynamics—an organization focused on providing independent guidance and oversight of Dynamics AX implementations, post-implementation reviews, and help to customers in defining a roadmap for the Dynamics AX platform. He held a leadership role for one of the leading Dynamics AX partners as the vice president of Dynamics AX delivery and oversaw Dynamics AX implementations throughout North America. He was awarded the prestigious Leadership Award twice during his tenure with the company. He has six Dynamics AX certifications, including financials, trade and logistics, and managing Dynamics AX implementation (Sure Step). In addition to more than a decade's experience of working on Dynamics AX, Yogesh has earlier experience with other business applications, including Dynamics NAV/GP and PeopleSoft. He has traveled extensively for global projects and has had the pleasure of visiting different parts of the world.

Acknowledgments

I would like to thank my mom for always being there and giving me lessons in honesty and being truthful that have helped me at every stage of my career.

I would also like to thank my wife, Ashwini, who has supported me at every step in life, bringing all the charm to my life. She has had the patience to allow me to take some personal time away to work on this book, pursue challenging projects, and travel like crazy, which have resulted in the many experiences mentioned in the book. Big thanks also go to the rest of my family, friends, coworkers, and peers in the industry for their input and inspiration.

My sincere thanks go to my coauthor and longtime coworker, JJ Yadav, and the reviewer, Stephanie Kroese, for their efforts and ideas in the making of this book. Special thanks to all the reviewers and Packt Publishing for providing valuable feedback and comments during the making of this book.

Finally, thanks to my bosses, clients, and the people who provided guidance in creating many success stories and helped me reach where I am in my career—Sandeep Walia, Pankaj Kumar, Anwar Jiwani, George Van Rijn, Sri Srinivasan, Kevin Scott, Henrik Bergholt, Paul Delahunty, Scott Ball, Petras Petroskevicius, Vivek Garud, Rohit Kulkarni, Anil Daga, and Dwarkanath Kasat.

About the Author

JJ Yadav has worked on Microsoft Dynamics AX for more than a decade as a solutions architect, project manager, technical lead, and developer. He started working on Axapta 3.0 as a developer with Euro Info Systems in India (now Tectura India). He has experience in leading and managing several Dynamics AX Global implementations and upgrade projects. His core technical expertise in Dynamics AX includes infrastructure planning, integration services, data migration, and workflow. He has extensive functional experience in financials, procurement, accounts payable, accounts receivable, inventory and warehouse management, and the service modules of Dynamics AX. Currently, he works as a senior technical project manager with Ignify in the central region of the U.S. on a leading Global AX 2012 R3 implementation project.

I would like to thank my family, friends, and coworkers for their support and inspiration. My sincere thanks to my uncle, Radhe Shyam, for his support during the most difficult time of my life; without his support and inspiration, I would not be where I am today. Finally, my beautiful wife, Khushboo, for supporting and encouraging me at every walk of life and all the patience and support during the hours and weekends that I spent writing this book.

My sincere gratitude to my longtime coworker and coauthor, Yogesh Kasat, for coming up with the idea of writing this book and making me a part of it. I would like to thank my reviewer, Stephanie Kroese, all the other reviewers, and Packt Publishing for providing valuable feedback and comments during the creation of this book.

About the Reviewers

Palle Agermark has worked as a developer and technical consultant with Concorde XAL and Microsoft Dynamics AX for more than 20 years. He worked at Microsoft Development Center Copenhagen for a number of years, primarily developing on the financial, accounts payable, accounts receivable, and unit test modules.

Currently, Palle works for one of Scandinavia's largest Microsoft Dynamics AX partners, EG, in Denmark.

He has been named a Microsoft Dynamics AX MVP for 2 consecutive years and blogs about AX at http://www.agermark.com.

Fatih Demirci (MCT) is a technical consultant, project manager, and Microsoft Certified Trainer. He graduated in computer engineering. He has been working professionally on Dynamics AX since 2006. During this period, he has worked for a lot of Microsoft partners, customers, and projects. He has over 10 years of consulting experience, playing a variety of roles, including senior software engineer, team leader, trainer, technical consultant, and project manager at Dynamics AX. He is a cofounder of DMR Consultancy, which is the most promising ERP consultancy company in Turkey, and he works with some of the most experienced and creative Dynamics AX professionals. Recently, he also reviewed another wonderful book, *Dynamics AX 2012 R3 Development Cookbook*, *Packt Publishing*.

He runs a professional and technical blog at www.fatihdemirci.net and shares his thoughts and readings on Twitter and LinkedIn.

> I would like to thank my family and friends for motivating me and always pushing me to do my best.

Stephanie Kroese is a solution architect and project manager with over 15 years of successful experience in managing IT organizations and leading projects, in which she delivered significant business value. She has a broad experience in the implementation, application, and delivery of ERP, strategic planning, and project management. For 12 years, Stephanie was the senior IT leader for a global battery manufacturer and was responsible for driving the strategic direction of the organization toward supporting business growth. In addition, she has spent over 7 years implementing various ERP systems—the last 4 of which focused on Dynamics AX—in certain global organizations as a senior consultant in project management, functional analysis, report writing, training, and technical roles.

Ravi Shankar Kumar is a passionate professional, who is able to contribute a unique blend of project management, delivery, sales, and exemplary problem-solving skills, along with a commitment to excel in any job. He has an eye for detail in ensuring that a project's mission and objectives are met within scope, budget, and schedule. Ravi has exceptional organizational skills to coordinate with and manage multiple stakeholders, along with the ability to work autonomously and prioritize his workload to deal with conflicting demands. An adept understanding of business processes and an organization's culture, combined with an aptitude for lateral thinking, enables efficient management of project risks and deliverables.

Ravi has been working in the IT industry since 2001, and his passion at work has been to assist companies to increase their usage of IT/ERP systems to improve productivity, manage change, and conduct better business for their customers, employees, and owners. He is a highly motivated and energetic person with a strong commercial and systems background, including extensive experience in analyzing business requirements and translating these into systems solutions. He is also particularly strong in the project management discipline and has a very good record of driving projects to their successful conclusion through the use of his interpersonal and organizational skills, including negotiations at the executive management level. Ravi has a consulting, functional, project management, and sales background and is flexible enough to be able to maintain a sense of humor under pressure. He is poised and competent with a demonstrable ability to easily handle cultural differences. In addition to this, he is also passionate about providing the best solutions in order to achieve business needs. Ravi is always keen to take up challenging assignments and deliver solutions to the customer's satisfaction.

Lastly, during several DAX 2012 and 2009 projects, he practiced communication on multiple levels, for example, from the CEO to a shop's ground staff. Ravi currently works with one of the top Big Four firms in India.

I would like to thank my fellow authors and Packt Publishing for giving me this opportunity. I look forward to many more publications! I would also like to take this opportunity to thank my mother, Shanti Sinha, and my beloved wife, Bharti Kumari, for their continued support during the long hours of reviewing this book.

www.PacktPub.com

Support files, eBooks, discount offers, and more

For support files and downloads related to your book, please visit www.PacktPub.com.

Did you know that Packt offers eBook versions of every book published, with PDF and ePub files available? You can upgrade to the eBook version at www.PacktPub.com and as a print book customer, you are entitled to a discount on the eBook copy. Get in touch with us at service@packtpub.com for more details.

At www.PacktPub.com, you can also read a collection of free technical articles, sign up for a range of free newsletters and receive exclusive discounts and offers on Packt books and eBooks.

https://www2.packtpub.com/books/subscription/packtlib

Do you need instant solutions to your IT questions? PacktLib is Packt's online digital book library. Here, you can search, access, and read Packt's entire library of books.

Why subscribe?

- Fully searchable across every book published by Packt
- Copy and paste, print, and bookmark content
- On demand and accessible via a web browser

Free access for Packt account holders

If you have an account with Packt at www.PacktPub.com, you can use this to access PacktLib today and view 9 entirely free books. Simply use your login credentials for immediate access.

Instant updates on new Packt books

Get notified! Find out when new books are published by following @PacktEnterprise on Twitter or the *Packt Enterprise* Facebook page.

For my son Neel, who brings me feeling of winning the world with his cute smile.

– Yogesh Kasat

For my precious children, Hrehaan and Mira.

– JJ Yadav

Table of Contents

Preface

The Microsoft Dynamics AX product has evolved into a formidable ERP platform that is suitable for large-scale and enterprise customers. Although it comes with richer functionality and better scalability, it also has additional complexity. This has translated into more challenging implementation cycles as many projects are now multicompany and multinational affairs. The keys for a successful Dynamics AX implementation in this type of complex environment revolve around strong project management and a clear understanding of what needs to be done in each phase of the project. Recent releases of the AX platform put many new tools in your toolbox; you need to understand the tools and select the corresponding techniques to ensure that your Dynamics AX implementation project is effective and successful.

Microsoft Dynamics AX Implementation Guide draws on real-life experiences from large Dynamics AX implementation projects. This book will guide you through the entire lifecycle of a Dynamics AX implementation, helping you avoid common pitfalls while increasing your efficiency and effectiveness at every stage of the project. This book focuses on providing you with straightforward techniques with step-by-step instructions on how to follow them; this, along with real-life examples from the field, will further increase your ability to execute the projects well. Upon reading this book, you'll be in the position to implement Dynamics AX right the first time.

ERP implementations are complex by nature because of their many moving parts, and leaders are expected to know of all the aspects. This book provides a summary of the various facets of running a successful Dynamics AX project without having to go through expensive and time-consuming training courses. The aspects covered include management, infrastructure planning, requirement gathering, data migration, functional and technical design with examples, go-live planning, and upgrade.

What this book covers

Chapter 1, Preparing for a Great Start, focuses on instituting effective project management, project governance, and resource alignment from the beginning of the project.

Chapter 2, Getting into the Details Early, focuses on the planning and execution of requirement gathering and Conference Room Pilot (CRP) sessions.

Chapter 3, Infrastructure Planning and Design, covers infrastructure planning, the architecture of production, non-production, and disaster recovery environments.

Chapter 4, Integration Planning and Design, covers integration planning, integration tools and frameworks available in Dynamics AX.

Chapter 5, Data Migration – Scoping through Delivery, discusses data migration requirements, managing data migration scope, and identifying tools and techniques for data migration and validation.

Chapter 6, Reporting and BI, covers common reporting and BI design principles and best practices.

Chapter 7, Functional and Technical Design, discusses planning and executing a functional design and a technical design. It covers tips and tricks with real-life examples of design patterns—both good and bad—to support the best practices recommended.

Chapter 8, Configuration Management, introduces you to tools and techniques used in managing configurations and moving them from one environment to another and managing configurations on larger projects to minimize conflicts and rework.

Chapter 9, Building Customizations, provides you with the best practices for customization and patterns that are recommended by Microsoft.

Chapter 10, Performance Tuning, helps you to understand architecture components that impact performance, performance and stress testing to catch issues ahead of time, and performance troubleshooting for post-production scenarios.

Chapter 11, Testing and Training, effectively manages and executes system testing and user acceptance testing. Its goal is to find issues and encourage business teams to stay engaged in spite of finding issues.

Chapter 12, Go-live Planning, defines an hour-by-hour go-live plan and reviews it with stakeholders.

Chapter 13, Post Go-live, shows you how to survive on a new system and use it to deliver value to the business.

Chapter 14, Upgrade, shows how to prepare for upgrades, upgrade planning, and preparing the business case for an upgrade. It even discusses the execution of upgrade projects and post-upgrade opportunities.

What you need for this book

You need to have the following knowledge to get the most out of this book:

1. A basic understanding of the ERP implementation process.
2. An understanding of IT project management and Software Development Life Cycle (SDLC).
3. Access to Microsoft Dynamics PartnerSource / CustomerSource and the Lifecycle Services (LCS) portal.
4. Knowledge of Microsoft Dynamics AX and the Microsoft Dynamics Sure Step methodology would be a plus point.

Who this book is for

This book is written from the perspective of a project manager, encompassing all the areas to create a successful Dynamics AX implementation. Solution architects, functional and technical consultants, business Subject Matter Experts (SMEs), super users, IT managers, and technology leaders who are in the process of planning or undergoing a Microsoft Dynamics AX implementation will also benefit from the insights provided in this book. The book will help you during every phase of the implementation with what to expect, the common pitfalls to avoid, and tips and tricks learned from our experiences. Most of these techniques are useful irrespective of the Microsoft Dynamics AX version. The Dynamics AX product has evolved since Microsoft acquired it, and while rich features and scalability have been added, there is also added complexity. We have tried to provide insights into relevant information for each phase of the project in a single resource to help manage this complexity. This book will be especially helpful to small/medium business customers that do not have the luxury to engage multiple resources with individual skillsets.

Every business has its unique business model and organizational culture, and that brings unique challenges for the ERP implementation. While going through this book, you will encounter many recommendations, guidelines, and experiences; however, you may need to fine-tune the recommendations as per your specific need based on the particular project size, timeline, business organization structure, and industry.

Conventions

ERP implementations are complex by nature due to so many moving parts, and leaders are expected to know all the aspects. This book provides a summary of numerous aspects that you need to know (without going through expensive learnings) to make your Dynamics AX implementation(s) successful. We will be jumping into management, functional/business, technical—code examples, infrastructure aspects and that is by design.

In this book, you will find a number of text styles that distinguish between different kinds of information. Here are some examples of these styles and an explanation of their meaning.

Code words in text, database table names, folder names, filenames, file extensions, pathnames, dummy URLs, user input, and Twitter handles are shown as follows: "For example, a new class created by the vendor ABC for the sales order import process should be named as `AbcSalesOrderImport`."

A block of code is set as follows:

```
while select * from custTmpLedger
{
    Info(custTmpLedger.Name);
}
}
```

New terms and **important words** are shown in bold. Words that you see on the screen, for example, in menus or dialog boxes, appear in the text like this: "The following screenshot displays **Customer transactions** grouped by customers."

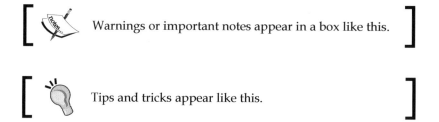

Warnings or important notes appear in a box like this.

Tips and tricks appear like this.

Reader feedback

Feedback from our readers is always welcome. Let us know what you think about this book—what you liked or may have disliked. Reader feedback is important for us to develop titles that you really get the most out of.

To send us general feedback, simply send an e-mail to feedback@packtpub.com, and mention the book title via the subject of your message.

If there is a topic that you have expertise in and you are interested in either writing or contributing to a book, see our author guide on www.packtpub.com/authors.

It is our honor and pleasure to present experiences throughout this book. We hope that peers in the Dynamics AX community and customers will benefit from this book. I would love to hear your implementation stories and any feedback for improvements. Please write to me on yogesh.kasat@realdynamics.com or connect with me on LinkedIn at https://www.linkedin.com/in/yogeshkasat. Visit us at www.RealDynamics.com.

Customer support

Now that you are the proud owner of a Packt book, we have a number of things to help you to get the most from your purchase.

Errata

Although we have taken every care to ensure the accuracy of our content, mistakes do happen. If you find a mistake in one of our books—maybe a mistake in the text or the code—we would be grateful if you could report this to us. By doing so, you can save other readers from frustration and help us improve subsequent versions of this book. If you find any errata, please report them by visiting http://www.packtpub.com/submit-errata, selecting your book, clicking on the **Errata Submission Form** link, and entering the details of your errata. Once your errata are verified, your submission will be accepted and the errata will be uploaded to our website or added to any list of existing errata under the Errata section of that title.

To view the previously submitted errata, go to https://www.packtpub.com/books/content/support and enter the name of the book in the search field. The required information will appear under the **Errata** section.

Piracy

Piracy of copyrighted material on the Internet is an ongoing problem across all media. At Packt, we take the protection of our copyright and licenses very seriously. If you come across any illegal copies of our works in any form on the Internet, please provide us with the location address or website name immediately so that we can pursue a remedy.

Please contact us at copyright@packtpub.com with a link to the suspected pirated material.

We appreciate your help in protecting our authors and our ability to bring you valuable content.

Questions

If you have a problem with any aspect of this book, you can contact us at questions@packtpub.com, and we will do our best to address the problem.

1
Preparing for a Great Start

Getting your project started requires a well-defined project methodology and a strong project manager. This chapter goes over some essential elements for getting your project set up for success.

In this chapter, we will cover the following topics:

- Project kickoff
- Project management and governance
- Agile methodology

Microsoft provides Sure Step and Lifecycle Services as the methodology for implementing their enterprise-level software. While we will reference a few Sure Step and LCS tools, principles, and documents, this is not a book on *How to Use Sure Step or LCS*.

Project kickoff

Prepare for a great start! Projects don't fail at the end; they fail when they start. Under this topic, we will learn how to prepare for the start of a project, which includes resource planning, understanding expectations and the commitments made, and engaging the stakeholders.

Managing customer expectations and commitments

To be successful, you need to understand the commitments made on your behalf by the sales team, and have access to the scope that the customer has signed off on. Additionally, at a high level, the project managers need to communicate these expectations to the entire team, consultants, and the customer team members alike. The following are some points to keep in mind for managing these expectations effectively:

- Schedule meetings with the sales and presales teams for knowledge transfer to the rest of the resources assigned to the project; ideally, the project managers should meet the main decision makers while the deal is being finalized.

- Document all the knowledge transfer items; you will need them for future reference and to bring the rest of the team members on board.

- Get all the documents related to the requirements that the sales team may have received, and have them uploaded on SharePoint (I will be referring to SharePoint often; as for most projects, you would be using it for as a common repository of documents).

- Understand the solution blueprint that was put together by the presales team, including any custom or ISV solutions that were shown as part of the solution during presales.

- Understand all the documented scope and the undocumented expectations that were set with the client.

- Understand the statement of work in detail. Get a good idea of what is in and out of scope, and clarify any vague areas.

- Understand the key players involved, their roles, their influence in the company/project, and their personalities. Basically, find out who the stakeholders of the project are.

- At this stage, everything looks very easy.

Tips for customers

The customers engaging on a Dynamics AX implementation should be hands-on and not sit back, waiting for the consultants to swoop in and do all the work. The customers should keep in mind the following tips to be proactive in getting the project off to a good start:

- **Getting comfortable with your partner**: Spend a lot of time working with your counterpart(s) from the implementation partner; learn about their tools, processes, and methodology.

- **Evaluate your people**: Skilled resources play a key role in your success. Spend time early on to evaluate whether the team you have can make it. Waiting too long to pull the plug on the resources is only going to burn your budget and impact the schedule. At the very least, raise your voice and let your partner know that you are concerned. A customer's project lead, with whom I worked in the past, would ask me within a couple of days of having a new resource on board, "Yogesh, do you think XYZ will make it? It's your call. Otherwise, you are paying for his expenses too". That project was very successful as the customer was always watching out and was very demanding to get the right resources on the project. Customers pay a premium rate for each resource and deserve to have the right resources to make the project successful.

- **Resource continuity**: It is a long ride and you need to ensure that you have resource continuity for the key resources, from beginning through to the end. Of course, there are unavoidable situations due to which you would have resource changes on the project—that's where the documentation plays a role. However, it does not replace the need to have resource continuity. To keep the good resources engaged for a longer term, be flexible with the onsite/offsite time or look for more local resources. You don't want to burn those resources with crazy travelling and lose them eventually.

- **Consider engaging an IV&V (Independent Validation And Verification Vendor)**: ERP implementations are complex, and each mistake could be expensive if not caught early on. Whether it is solution design, not having the right resources or methodology, or pushing back to the business on business processes, you need to catch them soon. Having an independent validator engaged early on would help uncover such issues and reduce the risk on the project.

Customer environment and culture

Every customer is different. Their business model, industry, and organizational culture have a huge impact on the way you run the project. For example, some environments move quickly, and you need to keep up with their speed. On the other hand, if you are doing a project for a public sector organization, you will have to slow down and go with their speed/processes. Some have a more mature IT organization than others (mature in terms of their IT processes, IT team, infrastructure, and so on). You need to understand the environment and the processes, adapt, and adjust.

- Engage with your customer early on to finalize the project governance and implementation methodology. Present them with your implementation methodology and align it to their needs.

- Understand their methodology wherever applicable. The customer may already have multiple scrum teams with their boards in a backlog tool, like JIRA or the Team Foundation Server. You can't just walk in and announce that from the next day onwards, they will be following this huge MPP project plan. You will be shot even before you are allowed to grab a seat.

Resources

No project can be successful without having the right people on your team. You need to have an *A* team to deliver on the complex project and transform the business for your customer. This goes for both the consulting team members as well as the client team.

Consulting team resource alignment

The following are some key points to be kept in mind while forming your consulting team:

- Identify the key roles needed on the project. Map the key roles and the individuals, along with their availability. You need a strong solution architect—someone who can see the big picture, a business analyst for each critical area (for example, if it is a retail implementation, you need to have an experienced retail business analyst), a QA lead, and a tech lead at the minimum to survive on the project as a project manager.

- Prepare a resource plan for the consulting team, and share it with your management. This is crucial to getting the right people at the right time.

Customer resource alignment

This is the most important project for the company, and it is one of the most complex ones as well; you need to ensure that the team is up to the challenge.

- Provide clear guidelines to the customer on what is required of a good team member to be assigned to the project, and what the commitment will be:
    - The team members must be knowledgeable and respected in their area of responsibility of the project; they must also be empowered to make business decisions on behalf of their organization.
    - Recommend the customers to shift responsibilities or acquire part time help during the project to free up the best resources. Business decisions should not be made by someone other than the core project team. Doing so could lead to rework, as decisions are usually reversed down the line.
- Similar to business, you need to secure the A+ resources from IT to work on the project.
- Make sure that the team members understand that the project would be challenging, and demand a lot of their time before they commit. Work with the executives to come up with compensation benefits upon the successful rollout of the project.

External resources

In addition to the consulting team and the customer resources, there are potential external resources that need to be considered. For example, if a key requirement is to integrate to a third-party solution, identifying and engaging resources from the solution provider at the start of the project will help keep these integrations from becoming roadblocks down the road. Share the high-level project plan with these resources and include them in your communication plan as well.

Establishing the team

Once all the resources have been identified, the project manager must bring them together as a cohesive team. The following are some tips and guidelines to building and maintaining a good, working team:

- Define clear responsibilities among the team members and document them in an organization chart. For example, John - accounts receivable, Tom - general ledger, Craig - accounts payable and fixed assets, and so on. Align the customer's resources on the organization chart (internal business analysts, business SMEs, infrastructure, project management, leadership team, and so on). The following diagram shows a sample organization chart:

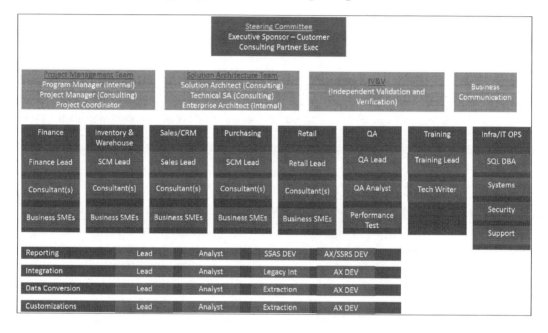

- Create a team environment and make sure that everyone is engaged. Work as a team and mandate no BMWs on the project (here, BMW stands for bitching, moaning, and whining).
- Start engaging with the team to understand the team assigned to the project and to identify the strong and the weak areas; you need to know who your problem children are so that you can pay more attention to them.

- Prepare a resource-onboarding checklist for the project. It should include getting access to the client VPN, environments, SharePoint, adding to the distribution lists, updating the organizational charts, the assignment of the development machines to the developers, any mandatory security trainings, and so on. Identify who to reach out to for initiating these steps. Smooth onboarding will help in making the resources effective as soon as they join the team.

- Every resource should have his/her own dedicated account (no sharing of accounts/passwords and no generic accounts like user1, user2, and so on).

- Watch out for the upcoming holiday schedules for the different locations where your project team members are based, and plan accordingly. Create a centralized calendar for holidays, and even vacations, for the project team. Update the key milestones and meetings on the project calendar.

- Align the internal IT resources/SMEs on the project organization chart prepared by the consulting PM. Ensure that you have good coverage for each area, and start working on filling the gaps through new hires, contractors, or by training the existing staff. This will help in smoother execution of the project, as your internal team will be involved with the decision making for the solutions. The team members will be able to help with the transition as they would already know the solution.

- Training the existing staff early on will kill two birds with one stone. Your customer knows the business already, and can add lot of value to the project team (it will also save the consulting dollars). Moreover, it will reduce their anxiety over job security post-implementation of the new system. It is worth the investment.

- Provide your project team access to customer source so that your team can go through the training material available there while the project planning is going on.

- Create a project in Lifecycle Services and grant access to the relevant project team.

- Build ground rules for your project in agreement with all the stakeholders. For example, if an e-mail conversation goes on for more than 10 threads, call for a meeting and close out.

The kickoff meeting

The project kickoff meeting is about setting goals and expectations. At the high level, clearly define and communicate the goals of the implementation and why the dollars are being spent. The following points outline the requirements for a successful kickoff meeting:

- Review goals with the key stakeholders and ensure that you have the goals defined in the order of priority.

- You may want to create a theme and remind everyone about the goals periodically such as in different milestone meetings. For example, protect the core - the goal is to sell, ship, and invoice the customer. (Everything else is negotiable).

- Communicating the goals clearly to the team will help keep everyone on track (and avoid any change requests that are not necessary). The kickoff meeting must convey the following to the entire team:
  - Project goals and scope
  - High-level solution overview
  - Project milestones
  - Project team structure and roles
  - Implementation methodology and steps to success
  - Project communication plan and risk management approach
  - Change control process

- Have the executives from both (partner and customer) sides engaged in the kickoff. Keep them engaged on the project as much as you can to help remove the roadblocks.

- Have all team members attend the kickoff meeting. With teams that are geographically diverse, you should utilize the web-conferencing technology or repeat the meeting for each team.

Project management and governance

A project manager needs to have a *fifty-thousand foot* view of all the moving parts on the project, and also be ready to get into the details where necessary. The project managers who can zoom in and zoom out are more successful than others. Those who are unable to do this fall into the following categories and their kind of behavior leads to project failure:

- Project managers who stay at too high a level and don't get into (or don't understand) details fail, because they don't have a sense of what is going on at the ground level of the project. These PMs can't assess the issues and fail to take corrective actions in time. Hence, the project fails.

- On other hand, there are project managers who come from a technical or consultant background, and often fall back into their comfort zone down in the details. PMs that don't look up out of the weeds will not only get in their team's way (affecting their morale), but will miss the unfolding bigger picture. In such a scenario, nobody has that *fifty-thousand foot* view, and the rest of the project team keeps running with no clear direction, leading to project failure.

In the following sections, we will cover the activities and deliverables that are important for project governance.

The project plan

Your project plan is a roadmap of the project outlining the things to be done, when they will be done, and by whom. When developing your project plan for the Dynamics AX implementation, the following details should be covered:

- Decide on a phased rollout over the big bang, and define your work-breakdown structure accordingly.
- Identify external dependencies as specific tasks in your plan. For example:
    - EDI testing with customers or vendors
    - Credit card processors
    - Dealing with the banks
    - Any other third-party providers
    - ISV solutions
    - Any other business project/projects that would impact the ERP rollout, such as a warehouse move, a new retail store, and so on

- Put together all the constraints on the plan—resource/holidays/any blackout dates for release (for example, you should avoid a major release for a retailer close to Thanksgiving or any other busy holiday season).

- Define the frequency for updating and publishing the project plan. Keep all the stakeholders posted with the updated plan and upcoming activities, activities that are behind schedule, and the plan for catching up.

Communication

Setting up your communication plan at the beginning of the project and reviewing it in the kickoff meeting is important for keeping the stakeholders engaged with the project. The following are some key components of communication management on any project:

- **Weekly status report**: It's extremely important to publish status reports with an accurate summary of the project every week. Utilize this as a tool to get attention from the sponsors for help. Share any bad news sooner and take corrective action. Sitting on the bad news is only going to make it worse.

 There is no IT project that is always green. If you are consistently showing a green status, there is something hiding in your blind spot. Don't be shy of marking areas red when it's time to do so.

- **Steering committee meetings**: Schedule them frequently to keep the executive stakeholders engaged. Engaging the stakeholders will help you clear the roadblocks and steer the decisions throughout the journey. Otherwise, they will be on your back when things are not going well and the budget has been burnt. You want them to be engaged when you want and not when have to. At the beginning of the project, you should work with the steering committee to set a timetable for the meetings, the format of the meetings, and the ways in which critical path issues and risks will be debated and resolutions defined.

- **Meetings on the milestone closure**: You can align the steering committee meetings to every important milestone. However, it becomes difficult to reschedule with any changes in the plan. You need to truly complete the milestones. Otherwise, you will end up carrying debt from the previous milestone into the next one. High debt means high risk to the project. Remember, you are not the government—keep your debt in control.

- **Issue log tracking**: Define a tool and a process for managing your issue log, and train the entire team on the process. Actively manage and publish the issue log with the due dates and owners from the beginning of the project.

- **Scheduling (effective) meetings**: Each meeting should have an agenda outlining the purpose or objective of the meeting, the high-level topics to be discussed with the assigned owners, and the time allotted for each topic. Try to have more frequent, but short meetings rather than long ones. Keep control over your meetings; ensure that they do not deviate from the topic, and don't let others derail your meetings. Keep the number of attendees to the meeting to the minimum—invite only those who are required to take the decisions at hand or those who need to be part of the project updates. This will keep the meeting under control. Use quick meetings to brief the team about project updates: even if you have sent e-mails, it does not mean that the message has been received; e-mails are the worst form of communication. The meeting minutes should be published after each meeting and should be brief, documenting the decisions and actions only.

- **Use of distribution list**: Set up e-mail distribution lists for communication/ updates related to the project. You may need multiple lists (project committee, SME's, technical teams, and so on) that will allow you to communicate with the relevant audience.

Change control

The stakeholders don't give you an open check book. To stay on track, you need to watch out for paths derailing your project, and manage them with a clearly defined change-control process.

- Set up a process for change request management, including the process for approval or rejection. Multiple levels of approval may not be a bad idea (for example, approval for estimation, approval for implementation, and so on).

- Very often, the change itself may not be big, but its impact on the overall project may be huge. The impact on the testing and training aspects need to be evaluated carefully in addition to actual design and development. Include all the components in your estimation template.

The timing of change is very crucial! I had a situation where the users wanted to change the sequence of the columns on the forms. Suggestions started coming in towards the end of the UAT. The changes that were requested would not have taken too much time had we received this feedback in the earlier rounds of UAT. However, allowing the changes to be made would've encouraged the rest of the business groups to come up with similar requests, would've required updates to the training material, and so on. We had to cleverly push back and add them to the business transformation list. These changes were made after the release, and by then, the business had learnt a lot more about the system and were able to provide better inputs on what they needed.

- Your solution architects are going to play a key role in supporting you in your decision to take on or push back the change request. Leverage them to help push back on the requests that do not add value.

- Sometimes, you may be in a tough spot when the business asks for changes. For the business it may be small change, but they can't envisage the big picture and the impact of the change on the project. Leverage the steering committee and present the cost/schedule impact.

 If your developers are directly working with the business, watch out for any new scope taken up based on the business feedback.

Budget tracking

You have a long way to go on the project, and you should make sure that you have enough fuel for the long ride. You can't wait till the end of your journey to check the fuel gauge; you would definitely run out of fuel.

- Keep a close watch on the planned budget to the actual, compare your projected burn rate, actual burn along with the projected earn, and actual earn.

- Make adjustments sooner—whether it's getting an additional budget or resource changes.

- Watch out for scope-creep items that were not initially planned (you don't want your project to be derailed if the person signing the check hasn't asked for it).

- Timesheets and invoice reviews are critical to managing your budget:
    - Carefully review your spend from the beginning, and understand where time is being spent. If there are not enough details in the timesheets, ask questions! It is like reviewing your credit card statement.

 Have your team break down the work done by key phase or milestones so that you can track your budget more granularly. That will help you make decisions on the steps you can take to correct overspending.

- Compare your initial projections of burn with what has been delivered.

 You will have to be extra careful if the consulting team is incentivized based on billable hours.

- **Follow up on payments/collections**: Timely payments by the customer show that they value the work you are doing for them. When there are delays in payment, most likely there is a problem with the delivery, and the sooner you address it, the more likely you are to put the project back on track.

The view from the top

As part of that fifty-thousand foot view of the ERP project, the project manager has to look out on the horizon for any outside factors that could impact the project. Here are some examples of things to be aware of for keeping your project on track:

- Use the latest service packs and cumulative updates for Microsoft Dynamics AX application, kernel, and SQL. Get them installed (have them on the project plan too) as soon as they are available. It will reduce your exposure to the issues that may exist in the standard product, and sometimes, provide an additional functionality that can be used by the business.

- Keep an eye out for upgrades or changes that are in the works for any ISV solutions that are part of your project or for any integration partners. Also make sure that the ISV solutions are updated to the latest cumulative updates.

- Be aware of other, competing projects that are in process at the organization, and of any pending projects that may be waiting in the wings. These projects could dilute your customer's focus and cause delays. Make sure that these potential conflicts are brought up in your steering committee meetings as a potential risk.

- Major changes to the customer's business environment: major customer losses or gains, raw material pricing changes, and an industry shakeup are all examples of external forces that can impact your project. Keeping a lookout for these potential risks will allow you to react and respond more quickly to them.

The Agile methodology

With Agile becoming more and more popular, many customers have adopted it as it allows you to react quickly to changing business needs. In my experience, I have seen Agile ERP projects being more successful than the waterfall method. Every customer has his/her own version of Agile though. Understand the customer's current process, and tweak it to the version that would work for the ERP project. For example, if they are creating all the tasks on the board and physically writing them down, you may want to switch to the electronic format for better collaboration with remote teams.

The following are some recommendations if you plan on implementing Dynamics AX via an Agile methodology:

- Plan the tasks 4-6 weeks ahead, and build a backlog of things to be done after the requirements or Gap/Fit sign off.

- It is very important to have unified tools and processes across the board.

- Generally, there is misconception about Agile; Agile does not mean *no documentation*. You need to enforce using standard templates for all the deliverables (for example, functional design, technical design, and so on), and do not take any shortcuts using the Agile methodology as an excuse.

- Schedule frequent reviews (demos) with the business owners for each sprint cycle.

- Break the implementation team into smaller scrum teams by relevant areas. You would have cross-functional dependencies across the teams.

Summary

As mentioned at the beginning of the chapter, projects don't fail at the end, they fail when they start. In this chapter, you learned about the things that are essential for a great start of your ERP-implementation journey. We discussed the importance of understanding the customer's expectations, environment, and culture. This was followed by learning how to plan resources and establish a team. You also learned about common project management and governance activities and about deliverables such as project plans, communication plans, change control, and budget tracking. In the end, you were given some recommendations for adapting the Agile implementation methodology and tips for project managers to keep the project on track.

In the next chapter, we will learn about the requirement gathering techniques and **Conference Room Pilot (CRP)**—early validation for the completeness of your requirements and solution.

2
Getting into the Details Early

We will be discussing the techniques that are helpful in the analysis phase along with a few examples. In this chapter, you will learn the following topics:

- Requirement gathering techniques
- **Conference Room Pilot (CRP)**: This is an early validation for completeness of the requirements and proposed solution

You need to dive deeper to understand what you are up against. One of the common reasons why projects fail to deliver on time is that the requirements keep on bubbling up at a later stage. You should ensure that you have the right resources on board before you start discussions on requirements. It is the foundation for your project. Projects will fail if the requirements are incomplete, if the right analysis was not done to understand them correctly, or if you neglect to push back on requirements that do not add any value. All these cases will result in more work (often rework) and will impact the quality and timeline of the project.

It becomes tough to fix such projects at a later stage, as things that were missed initially keep bubbling up throughout the journey and you are always reacting to them (of course, the business team gets frustrated with explaining the same things over and over again).

The requirement gathering techniques

Consultants use different techniques for gathering requirements. Each has value in certain circumstances, and in many cases, you need multiple techniques to gain a complete picture of the requirements. The following diagram shows some common techniques used for requirement gathering for ERP systems.

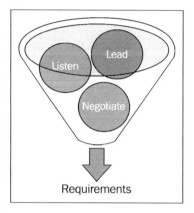

Listening is the first step in the requirements-gathering phase; you need to listen to the customer to understand what they need. We will now talk about the tools you can use at this stage to make listening or the information collection process smoother.

The tools to use at this stage

- Questionnaire
- Pre-existing business processes
- Calculations and examples
- Existing templates and formats
- Walkthrough of the existing system

Questionnaire

Prepare questionnaires to collect information and let the business SMEs fill them out. At this stage, you are giving them an opportunity to provide you with the details of what the business needs and with their view of the requirements.

- The questionnaire should be tailored for the client according to the his/her functional area and role.

- Microsoft Dynamics Sure Step provides you with a good starting point for questionnaires. You will have to tailor them considering the client business, scope, and the requirements knowledge based on the proposal and the client organization structure.

Here is an example of how the quality of your questions makes a difference. Suppose you are working with the client to understand the revenue recognition and deferrals process, one way of doing this is to go to the client, ask them to explain the entire process, and ask an open-ended question, such as "What would you like to have in the new system?". Another way is to understand the topic and put together good questions to engage the customer. The following table shows a sample of some questions or scenarios; I will take it to the customer and ask them for clarification/ examples and more inputs:

Revenue recognition and deferral questionnaire
Give me an example of the most common revenue recognition. For example, defer revenue to 12 months, starting today.
Do you have scenarios of deferring only a portion of the revenue (that is, if the revenue consists of 60 percent license and 40 percent services, then only services should be deferred)?
Renewal with the date in the past (start date in past).
Renewal with the date in the future (Start date in future).
Selling a future-dated contract.
Upsell of the product for the remaining period of the existing contract.
Rounding off – first or last month?
Proration calculations for the first and last month.
Complexities with uneven periods? (calculations by number of days in period? Applicable if you have 4-4-5 periods).
New sale with contract dates in the past.
Contract cancellation for the remaining period – reverse deferred revenue for the rest of the periods?
Contract cancellation with full refund – reverse deferred revenue for future, and recognize loss for past periods in the current period.
Batch invoicing for renewals and calculations of deferrals/recognition. Do you want every entry to hit GL or aggregated values?
Posting of deferral and recognition of a line discount.
Allocation of total order discount at the line level for deferral/recognition.
Migration of previously sold contracts (deferrals and recognition entries).
Cancellation of contracts sold prior to migration.
Contract cancellation with full refund for contracts sold prior to migration.

Revenue recognition and deferral questionnaire
Renewal of previously sold contracts.
Upsell on contracts sold prior to migration.
Replacement scenarios (?) – Need to cancel the previous line item and add a different line item starting today.
Integrations with the contract management system (where do you get the plan start and end dates from?)
Customer bought today, product launched in two months from now, for a year. Work starts in two weeks from now. When do you start recognition?
What happens when the launch date of a planned marketing campaign moves?
Variable billing per usage? (for example, cloud scenario, number of impressions in advertising business)
Are there any other scenarios we missed?
What are the key pain points in the current system?

1. This is something I learnt from one of my bosses; for which I must give him credit. Going with your detailed homework shows your knowledge about the topic and helps in gaining the customer's confidence that you understand it. At the same time, it also reduces the chances of missing out on any areas during discovery and the time the customer has to spend on explaining the process to you.

2. In this process, get examples of complex calculations (for example, revenue deferrals, royalties, commission, and pricing calculations are good candidates where you would need examples). Understand different scenarios and all the factors involved in calculations.

3. Understand the current business process flows (as is processes).

4. Ask for any work instructions or operations manuals that document their current process to help in understanding the current business process.

5. Get samples of the reports, especially external facing documents like invoices (sometimes customer invoices can become a project by themselves), checks, customer statements, packing slip, shipping labels, and so on, as applicable). Similarly, get samples of other templates, such as current fixed assets, import template, positive pay.

6. Schedule an existing-system walkthrough, especially for areas that are unique for the customer's business. Take screenshots and document the process. Clarify if any changes are to be made to the existing processes and provide recommendations for changes.

7. In global projects, engage the business SMEs to work with their counterparts from different locales to come up with unified processes.

Lead

Now that you have collected information from the customer, it's time to analyze and come up with your understanding of what they need. Document the requirements, open questions you want to discuss further and get ready to lead the requirements discussions.

It's time for you to dive deep into the requirements by engaging the customer and asking the right questions to extract the information that you need. Clarify conflicting requirements across the business groups.

Get business rules defined and validated in the form of flow charts. Each functional team should work together on the future state of a business flow. This will validate the completeness of requirements coverage, dependencies, and business rules. For example, the order review process will be as follows:

1. If new customer arrives, he/she will go to the *new ship* queue.

2. If order is for more than X dollars, it needs to go through the *big order* queue.

3. If the credit limit is exceeded or past due account, route to the *credit* queue.

4. If a special product (license purchase, and so on), it needs to go to the *merchandizing* queue.

5. If there's a customer tax exemption, route it to the *tax* queue.

6. A credit card order should go through fraud checks and to the fraud queue, if necessary.

The following diagram describes the process flow—I will go to business after analyzing several spreadsheets and the existing documentation about the current budget planning process and have them provide feedback on the requirement understanding.

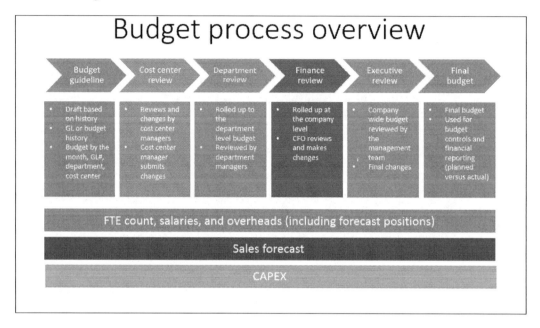

1. Understand the current process and document the pain areas; ask questions to clarify.

2. Avoid any discussion about solutions in the requirements meetings (you don't want the business to dictate the solution).

3. Do not spend time on discussing out-of-scope areas until the client has approved the change order. Do not let your project derail, if it is not approved to be in scope, it is not approved by the person who is signing the check.

4. Capture reporting, security, integration, and data migration requirements along with other requirements discussions. Non-functional requirements play a key role in shaping a project's success.

5. Avoid using Dynamics AX terminologies or acronyms (for example, posting profile, value models or DAX, OB, CRP and so on) during discussions with the business team. It may be your 10th Dynamics AX implementation, but most likely it is the first one for the client, and you will throw them off by using those terminologies.

Negotiate

As a consultant, you need to bring in the knowledge of the best practices in the industry, help customers improve their processes, and push back on requirements that do not add value to the business. As part of this negotiation, you will need to provide insights into why a specific feature is not needed anymore and what it can be replaced with in the new process.

Often, requirements are seen from the perspective of how it works in the current system. It does not always mean how it should work. What is worse, is that challenges/bugs in the current system become requirements to be implemented in Dynamics AX. Consultants accept these as requirements and provide custom solutions. Understand the problem you are trying to solve. Get to the bottom of the issue and provide a solution accordingly. In most cases, customization is a lazy way of providing solutions as an analyst; you are just taking the solution from the existing system and pushing your work to the developer in terms of customization.

Here are a few examples of requirements for which you should push back:

1. I had a customer requirement to post an out-of-balance general journal entry. Dynamics AX doesn't support it. The reason why the users were asking for this to be a requirement was because the previous system had a bug that would post an out-of-balance entry in certain scenarios and then accountants had to use this *feature* to correct it.

2. A customer wanted a very complex workflow to be created. Every taxi expense greater than $30 had to go through multiple approvals, all the way to the CEO. All of that was being done when they were handling expense approvals on paper, and was okay till then. We had to explain the complexity they were adding (in terms of implementation and, more importantly, ongoing support) by building a complex workflow. The question is not whether Dynamics AX can handle it; you need to ask what value it would add and whether the efforts are justified. It was a tough battle to win, but it was worth fighting for and we won it in the best interests of the customer.

3. Another customer requested changing the unit price field to 8 decimal places. They were selling some products in the quantity of 1 million units and the per unit price would come to 8 decimals in reporting. Hence, the person who was writing reports in the data warehouse requested the change in the ERP to save reporting efforts.

There are many examples like this; poor analysis will add more customization. Every time you get a requirement that needs customization, try to think how other Dynamics AX customers are using it. Why did Microsoft not build the feature? You will then find the pointers to push back. Having said that, there may be some legitimate needs for customization though.

These types of requirements keep coming back hence, you should document them in your **Business Requirements Document (BRD)** with the priority of *Out of Scope*.

In some situations, you run into strong personalities from a customer/business SME and they might be reluctant to accept the provided recommendations. You should document your feedback in BRD/Gap Fit documents as *Strongly not recommended*. For example, in one of the projects, I was involved in a review capacity. The customer wanted to see on-hand information of different variants of the product in columns (because they were used to seeing it that way in the previous system). Dynamics AX 2009 used to store them as rows and it was going to be a major change in the core feature of Dynamics AX. I documented all the reasons to avoid it. Eventually, there were issues with the feature and initial documentation of the pushback was helpful.

Your goal should be to simplify the processes and go with the industry standards. Your efforts in this exercise are to protect the interests of your customer and the project; don't be shy in pushing back.

Conference Room Pilot (CRP)

A picture is worth a thousand words. Similarly, a good CRP is an effective way of communicating the solution in a language that business SMEs will understand. It will help confirm your understanding of the requirements and get an early feedback on the proposed solution.

Why is CRP needed?

Use **Conference Room Pilots (CRP)** to model business scenarios, get early feedback on the solution, and progressively refine the scenarios through a series of CRP workshops to gain the business SME's acceptance, as shown in the following diagram:

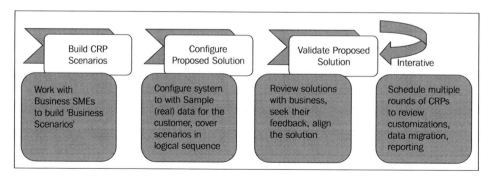

Considerations for CRP success

Followings are the key considerations for successful CRP:

1. Focus on modeling business scenarios rather than individual requirement fit-gap.

2. Dynamics AX is a very configurable solution. You may have multiple options to choose from in the solution. Present those options to the business and help them pick the right solution.

3. Identify missing requirements through solution review and solution gaps.

4. Schedule multiple CRP iterations as you progress through the solution process. This will help to get an early feedback from the business and address training earlier and make your UAT much smoother (as the business will see the solution multiple times before UAT).

5. CRP workshops bring business, IT, and delivery teams in sync with the solution.

6. It helps you to keep the business engaged in the project; business involvement is the key for success of a project.

7. Ensure that you communicate your goals for every round of CRP. The SMEs may watch half-baked solutions in some cases; you should make sure that expectations are set upfront.

8. Make sure that you have all the process owners (decision makers) in the CRP. You don't want to delay the design acceptance by hearing something like, "This looks ok to me, but I can't really sign on it without Mary in accounting saying that this gives her the information that she needs". Make sure Mary is there too!

9. Conversely, you don't want so many people in the CRP that you get easily taken off-track by too many opinions. Carefully evaluate who the process owners are and limit participation to those SMEs.

The CRP execution

Consider following points during the CRP execution:

1. **Scenario:** Engage with business SMEs to identify critical business scenarios, cover all key processes, and put them into logical groups and sequence.

2. **CRP planning**: CRP is one of the most important milestones (your first key deliverable for the business team and their first exposure to Dynamics AX too). You need to make sure there is enough time for environment setup, data imports, and cross functional reviews within the team before you review with the SMEs.

    ○ **Define a clear agenda**: Mention the topics and scenarios that need to be presented. Organize topics in a logical sequence, so that you can present a complete story.

    ○ Data migration for the CRP and any other DEV efforts that are required for the CRP will be on a critical path. Deploy resources and have them started early. It is critical to use customer data, rather than using a demo data for the CRP.

3. **Basic customizations for showing UI for critical changes**: This will allow the SMEs to visualize the changes that you have proposed and to get their feedback.

4. **Prepare documentation**: This contains the CRP presentations along with the relevant screenshots or videos using an application like, **Task Recorder**. This is helpful for the business team to refer to it later or to review with their teams.

5. Have business analysts review the CRPs with the respective business owners offline to get their buy-in (they will help you drive the CRP demos and make CRP much smoother).

The Fit/Gap analysis

One of the key deliverables from the analysis phase is a Fit/Gap document. CRP allows you to review the business fit of the standard processes configured within Dynamics AX and also gets the feedback on the proposed solutions for Gaps.

- You can leverage the business process modeler in Microsoft **Lifecycle Services (LCS)** for complete business processes. Having this created in LCS means that the overall business process is analyzed, and providing access to the LCS project increases knowledge of the gap.

- It is important to remember that this is a FIT gap session and Fit should also be analyzed.

- Often at times, you will find gaps listed that aren't really gaps, as the solution can handle the requirement.

- Another time to revisit and negotiate items that are causing a lot of customization work and can be avoided.

The implementation strategy

On global rollouts, single-instance versus multi-instance is a key implementation decision. Leverage the following pointers to decide:

1. Localizations / countries / legal requirements
2. Security, data privacy / SOX
3. Connectivity (network latency) / performance
4. Maintainability / deployment / downtime for maintenance
5. Risk management for solution conflicts
6. **Costs**: licensing, support, upgrade
7. Shared services, intercompany transactions, master data management

Factors	Single Instance Global instance	Multiple Instance Regional/country specific
Decision making	Top down; from HQ to subsidiaries	Individual control, more control with subsidiaries
Shared processes	• Centralized, shared services model • Close collaboration – Master data management, intercompany trade	• Decentralized processes
Software licensing	Centralized, cost effective	Decentralized, may be same or different platforms
Software deployments	• Centralized • Downtime challenges, latency & connectivity considerations	• Local deployments • Less of downtime and latency issues
Flexibility	Similar business model and unified processes	Diversified portfolio and operating models, easy for divestitures/company split

Key deliverables from the analysis phase

Following are the key deliverables from the analysis phase:

- **Business Requirements Document (BRD)**
- Implementation strategy
- Solution blueprint and Fit/Gap
- List of change requests and disposition (approved versus rejected or deferred)
- **Project plan baseline**: Alignment to the project plan based on the approved changes coming out of the CRP and updated BRD

Summary

With this chapter, we started the analysis phase of the project. We learned about requirement gathering tools and techniques. We learned how you can use the basic principle of listen, lead, and negotiate to successfully gather the requirements. We discussed the importance of the conference room pilot and important considerations for planning and executing the CRP sessions. We also learned about other deliverables from the analysis phase such as Fit/Gap analysis and implementation strategy.

In the next chapter, we will learn about another key process in an implementation project—infrastructure planning and design.

3
Infrastructure Planning and Design

The infrastructure planning and design process typically starts during the requirements gathering phase of the implementation project. This process is led by the solution architect, project manager, and the customer IT team.

Unless software is supported by the right hardware, it will never be able to reach its full potential. Sizing the infrastructure is laying the groundwork for success. Sizing the right hardware is not only important for getting an accurate budget for your Dynamics AX project, but also vital to how the system will function and perform after the implementation and for years to come.

This chapter will cover the following topics:

- Dynamics AX components and architecture
- Capacity planning and infrastructure estimation
- Planning system topologies
- Industry best practices and recommendations

The Dynamics AX components and architecture

The key to planning an effective design is to understand the architecture and components of Dynamics AX. A clear understanding of the architecture will help you decide on the different components that you will need in your implementation and the hardware required for all the components. The following diagram from the Microsoft TechNet System architecture page shows the high-level logical view and various components of Microsoft Dynamics AX system architecture:

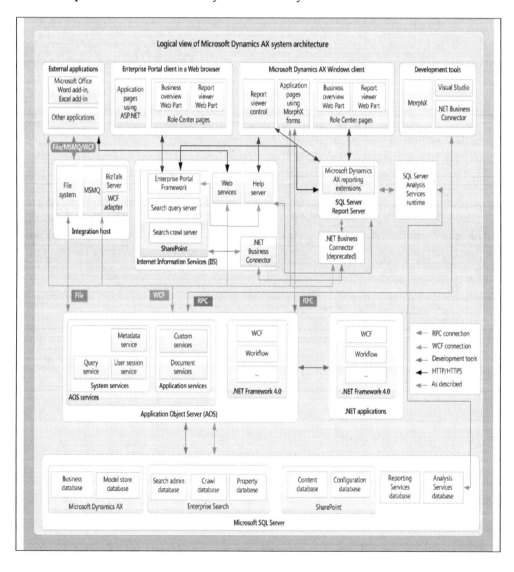

Databases

There are three types of databases in Dynamics AX and are explained as follows:

- **Business database**: This is the transaction database for Dynamics AX.

- **Model database**: This database stores the application elements. These elements include standard code and customizations.

- **Other databases**: These are the content and configuration database for SharePoint, Enterprise search databases, reporting services, and analysis services (OLAP cubes) databases for **Business Intelligence** (**BI**) and reporting.

The middle tier

The middle tier of Dynamics AX consist of following components:

- **Application Object Server** (**AOS**): This is the middle tier for a three-tier Dynamics AX architecture. As per the implementation strategy, you might need multiple AOS servers to balance the load. The AOS performs the following operations:
    - It controls the communication between AX clients, databases, and applications
    - It executes the business logic of the Dynamics AX application
    - It handles the required connectivity, security, and connection management

- **Services and Application Integration Framework** (**AIF**): This integrates Dynamics AX with the other systems. AIF services can be hosted on AOS or IIS.

- **Workflow system**: This can be used to create individual workflows and business processes and it runs on AOS.

- **Enterprise Portal**: This is the web portal of AX; commonly referred to as **EP**, it extends common AX functionalities for customers, vendors, and employee self-service. An enterprise portal requires the following components.
    - IIS
    - Microsoft SharePoint Foundation or Microsoft SharePoint Services

Reporting and BI

The following components provide reporting and BI capabilities for Dynamics AX application:

- **SQL Server Reporting Services**: This is used as the primary reporting platform for Dynamics AX. All the reports are deployed and executed on SQL reporting services. Dynamics AX reporting extension provides connectivity between AX clients, AOS, and reporting services.

- **SQL Server Analysis Services**: This is used as the primary BI solution. All the Dynamics AX BI cubes are deployed and executed on the SQL Server analysis server platform.

Client

There are three types of clients for Dynamics AX 2012 R3, explained as follows:

- **The Dynamics AX client application**: This is a windows application which provides rich user interface for AX application

- **Excel Add-in**: This add-on allows the users to access the Dynamics AX data through Excel

- **Enterprise Portal**: This provides web user interface for Dynamics AX

The Help server

The Help server does what it says, it hosts the help content. The Help server is hosted on IIS.

Capacity planning and infrastructure estimation

You cannot determine appropriate hardware resource requirements without first creating a measurement standard for using that hardware resource. In this section, we will learn the information that we need to effectively estimate hardware requirements and how to use **Microsoft Lifecycle Services (LCS)** to create a usage profile and infrastructure estimates.

Capacity planning

Capacity planning or generating a usage profile is the process of collecting data required to understand the current and the projected use of the system to be implemented. The Microsoft Lifecycle Services portal provides a data gathering tool, **Usage Profiler,** to help you describe your current and projected usage of Dynamics AX.

Before you use Microsoft Lifecycle Services to create a usage profile, you need to gather the information in the next section for your current implementation.

The deployment details

In this section, gather the deployment-specific information as described in the following table:

Hosting	Answer
Will the deployment be in a hosted environment?	No
Virtualization	
Do you plan to use virtualization in the proposed deployment?	Yes
Organizational structure	
Does your organization's structure include multiple organizations?	Yes
How many legal entities are present?	10
How many subsidiary entities are present?	3
The total number of concurrent users	400
Across the enterprise, what is the peak number of concurrent users?	200
Global deployment	
Will Microsoft Dynamics AX be deployed in more than one country? List all the countries.	No, US only
Do we need to deploy it multiple languages? List all languages.	No, English (US) only
Components	
Will a workflow be used?	Yes
Will you use the Office Add-ins for Microsoft Dynamics AX?	Yes
Will Microsoft **SQL Server Reporting Services (SSRS)** be used?	Yes
Will Microsoft **SQL Server Analysis Services (SSAS)** be used?	Yes
Will any reporting solutions other than Microsoft Dynamics AX Reporting be used?	Yes, Management Reporter

Reports

Describe reports on the basis of whether they are operational, management, or offline, their complexity, frequency, and the related business process.

Name	Description	Type	Complexity	Frequency	Related business process
Trial balance	Trial balance	Management	High	Daily	Ledger
Purchase order	Purchase order report	Operational	Low	Ad hoc	Purchase order
Purchase receiving log	Purchase receiving log	Operational	Medium	Ad hoc	Purchase order

Operating sites and schedules

Operating sites are the locations at which your organization is running Microsoft Dynamics AX. You'll need to provide a name, whether the location is remote or onsite, upload and download bandwidth, and your WAN connection latency. Use the work schedule to enter peak concurrent users per hour:

Name	Location	Upload bandwidth (Mbps)	Download bandwidth (Mbps)	WAN connection latency (milliseconds)	Time zone	Schedule
US – Chicago	US – Chicago	100 Mbps	50 Mbps	100	US Central	8 a.m. to 6 p.m.
US – Washington	US – Chicago	100 Mbps	50 Mbps	100	US Central	8 a.m. to 6 p.m.

The ISV products

Enter the ISV products in your environment, and the estimated transaction lines per hour:

Name	Estimated peak transaction lines per hour
Sales Tax Calculation and Reporting ISV	1000

Customizations

This describes the planned customizations in terms of peak transaction lines per hour, and the related business process.

Name	Related business process	Estimated peak transaction lines per hour
Revenue recognition	Ledger	1000
Commission calculation	Sales	1000

Integrations

This describes the planned integrations in terms of peak transaction lines per hour, and the related business process:

Name	Description	Related business process	Estimated peak transaction lines per hour
Sales order integration	Web orders	Sales	2000
EDI Integration of PO	Purchase orders integration	Purchase	100

The batch process

This describes the batch processes in terms of transaction lines and recurrence:

Name	Transaction lines	Recurrence interval value	Recurrence type	Time zone	Start time	Duration (hours)
Sales order invoicing	1000	1	Day	US – Central	8:00 p.m.	1
Purchase order confirmation	100	2	Hours	US – Central	8:00 a.m.	.5
Sub-ledger transfer	1000	1	Day	US – Central	9:00 p.m.	.5
AIF message processing	1500	1	Hours	US – Central	8:00 a.m.	.25

Using Lifecycle Services – Usage Profiler

Once data is collected, you can use the Lifecycle Services Usage Profiler tool to enter the data or download it, fill data, and upload it. Follow these steps to create a usage profile for your project:

1. Login to the LCS portal at `https://lcs.dynamics.com`.

2. Select your **Project**.

3. Select **More Tools | Usage profiler**.

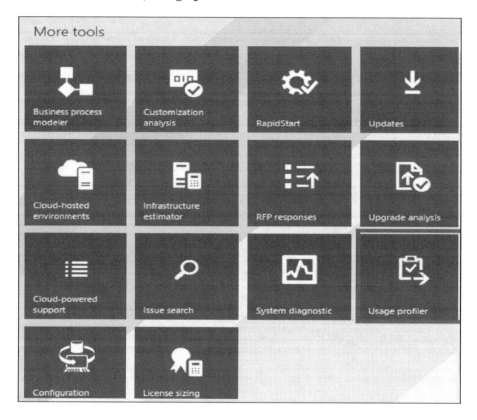

4. Enter the data using the tool or download the Excel template and upload the data. Use the horizontal scroll bar to see and enter all other details in the **Usage profiler** tool.

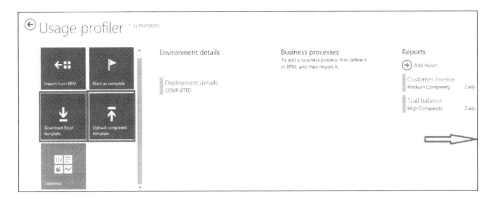

5. Mark Usage Profiler as **Complete** when all the details are entered.

Infrastructure estimation

The Microsoft Dynamics LCS Infrastructure estimator provides an automated, rough first estimate of the hardware needs of an environment. Estimates can be provided for environments that are on your premises or on the cloud. As pointed out, the LCS Infrastructure estimator tool provides a rough estimate based on the usage profile data entered in LCS, and these estimates need to be reviewed by the system architect on your project. You also need to consider hardware requirements for your disaster recovery site and any other non-production environments.

The following steps explain how to use the LCS Infrastructure estimation tool to create an infrastructure estimation:

1. Log in to Lifecycle Services.

2. Select your project; on the project home page, and click on the **Infrastructure estimator** tile.

3. Click on **New estimate**.

4. Select the type of environment that you are creating an estimate for, like for example, **Production**.

5. Enter a name for the estimate, and select whether the environment will be hosted on the premises or in the cloud.

6. Enter other information as needed. The following table describes the additional information that you may need to provide depending on the type of environment that you have selected:

Environment	Parameters
Development	• Number of developers • Version control system
Production	None
Test	• Type of testing • Number of computers
Training	Number of computers

7. Create an estimate for all the environments that you need.

8. The following screenshot displays the list of environments created and the corresponding hardware estimate:

Planning the system topology

Environments for development, testing, and production should be carefully optimized for throughput, response time, scalability, and availability. Under this topic, we will learn about the recommended system topologies for production and non-production environments.

The production system topology

The following diagram shows a layered system topology for large-scale implementation projects:

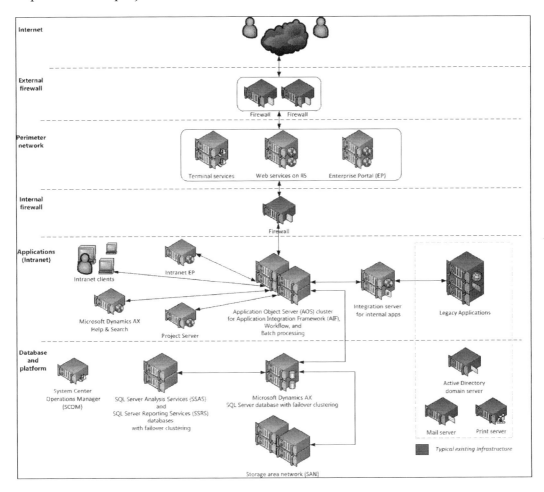

In the preceding diagram, servers are divided among three main layers. The following table explains the different layers, recommended servers, and their purpose:

Layers	Server	Purpose
Perimeter network layer	Terminal service cluster	This provides VPN access to authorized users.
	Internet Information Services (IIS)	This provides access to services for AX through the IIS feature.
	Internet Information Services cluster (IIS cluster)	This provides Enterprise Portal Support for AX.
Applications layer	AOS cluster	This provides connection to the end users using AX Windows client. Also, it provides functionality for AIF, workflow, and batch processing tasks. It is recommended that separate AOS clusters need to be created for AX client users, EP users, and batch processing.
	Integration server clusters	This provides connection to the internal systems.
	Dedicated servers	This provides internal client's access to the Enterprise portal, Help server, search server, and project server.
Database and platform layer	Microsoft SQL Server Failover cluster	This provides storage and support for AX databases. Also, it provides support for additional database requirements.
	SQL Server Failover cluster for reporting and BI	This provides support for deployment and execution of Dynamics AX reports and BI cubes.
	Storage Area Network	This provides support for data backup.
	System Center Operation Manager (SCOM)	This provides support for system monitoring.
	Active Directory Domain Controller	This provides support to deploy AX components.

The system topology shown in the preceding diagram is only an example; the solution architect needs to work with the internal IT and network teams and design an appropriate system topology based on the components that you need in your project, and other requirements such as availability, throughput, and scalability. Follow the latest recommendations and best practices from Microsoft and other experts when working on production infrastructure design.

The nonproduction system topology

The following diagram represents non-production environments, such as the test and training environments:

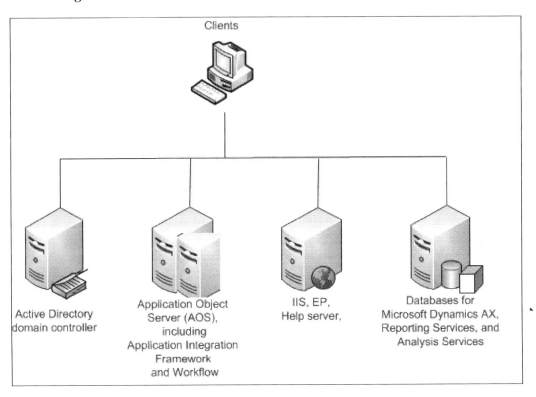

The following table describes how the computers in this sample topology are used:

Server	Purpose
Active Directory domain controller	This is used to deploy the Dynamics AX components.
Application Object Server (AOS) cluster	This is used to separate server for AX client, batch processes, and enterprise portal.
Web server	This is used to deploy IIS, EP, and Help server.
Database server	This is used as a common database server for Dynamics AX databases, Reporting services, Analysis services, and SharePoint database.

Cloud deployment

The cloud simplifies many challenges such as lead time, scalability, disaster recovery, and so on.

The cloud services

In general, the following cloud services are offered by the Dynamics AX partners:

Type of service	Description
Software-as-a-Service (SaaS)	Here, infrastructure, application, and data, everything is managed by the vendor.
Platform-as-a-Service (PaaS)	Here, the vendor manages the infrastructure and the Operating System. You only have to worry about managing your application and data.
Infrastructure-as-a-Service (IaaS)	Here, the infrastructure is managed by the vendor and you manage the operating system, application, and data.

The following diagram shows the difference between the various cloud services:

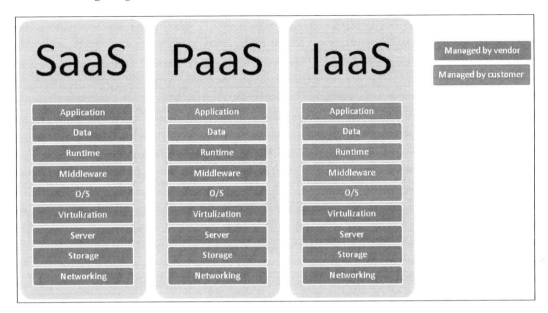

Several Microsoft Dynamics partners provide these services. You can review the cloud partners and see which engagement makes more sense for you. PaaS and IaaS are the most commonly used offerings for Dynamics AX 2012 R3.

Microsoft Dynamics AX 2012 R3 on Azure

The cloud is a key strategy for Microsoft as an organization, and the Dynamics AX R&D team is making huge investments to simplify Microsoft Dynamics AX cloud deployments. Microsoft Dynamics AX 2012 R3 can be deployed on Microsoft Azure virtual machines. When you deploy Microsoft Dynamics AX on Azure, it's basically an IaaS offering. This means that Azure provides the virtual machines, storage, and networking capabilities. You must manage and secure the operating systems, applications, and the data installed on the virtual machines.

Microsoft has simplified the deployment of Dynamics AX 2012 R3 using the **Lifecycle Services (LCS)** Cloud-hosted environments tool. When you use the Cloud-hosted environments tool to deploy, you'll need to select the type of environment that you want to deploy on Azure such as a demo or development/test environment. Based on your selection, the Cloud-hosted environments tool provisions the appropriate number of virtual machines on Azure. These virtual machines have AX 2012 R3 components—and all of their prerequisites—already installed on them.

Follow these steps to create cloud-hosted environments for your project:

1. Log in to the LCS portal at `https://lcs.dynamics.com`.
2. Select your project.
3. Select **More tools | Cloud-hosted environments**.
4. Provide the Azure subscription ID.
5. Download the security certificate and upload it on the Azure management portal.
6. Select the type of environment such as demo, development/test, or production environment and deploy.

The following screenshot shows a list of the Dynamics AX environments deployed on Azure:

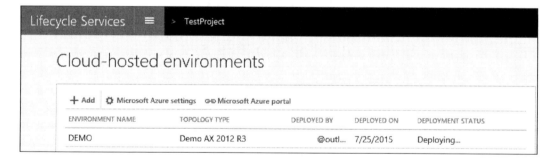

The following diagram shows the architecture of the Microsoft Dynamics AX deployment on the cloud:

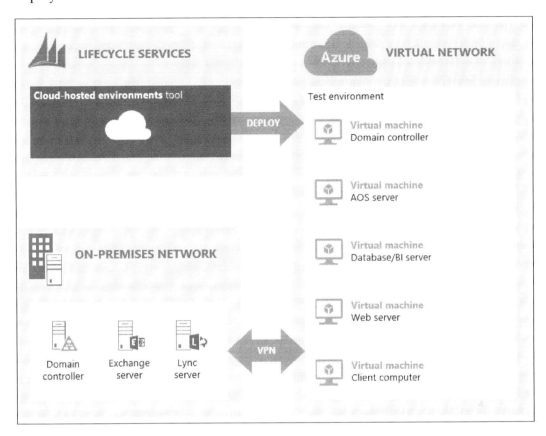

Industry best practices and recommendations

The following are a few industry best practices and recommendations for Dynamics AX infrastructure planning.

Planning

- Once you have the infrastructure design in place, you need to ensure that you have a plan to deliver the environments as per other milestones.

- There could be a long lead time in getting the budget approvals, the procurement process including lead time from Vendor, OS installation, and so on.

- Add tasks for infrastructure deliverables to the overall plan and have the lead time defined for the infrastructure team to deliver those tasks for your project.

The SQL server

Most of the performance issues arise from bottlenecks on SQL:

- Utilize the latest supported SQL Server version for Dynamics AX databases to utilize the latest SQL Server features.

- The Dynamics AX database has intense storage requirements and it should not be mistaken for any other OLTP database. Utilize the Microsoft recommendations on storage planning and configuration. The following blogs at Microsoft contain useful information on this topic:

Blogs links	Details
`https://technet.microsoft.com/` `EN-US/library/dd309734.aspx`	This is a Microsoft TechNet article on SQL Server Storage Settings.
`http://blogs.msdn.com/b/axperf`	**Microsoft Dynamics AX performance team**: This contains several blogs on storage setting best practices and recommendations
`http://blogs.msdn.com/b/axsup-port/`	**Microsoft Dynamics AX support team**: This contains several blog topics on infrastructure estimation and hardware sizing.

- Dynamics AX 2012 extensively uses `TempDB` and in-memory processing of data for performance optimization. In SQL Server 2012, `TempDB` is supported on the local drive which gives you an opportunity to store the `TempDB` files on **Solid State Drives (SSDs)**. This can improve the performance for I/O access to `TempDB` and avoid any contention.

- Plan for high availability by using failover solution on the SQL Server instance for the recovery strategy. SQL Server 2012 supports the *Always on availability group* feature to synchronize the primary instance to up to four secondary replicas.

- Plan for future expansion. For example, leave room for expansion in case you have to add more RAM or CPUs at a later stage.

The AOS server

- Plan the AOS servers for different purposes and redundancy. Use Windows Load Balancer or the Dynamics AX built-in load balancer functionality and create a cluster for user AOS, integrations, and batch processes.

 You can combine some of these depending on your load. For example, user AOS can be used a batch server for nightly batches.

- Try to minimize the number of AOS servers by having additional resources on the servers.

 Instead of having six AOS servers for users, I would get away with two powerful ones. In the previous versions of Dynamics AX, there was a limitation for scaling the AOS server and customers needed multiple AOS servers. With Dynamics AX 2012, that's not the case anymore. One of my customers was able to downsize from 18 AOS servers to 6 with Dynamics AX 2012. The lower number of AOS would help with the AOS licensing cost, maintenance, and troubleshooting.

- Do not oversize the AOS server resources either. The Microsoft recommendation is to limit the AOS server to maximum eight CPU cores and 16 GB physical memory.

- Virtualization is recommended for AOS servers as it helps to reduce maintenance costs and allows high availability.

- Monitor the AOS server hardware utilization during tests and performance testing to evaluate if the performance meets the required benchmarks.

Reviews

- You need to have somebody else to review the environments (other than the resources who built it—leverage your partner, Microsoft Premier Support team, or external consultants) once the hardware has been procured and set up. SQL, network, OS, AOS, hardware, storage, security, and others are very important aspects of your environments and need to be reviewed thoroughly.

- You have architected the infrastructure well enough, spent enough to buy all the high-end hardware. Now, the last thing you want to realize is that you haven't configured it well or you are not using all of its features.

We had a funny incident during one of the projects. We brought in a consultant to review the hardware and the network. They found that the network speed between AOS/SQL and the other application was slower. Getting into details, they found that all these servers were connected through a 100 MB switch while 1 GB switches had been bought, but were sitting on the floor at the data center since more than five years. Isn't that funny? But it happens all the time. The infrastructure teams have the highest number of critical projects running all the time with firefighting situations which demand off-hours work. There is always a possibility of missing out on such things.

Summary

In this chapter, we went through the Dynamics AX system architecture and learned about the different components in there. We learned about the information that we need for capacity planning and infrastructure estimation, how to use Microsoft Lifecycle Services to create a usage profile, and to roughly estimate the hardware requirements for your implementation project. After getting rough estimates for the hardware, we went through the different system topologies for production and non-production environments. Finally, we explored the industry best practices and recommendations related to infrastructure planning.

In the next chapter, we will learn another key aspect of ERP implementation projects—integration planning and design.

4
Integration Planning and Design

ERP is in the middle of the ecosystem of business facing applications, and Microsoft Dynamics AX will need to directly or indirectly integrate with other applications. Accuracy and timely update of this information is very important for business success and growth. This chapter is about integration planning, understanding integration technologies, and integration design/development.

In this chapter, the following topics are covered:

- Integration planning
    ○ Integration scenarios
    ○ Integration requirements

- Integration technologies
    ○ **Application Integration Framework (AIF)**
    ○ **Data Import/Export Framework (DIXF)**
    ○ Microsoft .NET Framework
    ○ Third-party integration solutions

- Integration design and development
- Best practices and recommendations

Integration planning

Planning is an important part of any data integration effort. Data integration planning requires identifying integration scenarios and the high-level requirements of integration. This topic covers common integration scenarios and the common questions to be asked for gathering integration requirements.

Integration scenarios

Every project is different. So, integration requirements will vary depending on the scope and the needs of the specific project. However, there are some common areas where most of the businesses have processes that require integration. The following table shows the common integration points and possible scenarios:

Integrations	Possible scenarios
Customers	Customers need to be maintained in the CRM system which needs to be synced with the ERP system.
Sales orders	Integrating web orders with the ERP system that includes delivery notification, invoicing, and payments or with customer systems directly (for example, EDI integration).
Product and inventory (on hand)	Receiving product data from a PLM system. Sending the product-and-inventory-on-hand data to external systems or customers. For example, e-commerce, Amazon, Marketplace, and so on.
Price list	Sending product price list to external systems or customers. For example, e-Commerce, marketplace and so on.
Sales tax	Sales tax integration with sales tax solutions (To calculate the sales tax based on the product, customer, ship to, price, and other relevant parameters).
Purchase orders	Purchase order, including ASN and AP invoice, integration with the vendor systems.
Employee and positions	Receiving employee and reporting relationship from the HR system or sending employee information to the payroll or expense systems.
Chart of accounts and financial dimensions	Sending the chart of account and financial dimension data to other internal systems like the payroll system, expense system, and others.
Exchange rates	Downloading daily exchange rates from exchange rate providers, such as Oanda.
Payment integration with banks	Sending AP payments such as check, ACH, wire, and so on, to the banking systems or automating bank reconciliations.

Integrations	Possible scenarios
GL integration	Importing GL journal entries occurring outside of Dynamics AX system such as expense, payroll, loan accounting systems, or other divisions using a different accounting system (acquisitions).

Integration requirements

In a typical integration scenario, the implementation team works with the business users, internal IT, and in some cases, representatives of the applications identified for integration to determine the requirements in detail. The following questions must be answered and documented in order to have a successful integration solution. Often, the answers to these questions are not clear-cut and will require modeling of the different scenarios to develop the best solution. That being said, starting this process early in the project is the key.

Questions	Example values	Effects on design
What type of data needs to be integrated?	Sales orders, purchase orders, and so on	This will help you to determine if you can use any existing document services or need to create a new one.
What kind of integration type will the other applications support?	XML, Web services, flat file, .NET Interop	This will help you to determine the technology to use.
What is the availability of the systems that are being integrated? What are the requirements of real-time data exchanges?	Asynchronous or synchronous	This will help you to determine the integration technology and configuration requirements.
Is the integration based on the **pull** model or the **push** model?	Pull, push, event-driven	This will help you to determine the customization and configuration of the exchange event.
What is the volume of transactions?	Number of transactions (daily, weekly, monthly, yearly)	This will help you to determine the scale of integration, suitable integration technology, and deployment options.
What will be the frequency of data exchange?	Timing per second, minute, hour	This information helps you to determine how to configure the integration solution.

Questions	Example values	Effects on design
What business rules are associated with the data?	Sequence of events and exception handling	This will help you to determine the customization requirement for the document exchange.
Does the data need to be transformed? Will the transformations be performed before data is sent or when data is received?	Extent of transformation—field level mapping, value mapping, and flat file to XML or vice versa	This will help you to determine whether AIF value mapping, .NET transformation, or XSLT transformations need to be used.
If integration needs to update Dynamics AX, how will the changes be updated?	Full, incremental	This will help you to determine the configuration or customization requirement on exchange.
Is the external system an in house system or an external trading partner?	Security and encryption requirements	This will help you to determine how the users and security need be configured.

Synchronous or asynchronous

One of the key decisions to be made is whether integration should be real-time (synchronous) or asynchronous. The following table analyses both the messaging approaches and describes the scenarios when one should be selected over the other:

	Pros	Cons	Good for	Examples
Synchronous	• Fail-safe communication • Error/ exception handling	• Tight coupling between systems • Block sender until receiver is finished • Network dependency must be available	Transaction processing across multiple systems	Mobile app/ handheld for PO receiving, SO picking, Inventory counting, and so on.
Asynchronous	• De-coupled systems • Does not block sender • Network need not be available • Messages can be queued	• Reliability • Error/ exception handling	• Publish and subscribe • Request reply • Conversation	• GL integration • SO/PO Integration • Master data integration

Asynchronous messaging architectures have proven to be the best strategy for an enterprise integration because they allow for a loosely-coupled solution that overcomes the limitations of a remote communication, such as latency and unreliability. The issues of reliability and exception handling in asynchronous messaging can be overcome by utilizing request/response and logging features in the Microsoft Dynamics AX AIF Framework.

Integration technologies

As enterprises move toward using more and more specialized applications rather than having an ERP do everything for them, you need a robust framework and strategy for managing integrations within the ERP system. Dynamics AX provides many such robust frameworks and functionalities to integrate with third-party applications using modern techniques.

The following section outlines the commonly-used integration technologies in Dynamics AX. It is important to make sure that the technical analysts and developers in your project are familiar with these technologies, so that they can support the design process and identify the best integration solution for your project.

Application Integration Framework and services

AIF (**Application Integration Framework**) is the de facto integration methodology to integrate Dynamics AX with third-party applications and is a built-in infrastructure into the Dynamics AX platform.

AIF enables companies to integrate and communicate with the external business processes and partners through the exchange of XML over various transport media. AIF can be used to implement both business-to-business and application-to-application integration scenarios.

The AIF architecture

The following diagram shows the high-level AIF and services architecture. As shown in the diagram, AIF and service are based on **Windows Communication Foundation (WCF)** and are hosted on AOS. AIF web services can also be hosted on IIS. The AOS-hosted services are available to users and applications across Intranet. To consume these services over the Internet, you must host these services on **Internet Information Services (IIS)**.

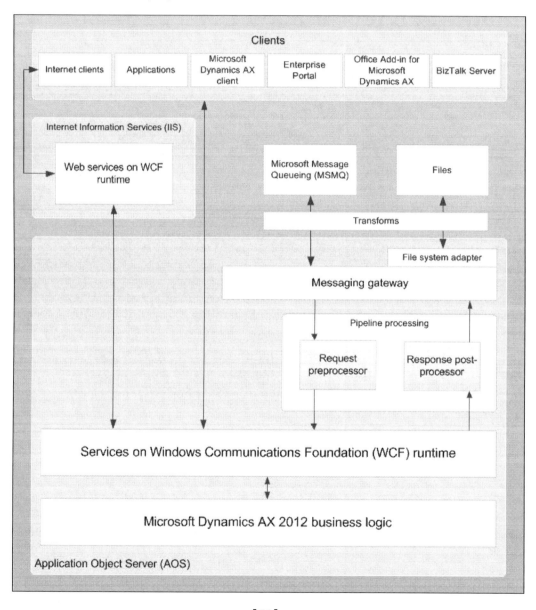

Key concepts in AIF

The key concepts in AIF include the following:

- Services
- Adapters
- Message processing

Services

The different types of services AIF provides, are as follows:

- **System services**: As the name suggests, system services are used for querying system related data and not for data integration as such. System services include the query service, the metadata service, and the user session service.

- **Document services**: Document services represent a business entity which, is used as an integration point. For example, *Sales order* is considered a document even though it comprises multiple tables such as *SalesTable*, *Sales line*, and many others. There are around 70 standard document services in AX which can be utilized or customized for specific integration requirements.

- **Custom services**: Microsoft introduced a new programing model in AX 2012 through which a developer can convert the X++ business logic to a service. There are several custom services delivered out-of-the-box in Dynamics AX. For example, in AX 2012 R3, the warehouse web application utilizes custom services to interact with Dynamics AX. The custom services shipped with Dynamics AX can be utilized as a reference for building other custom services.

The following table compares document services and custom services and explains some of the example scenarios to determine the appropriate programing model for your integration requirement:

	Pros	Cons	Good for	Examples
Document services	• This is based on query entity and supports the create/read/update/delete queries • This handles complex entity requirements like table relations, polymorphism, date effectivity, and so on. • All integration stack elements such as pipelines, transforms, and schema constraints can be applied to document services. • Schema validation and data validation is performed by the framework.	• Performance overhead due to complex framework • Tight coupling between the service contract and the underlying query-table schema.	• Complex document exchange.	• Create/read/update sales orders.
Custom services	• This is based on data contract defined by developers and the service contract can be controlled. • An existing business logic can be utilized and exposed as a service. • This is good for simple entity requirement. • This is good for performance. • This is good for an action triggered by third-party applications such as PO receiving/posting, packing slip, and so on.	• You need to write a lot of code to handle relations, polymorphism, date effectivity, and so on. • Schema constraints and value substitutions are not honored for custom services. • Schema validation and data validation need to be handled in code.	• This is good for mobile app integration as these are fast and simple service contracts. • This is good for read operations where output requirement is simple. • This is good for simple business entities as a service. • This is good to expose custom logic.	• Create/update/delete/submit expense report. • Approve/reject workflow.

Adapters – transport mechanism

Adapters represent the transport mechanism for message transmission between Dynamics AX and the integration application. Dynamics AX 2012 provides the following out-of-the-box adapters for message transmission:

	Adapters	Protocols	Good for
Synchronous	HTTP adapter	This uses an HTTP or HTTPs transport.	Synchronous Integration with non .NET Applications
	NetTCP adapter	This supports over the **Transmission Control Protocol (TCP)** transport. This adapter corresponds to the WCF-NetTCP binding in **Windows Communication Foundation (WCF)**.	Synchronous integration with .NET-based applications.
	Windows Azure Service Bus adapter	This enables to publish the AX 2012 services by using the Windows Azure Service Bus.	Integration with cloud applications.
Asynchronous	MSMQ adapter	This supports queuing by using message queuing as a means of transport.	Asynchronous integration using MSMQ.
	File system adapter	This supports asynchronous exchange of documents through file system directories.	Asynchronous integration using file system.

Message processing

Generally, integrations are designed either around the source system or the target system schema. This is basically called as adding system dependency to your integration. The recommendation is to keep the integration schema in a generic format. The key benefits in keeping the schema generic are as follows:

- This encapsulates the integration schema from the source or target system

- This minimizes the impact of changes (upgrade or changes) happening in the source or target system

- This increases the extensibility of integration—if another system needs to be integrated with the same data, the same schema can be used

- This eases troubleshooting and support—it would be easier to understand the generic schema from troubleshooting and support perspective than system-specific schema

AIF provides the following two powerful features to manage messages transformation and value substitutions:

- **Transforms**: This provides the ability to transform messages using XSLT or .NET code. Transforms apply only on asynchronous exchanges.

- **Pipelines**: This can be used for both synchronous and asynchronous exchanges. Pipeline supports messages transformations using the following transforms:

    ○ XSL transforms

    ○ .NET assembly transforms

    ○ Value substitution

The following diagram shows how data moves through an inbound integration port and the application of transform and pipelines:

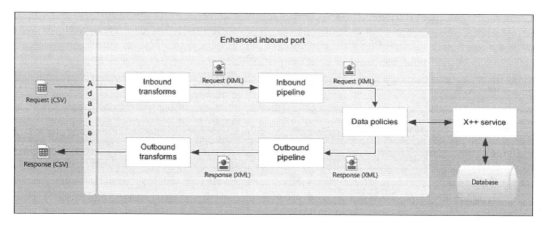

Cloud-based integration

The AIF Service Bus adapter provides a simple process for developers to build compelling companion applications, which are highly integrated with Dynamics AX. To build a cloud-based application for Dynamics AX, you need the following additional components:

- Microsoft Azure Service Bus

- Microsoft **ADFS (Active Directory Federation Services)**

To build a cloud-based application, the following are the high-level steps that a developer needs to perform the following steps:

1. Configure Windows Azure.
2. Publish AX services using AIF.
3. Develop client app to work with the Service Bus.

The next diagram shows a high-level system architecture outlining how Microsoft Azure Service Bus, ADFS, and Dynamics AX AIF interact when used together for cloud-based applications.

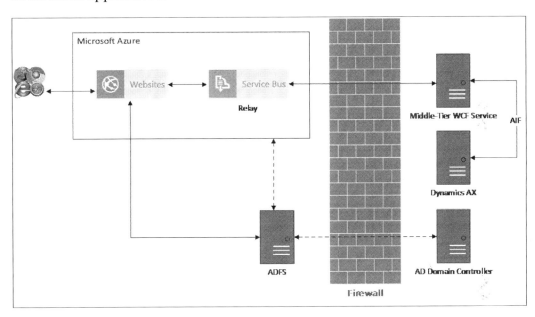

The Microsoft Dynamics AX 2012 Data Import/ Export Framework

The Microsoft Dynamics AX 2012 Data Import/Export Framework is an extension that helps you import and export data in Microsoft Dynamics AX. Primarily DIXF is designed for configuration and transaction data migration but the robust framework and extensibility makes it a perfect fit for high-volume asynchronous integration scenarios with small enhancements. Use of DIXF for data migration purpose is explained in *Chapter 5, Data Migration – Scoping through Delivery*.

The following sections explain some common integration scenarios where DIXF can be used as an integration solution.

An ad hoc manual file import/export

We often encounter integration scenarios where a particular data entity needs to be exported or imported manually by the business users. The traditional way of supporting such an integration is by writing X++ classes to import or export specific data files. DIXF provides a robust framework to handle such manual integration scenarios by extending the framework to the applicable business area. For example, a company payroll is generated by a third-party system and at the end of the month, the accounting team receives a consolidated GL entry file, which they want to import in Dynamics AX. DIXF can be used for such a requirement by considering the following scenarios:

- Create a processing group and a map source data file with the **DMFLedgerJournalEntity** table

- Modify the mapping document and setting the default data mapping, such as journal name and voucher number

- Set up the role for the processing group, and select appropriate security roles and entities

- Now, the accounting team can use the DIXF module to import the GL entry file as a general journal entry

Automated asynchronous integration

How this framework can be leveraged and extended is answered at a high level in the following three steps:

1. Extend the framework to act upon the data changes only when the source system notifies it. For this, you can customize some of the core DIXF classes to introduce this integration concept. The framework classes that need to be changed are `DMFStagingWriter` and `DMFEntityWriter`.

2. Extend the DIXF Framework to map the integration point with the processing groups and entities. Here, the DIXF processing groups and entities are to be extended to build that relationship/hierarchy.

3. Extend the DIXF to provide a feedback mechanism for the source systems to be notified of success, failures, and error logs.

The following diagram depicts the solution idea:

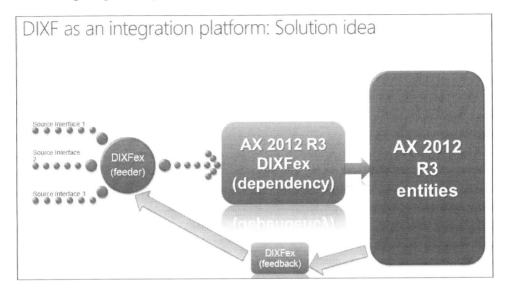

It is important to know that Microsoft is investing heavily in DIXF and it will be the key integration tool for asynchronous message processing in Microsoft Dynamics AX 7.

Master data management

Master data management (**MDM**) is a new feature in Dynamics AX 2012 R3 which can be used to synchronize master data across multiple instances of Dynamics AX 2012. MDM uses Microsoft **SQL Server Master Data Services** (**SQL MDS**) as the central data store and AX 2012 Data Import/Export Framework entities as the unit for data synchronization. MDM is preconfigured to support synchronization of the customers, vendors, employees, global address book, and product entities. You can also create customizations to support other Data Import/Export Framework entities in MDM.

The following diagram shows the high-level architecture of an MDM:

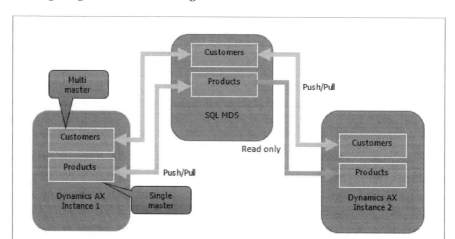

The following are the key features supported in MDM:

- **Single-master or multi-master**: Using MDM, you can configure a single-master environment, where, only one instance can push the updated data to SQL MDS, and all other instances are read-only. You can configure a multi-master environment, where all AX 2012 instances can update the master data records. In case of a conflict, SQL MDS can be used to manually resolve it.

- **Synchronization scheduling**: You can create a synchronization group to manage multiple entities and define synchronization schedules.

- **Data filtering**: Appropriate data filters can be applied on entities to filter the data which can be synchronized. For example, if you want to synchronize only a subset of vendors across multiple instances, you can define such a filter at the entity level and synchronization will happen only for the filtered dataset.

- **Customization support**: MDM can be extended to any other DMXF entity by adding a script to SQL MDS. Technically, an MDM can also be extended to synchronize master data between Dynamics AX 2012 R3 and a third-party application like e-Commerce solutions.

.NET Framework – .NET Interop

Dynamics AX can be used to consume the business logic developed in common .NET programing language. You can also build business logic in other programing languages, such as C# and Visual Basic, and use Dynamics AX objects such as tables, classes, and enums as proxy objects.

The .NET Business Connector

The .NET Business Connector enables you to build software applications that integrate with Microsoft Dynamics AX. You can access data or start a business logic. The .NET Business Connector is not a recommended integration technology for the following two reasons:

1. The .NET Business Connector is deprecated from AX 7 the future version of Dynamics AX.

2. The .NET business connector uses RPC as a communication protocol which is considered *chatty*, and it is not suitable for high-volume integrations.

The third-party integration solution

There are several vendors that provide specialized integration solutions with Dynamics AX such as EDI solutions, sales tax, and AP automation. These integration solutions typically utilize AIF or other integration technologies supported in Dynamics AX and extend the solution to implement common industry integration points with various products. The following table lists a sample of third-party integration solutions:

Vendor	Category	Specialized use
Data Masons	EDI	**End-to-End EDI solution**: This includes predefined EDI maps, data transformation, Integrations with trading partners, Integration with Dynamics AX.
Vertex, CCH, Avalara	Integration with Sales tax solution	This integrates between Dynamics AX and tax solution, transactions like sales order inquiry, invoice posting, project invoices, free text invoices, and so on.
Sandler Kahne Software	Banking	This includes lockbox, wire, bank reconciliation with banking institutions.
Red Maple	Credit card	This includes enhanced credit card services and integration with payment processors.

 These are not necessarily the recommended solutions, but are just a few examples of the options available at the time of publication.

Connector for Microsoft Dynamics

Connector for Microsoft Dynamics is an integration tool for connecting the Microsoft CRM application with any Microsoft Dynamics ERP system. The following diagram shows the high-level architecture of Connector for Microsoft Dynamics. As shown in the diagram, Connector for Microsoft Dynamics is a standalone integration component and provides connectivity between Dynamics CRM and the Dynamics ERP system through web services:

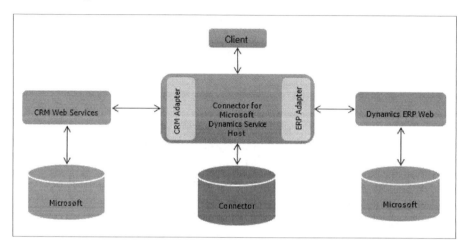

Connector for Dynamics, along with Dynamics AX, provides the following integration entities out of the box. Additional entities can be added though customization:

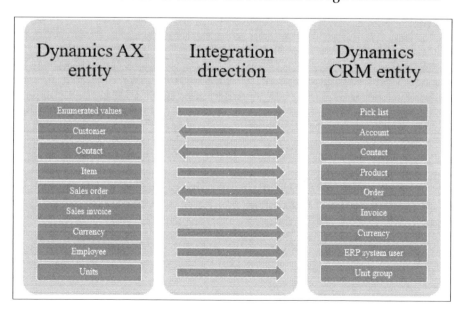

The following are the key features of the Connector for Microsoft Dynamics:

- Robust integration
- Easy installation and configuration
- Scheduling
- Logging
- Retries
- Support for customizations in source and destination systems
- SDK available for creating adapters to and from third-party systems

Integration design and development

Once you have all the detailed integration requirements, an integration specialist works with business analysts, developers, and system administrators to create a detailed design. The following topics in this section explain the process of designing an integration solution.

Selecting the right integration technology

It is important to select the best suited integration technology for each of the identified integration requirements. The following table compares integration technologies to help you determine the suitable integration tool as per your requirements:

	Pros	Cons	Good for	Examples
AIF	<ul><li>Robust framework</li><li>Out-of-the-box services</li><li>Administration and monitoring</li><li>Scalable</li><li>Secure</li></ul>	<ul><li>Framework overhead</li></ul>	<ul><li>Document-based exchanges</li><li>Transaction processing across system</li></ul>	<ul><li>Create/update sales orders</li><li>Create customers</li><li>Send Product details</li><li>Send Price details</li><li>Send AP payment data</li></ul>
DIXF	<ul><li>Robust framework</li><li>Future async integration methodology for dynamics AX</li></ul>	<ul><li>Needs extension to automate and administer the process</li></ul>	<ul><li>High-volume integrations</li><li>Master data synchronization</li></ul>	<ul><li>GL Integration</li><li>Expense report import</li><li>Master data sync</li></ul>

	Pros	Cons	Good for	Examples
.NET Framework	• Utilizes the power of .NET programing languages		• Add on solutions • Integration with .NET apps	• Transformation components • Integrating with specialized SDK such as OCR*
Business Connector	• Exposes Dynamics AX business logic • Utilizes the AX security framework	• Phasing out • Uses the TCP communication protocol	• Application extension	• Application for handheld devices
Third-party Integration Solution	• Specialized end-to-end solution	• Special scenario only	• Specialized third-party applications	• Sales tax • AP automation • EDI Integration • Banking • Credit card

Developing a high-level conceptual design

Developing a high-level conceptual design diagram is important to explain the different integration points and directions. The following diagram shows an example of a conceptual integration design between Dynamics AX and a B2B e-commerce application:

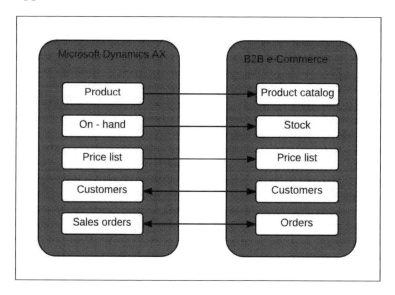

The following table explains the integration points shown in the preceding diagram and the recommended integration technologies:

Integration point	Description	Recommended solution
Product	Products and attributes will be stored in Dynamics AX and synced nightly with an e-commerce application as a flat file.	• DIXF • AIF using file system adapter
Product on-hand	Product on-hand needs to be shared with the e-commerce application in real-time.	AIF Web Service
Price list	The price list will be mastered in AX and will be updated on the e-commerce application on a nightly basis as a flat file.	• DIXF export • AIF document services using file system adapter
Customers	The customer can be created or updated either on the e-commerce website (such as address) or updated in DAX (such as credit limit) and synced in both the systems.	• DIXF – master data management • AIF document services using create, update, read operations
Sales orders	Sales orders will be created in the e-commerce application and created or updated to AX. Sales order status updates such as shipment confirmation, invoices, and payment application need to be synced to the web application.	• AIF web services • AIF document services using Queue-based adapter such as MSMQ

Defining field mapping

Defining field-level mapping for each integration point includes data type, field length, applicable values, and validation logic for each field. The ensuing table shows customer integration between Dynamics AX and an e-commerce application as an example:

AX Field name	Data type	Requirement	Default value	E-Commerce Field	Description
CustTable.AccountNum	NVARCHAR(20)	Mandatory	Number sequence	Account.Id	This is a unique identifier for the customer record
CustTable.CustGroup	NVARCHAR(10)	Mandatory	Web	NA	This is used to define accounting setup in Dynamics AX
DirParty.Language	NVARCHAR(10)	Mandatory	en-us	NA	This stores the customer's language
DirParty.Name	NVARCHAR(60)	Mandatory		Account.Name	This stores the customer's name
DirPartyPostalAddress.IsPrimary	Boolean	Optional	Yes	NA	This is a Boolean value where it is confirmed whether this address customer's primary address.
DirPartyPostalAddress.CountryRegionId	NVARCHAR(3)	Mandatory	USA	Account.Country	This stores the customer's country code
DirPartyPostalAddress.State	NVARCHAR(20)	Mandatory		Account.StateCode	This stores the customer's state code
DirPartyPostalAddress.County	NVARCHAR(20)	Optional		Account.County	This stores the customer's county code
DirPartyPostalAddress.City	NVARCHAR(60)	Optional		Account.CityName	This stores the customer's city
DirPartyPostalAddress.ZipCode	NVARCHAR(10)	Mandatory		Account.PostalCode	This stores the customer's zip code
DirPartyPostalAddress.Street	NVARCHAR(250)	Mandatory		Account.Address 1 + Account.Address 2	This stores the customer's street address

Development, configuration, and testing

The next step would be to do the required development, configuration, and testing the integration. The following are some helpful tips for developing integration solution:

- Utilize the existing code and functionalities for integration; extend as needed.
- Keep the message format generic as far as possible, so that the same integration point can be used with other applications, if needed. Use the XSLT transformation or other transformation tools to transform the messages in an appropriate system schema.
- Build an error handling and notification mechanism to monitor the failure. Keep a closed loop; there should be a mechanism to notify other applications of the success or failure of message processing.
- Develop the test data and a unit test scenario; perform unit testing before end-to-end integration testing.
- Develop test simulation, if possible, for system testing. This can save a lot of time during the end-to-end testing.
- Perform load testing by generating a large set of data. Many times, integration solution fails on the production load as the development or test environment does not have sufficient data to simulate the production load.
- Prepare a test plan including the positive and negative scenarios. Test all exceptions and boundary scenarios. Test the end-to-end business process on integration data to avoid any fallback impact in the production environment.
- Develop a security and deployment plan for integration solutions and test deployment and security in the test environment before moving to production.

Best practices and recommendations

Here are a few considerations to keep in mind while designing your integration solution for Dynamics AX:

1. Simplify the overall architecture and try to reduce the number of integrations between applications wherever possible. It is one of the areas that cause recurring issues in production.

2. Define clearly the master system for each data element, even though you may have it stored at multiple places. In some cases, this may have to be defined at the field level. For example, a customer master is stored in CRM and Dynamics AX as well. CRM might be the master for all the customer information except credit limit.

3. Ideally, you should avoid duplication of data across multiple systems, although in some cases you cannot avoid it for business reasons or for systems to work. For example, customer records are required in both, the CRM system and Dynamics AX. However, you can opt not to integrate the CRM-centric customer information that may not be needed in Dynamics AX.

4. Understand and document business SLAs for each integration; think through the impact in extreme situations.

> One of my customers had the inventory getting refreshed into their e-commerce system every 2 minutes. It was okay until the Black Friday weekend. During that 2 minute window, they oversold a product that was being sold below its cost (they only wanted to get rid of the on-hand stock). However, the customer ended up buying more to fulfill the additional orders that were received due to the delays in inventory updates. It is important to understand SLAs and the business impact while designing integrations.

5. Using the AIF adapter framework, you can create a custom adapter. Several Dynamics AX customers use custom adapters like FTP, EDI, SQL adapter, and TIBCO adapters used with the AX AIF framework. Our recommendation is to build any such custom adapters if that suits your integration requirement better than these out-of-the-box adapters.

Summary

In this chapter, we learned about the tools and techniques for integration planning and design. We started with understanding the common integration scenarios on ERP implementations and gathering integration requirements. Subsequently, we learned about the available integration technologies in the Dynamics AX application and sample scenarios for recommended use. Depending on your requirements, there are several integration options to choose from. However, AIF is the most commonly used integration option. In the end, we learned about the common industry best practices and recommendations related to integration planning.

In the next chapter, we will learn about another complex but underestimated area of the ERP implementation project—data migration.

Data Migration – Scoping through Delivery

Data migration is usually the most complex and underestimated area of any ERP implementation. This chapter makes you understand data migration requirements, managing the data migration scope, identifying the tools and techniques for data migration, and data validation.

The following topics are covered in this chapter:

- Understanding data requirements and challenges
  - Defining what data needs to be migrated
  - Source systems involved

- Managing the scope of data migration
  - Questions to ask during scoping
  - Leading data migration requirements
  - The battle of history

- Tools, techniques, and development considerations
  - Data extraction and cleansing
  - Using the data migration framework
  - Building a repetitive process

- Data validation
  - Testing scripts
  - Engaging business for validation
  - Using migrated data during testing

Managing scope – simplifying data migration through rightsizing the scope

Rightsizing the scope is the first step towards successful data migration. Often, customers have either not considered data migration at all or have unreasonable expectations regarding the requirements. Even if the original sales proposal has explicit data migration requirements that have been identified, many of the project team members and stakeholders may not be aware of what was specified or may not agree to the mentioned scope. Hence, it is important to facilitate a scoping exercise with the project team and document the mutually agreed results.

The following section covers a few tips for the scoping of data migration and educating the business stakeholders.

Questions to ask during the scoping exercise

The following set of questions can be asked during the scoping exercise:

1. What do I need to keep the business running? Define the business goals with that question in mind, and then approach the issue of what information needs to be migrated to meet these goals or what solutions can be provided to meet the goal without migrating the data. For example, I need to be able to collect my receivables and run aging for customers—that's the business goal. This means you need to only migrate Open AR for the customers along with the due date.

2. Is there an alternate way to live without bringing the existing data over? Reporting out of legacy system or a data warehouse and defining a manual process, if it is going to be used only for inquiries over a short period of time, are some potential alternatives.

3. Every record that needs to be migrated comes at a cost. Is this cost justified? It's not a question of whether it can be done. Is it worth it?

4. Do you trust the data present in the legacy systems? Do you want the new system to have the same issues that you are trying to solve in the current system?

5. How many records are involved? Ensure that the ball park numbers of record counts are defined for each area during scoping/requirements (for example, 4 million products, 200,000 customers, 2000 open orders, and so on). This will help you select the right tools.

6. How often will you be asked to retrieve this data?

7. Identify the business needs clearly. You can avoid the cascading effect and carve out the critical pieces of data that you need frequently, to limit the scope. For example, just migrating the open balance of each customer invoice rather than trying to bring the complete line item detail requires less effort. If a customer service needs the invoice line detail to research a customer issue that happens once a month on an average, the detail generally would not be worth the effort to try to migrate it.

With one of the best CIOs that I worked with, negotiations always started at point zero. This strategy worked well to condense the huge data migration requirements that the business had come up with, to a minimum of only what they needed (only open records).

Leading the data migration requirements sessions

Do your homework on the proposed data migration and validate your assumptions with the business rather than asking the open ended question "What data do you want to migrate?" The following table is an example that you can use as a starting point to help validate the decisions to be agreed upon in a data migration requirements session:

Functional area	Guidance for scoping
General ledger history	Prior years' history: periodic balances for 2 years
	Current year — till date, periodic balances
Customers	All the active customers (and addresses)
	Has performed a transaction in the last 18 months or has an open balance or has any open sales orders
Vendors	All the active vendors (and addresses)
	Has performed a transaction in the last 18 months or has an open balance or has any open purchase orders
Products and prices	All the active products and prices
	Products created in the last six months or has stock in-hand or has open purchase, sales or production orders or was sold in the last 12 months
	Prices: All active and future prices for customers and vendors (Trade agreements and Sales / Purchase agreements in Dynamics AX terminology)

Functional area	Guidance for scoping
Open AP	Migrate all open documents—invoices, payments, debit notes
	Key fields: Vendor ID, open amount, description, due date, invoice number, document number, document date (original invoice date), method of payment, PO/reference, or any other information that you need in order to pay the vendor
	You should be able to run vendor aging and pay vendors (1099 reporting considerations)
Open AR	Migrate all open documents—Invoices, payments, credit notes
	Key fields: Customer ID, open amount, description, invoice number, original date, due date, method of payment, customer PO number, and reference to sales order number
	You should be able to run customer/AR aging and collect payments from the customers
Inventory (On Hand)	Migrate on-hand inventory for each product by dimensions
	Are your product's numbers changing? (That would mean changing labels in the warehouse)
	Cost for each lot and dates for batch numbers
	Review the impact on inventory costing
Open Orders	Open sales orders and open purchase orders—orders that are not yet delivered
	Discuss the returns (you may need to refer to the old system for a short period of time)
	Orders that are delivered but yet not invoiced
Bank Balances	Last-reconciled balance
	Unreconciled transactions
Fixed Assets	**The active assets**: Assets that are in possession and in the books
	Key values: Fixed asset number, acquisition price, accumulated depreciation till date, remaining periods, acquisition date/ put-in-service date, date depreciation last run, serial number, assigned to, dimensions, and so on
	Do you need to keep track of tax book values?

Additionally, you can leverage the Dynamics AX data migration requirements spreadsheet within Microsoft Sure Step to identify and plan to migrate your data. This spreadsheet is intended for the consulting team to use internally. However, it can also be used as a tool to facilitate the data migration requirements gathering and can subsequently be used throughout the project lifecycle to confirm whether each migration data element has been identified, and that the process has been defined, developed, and tested. The following table image shows an example of the columns and data that are important for the scoping session. Additional columns help you manage the development, testing, and final move to the production system:

Functional Description ▼	Master or Transactional ▼	Approach ▼	Target	Source(s) ▼
Open vendor invoices	Transactional	DIXF	Load data into Accounts Payable > Journals > Invoice Journal > (type of invoice journal) and post	Legacy system: vendor name, convert to new AX number, 1099 data
Vendors	Master	DIXF	Accounts Payable > Common forms > Vendors > All Vendors Procurement and Sourcing > Common Forms > Vendors > All Vendors	Legacy sytem: Vendor name, address, terms for vendors paid in last two years
Customers	Master	DIXF	Accounts Receivable > Common forms > Customers > All Customers Sales and Marketing > Common Forms > Customers > All Customers	CRM system: customers with open orders; name, address, terms, sales channel

The battle of history

As I stated at the beginning of this chapter, business stakeholders often expect their shiny, new Dynamics AX system to have their historical data from their legacy system. Anything less would mean that they have less information now rather than more, right? Part of the data migration planning process is educating the business stakeholders on the cost of that mentality and focusing the business on the information, which is driving business decisions, servicing customers, and providing analysis.

In principle, you should avoid migrating historical transactions, such as posted sales invoices, posted purchase orders, individual general ledger transactions, inventory transactions history, and so on. The effort to cleanse and transform the data for Dynamics AX is an expensive proposition and takes the resources away from the goal of designing and developing improved processes within Dynamics AX. More importantly, most of this data doesn't really drive the business decisions or even worse, it provides inaccurate views of the business due to bad data and/or processes from the legacy system.

Certainly, the historical transactional data is needed for either regulatory, business analysis, or customer satisfaction reasons. However, there are other solutions available rather than agreeing to migrate the legacy data into Dynamics AX tables. Some cheaper solutions that I have used in the past to satisfy customer needs around history are given as follows, and can be used depending on the size of the dataset and the requirements around how the data will be used:

- Run the reports and save them in a shared folder or on a SharePoint site as a PDF file. This will be useful for reports that must be kept for regulatory purposes such as financial statements.

- Export the data to Excel or Access to a read-only folder that only specific users can access. Smaller datasets where you want to query, filter, or sort the data in different ways are a good match for this.

- Leverage an existing data warehouse to meet the reporting/analysis requirements.

- Set security on the legacy system to read-only and do historical lookups there. Make sure that support contracts and an exit strategy are part of any discussions around this option so that the customer is not paying for multiple systems indefinitely. This is a good option for a stable legacy system where support is still available (without paying a hefty annual support price) and also helps ease the transaction for the legacy system support vendor.

- Create new AX tables that replicate legacy data tables and pull in the data without having to do a mapping or cleansing process. Reports or inquiries can be developed over this data, which is often cheaper than the programming required to clean and normalize the data to AX requirements.

The design and development phase

During the design and development phase, you will need to work on data migration actively. The key steps during this phase include data mapping and transformation for the identified migration elements, creation of tests and a go-live plan for migration as well as developing the scripts, templates, and test datasets for migration.

Data mapping and transformation

The following are the key steps for managing the data mapping of the source and target systems:

- Select source systems to use for migration. If the data is stored at multiple places in a legacy system, you should pick the cleanest one to extract a copy. Consider the update timings in the source and add dependencies in the go-live plan to get the source data updated prior to starting the extraction.

- Define field mapping between the legacy systems and Dynamics AX, along with any transformations that need to happen between the extracts and the import processes.

- Identify the areas that need data cleansing; have the data cleansing efforts started early on. Define rules or have them addressed in the source systems (for example, bad addresses, phone numbers, and so on).

Planning the data migration

During the design and development phase of the project, you should develop the overall plan for migrating the identified data elements. The following is a list of items to consider when developing your plan:

- **The data migration environment**: Plan for an environment to run data migrations iteratively. You don't want the test environment to be messed with every week, while the data migration team is still trying to stabilize the data migration processes.

- Plan for multiple cycles of data migration that are a few weeks apart. This allows time to validate the data, fix issues, and improve the performance of the migration processes.

  - Business resources will be required to help extract and validate the data for each cycle. They may need to help cleanse the data if you run into issues from the legacy data.

  - IT resources will be required to extract, import, and validate data. It is a good idea to train and utilize junior resources in the data conversion execution process as it is an iterative process and have experienced resources to focus on improving the process based on the feedback received from data validation.

  - Data quality in the source system has a huge impact on the number of data migration iterations that you have to perform during tests.

- Complete a full data migration prior to starting system integration testing, UAT, and training. These migrations should be performed by following the data migration process documentation, and the time for each step needs to be recorded. As part of this process, have the migrated data validated by the business prior to starting the tests in these environments.

- Come up with iterative/automated processes, which include data extraction from the legacy systems. This makes the cycle time for data migration shorter, improves the quality, and provides consistent results (for extraction, you may be lucky to get away with the reports that the business uses. For example, if a business uses a detailed AR aging report, you can use that report as an input for migration rather than building a separate job for data extraction).

- The team should record the timing for each process and arrange dependencies and processes that can be run in parallel. As noted earlier, using the Sure Step data migration requirements spreadsheet can aid in documenting this.

- Document the migration process end-to-end, from data extraction and intermediate validation to migration (the development team that writes the code should not be the one executing it). With a documented process, you can engage the junior team members to execute the repetitive data migration processes. You can save the senior resources to work on other parts of the project.

- **Visual communication for stakeholders**: Demonstrate a visual presentation of the data migration process to communicate its progress.

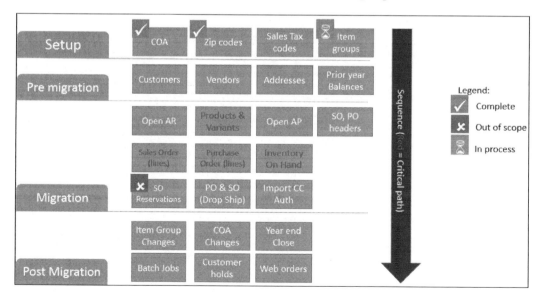

Selecting the tools for data migration

In this section, we will talk about the most commonly used tools including **Data Import/Export Framework (DIXF)** shipped with Dynamics AX. Microsoft has made huge investments in the Data Import/Export Framework, and this has been a big step in solving the challenges in data migration. Although the introduction of stable and rich features in DIXF has reduced the need for other tools for migration, we will discuss several options for migration.

How do I select the right tool?

There are several factors that you should consider:

- Do you have something to reuse (integrations, or import builds for the project)?
- How much is the data volume? Hundreds, thousands, or millions of records?
- What kind of validation or transformation is required?
- What is the format of the source data? CSV, SQL, Flat files, and the like?
- How much downtime is available for migration? This would drive the investments that you need to make in building additional features rather than using the standard tools that are available.
- What is the trade-off between validations and import time, and the quality of the source data?

Data migration versus data entry

It is often easier to simply enter the data than to migrate it, provided that the dataset to be migrated contains only a few hundred records that can be entered in a timely manner and with relatively few errors. Part of the consideration of whether to manually load the data is the required timing—if you can do it ahead of time or post-release, manually entering the data is a good method. If the data load needs to take place during the downtime and on a critical path, then it could be tricky.

Data import features developed on the project

Going forward, you might have to use custom features for imports like the general journal upload and fixed assets import. Try to leverage similar import programs for data migration.

The Data Import/Export Framework

The Data Import/Export Framework (DIXF) is an extension module to help export and import data in Dynamics AX. DIXF is now an essential part of Dynamics AX R3. It can be installed explictly and used with Dynamics AX R2 and the RTM release as well.

The common pattern for the use of DIXF is shown in the following diagram:

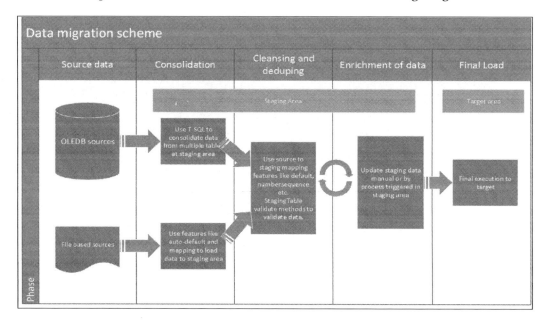

The framework is commonly used in the following areas:

- Master data, open orders, on-hand inventory, and balances
- Moderate to high numbers of records (a few thousand to a couple of hundred thousand records)
- Low customization

The framework is not recommended in the following areas:

- Highly customized areas
- A huge volume of data (then you need to bypass the Dynamics AX business logic)

Terminologies

Let's first understand the common terms used with DIXF. They are explained as follows:

- **Source**: This is the external data source from where we want to import data into Microsoft Dynamics AX 2012.

    ◦ **File**: Text (delimited and fixed width), Microsoft Excel, and XML

    ◦ **ODBC**: Database , Microsoft Excel, Microsoft Access, and so on

- **Staging**: This is the intermediary table inside Microsoft Dynamics AX 2012.
- **Target**: This is the entity inside Microsoft Dynamics AX 2012 for which we want to import data from an external data source. For example, customer, vendor, and so on.

Architecture

The following diagram shows the architecture of the Data Import/Export Framework. It can basically be understood as a **Source** | **Staging** | **Target** process:

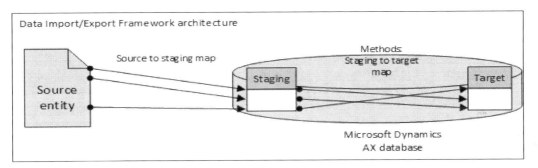

The Data Import/Export Framework creates a staging table for each entity in the Microsoft Dynamics AX database where the target table resides. Data that is being migrated is first moved to the staging table. There you can verify the data, and perform any cleanup or conversion that is required. You can then move the data to the target table or export it.

The import/export process

The following diagram shows the steps that are required to import or export data in Microsoft Dynamics AX:

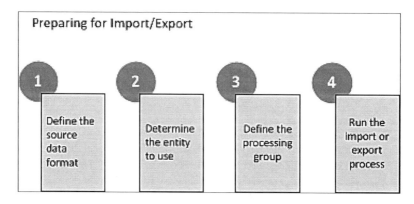

1. Determine the source of the data to export or import, and create a source data format for the data. For export, the source is **AX**. For import, you can use any of the following sources:

    ○ **AX**: This imports data from another Microsoft Dynamics AX instance

    ○ **ODBC**: This imports data from other databases such as Microsoft SQL Server or Microsoft Access

    ○ **File**: This imports data from a fixed-width or delimited text file, XML file, or Microsoft Excel file

2. Determine the entity to associate with the data. This entity can either be the source of the export data or the target for the import data. You can also use an existing entity or create a custom entity. There are 150 out-of-the box entities and the list is increasing continuously.

3. Determine the entities that should be imported or exported together, and put all these entities in a processing group. A processing group is a set of entities that must be processed in a sequence, or that can logically be grouped together. The entities in a processing group are exported together, or they are imported together from source to staging and then from staging to target. In a processing group, you also associate each entity with a source data format.

4. Use the processing group options to either import or export data.

5. For import, you first import the data to a staging table where you can clean or transform the data as required. You should validate that the data appears accurate and that the reference data is mapped correctly. You then migrate the data from the staging table to the target table. You should validate that the entity appears accurate in the target table.

A summary of key features

- Compare and copy entity data across legal entities.

- **Entity types**: The different types of entities are entity, composite entity, and flat table.

- **Mapper control**: This allows flexible mapping, supports complex transformations, and the *m:n* cardinality between the target entities as shown in the following diagram:

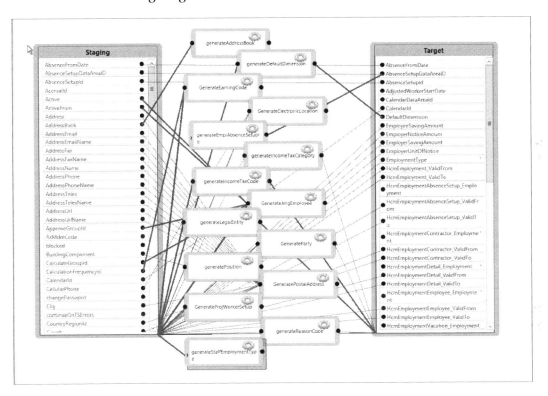

- Parallel execution support from staging to target using task bundling.

- Folder as input for running periodic import with functionality to move the files to different folders (in-process, error, and completed).

- **Error handling**: This includes skipping error rows and errors stored in XML files.

- Merging data into a single-source column and split during transformation, for example, financial dimensions.
- Multiple source columns can be used to create records in multiple tables, for example, an address book.
- Use Data Import/Export Framework as an **Application Integration Framework (AIF)** service to export data to a file. This feature will allow you to leverage the data migration code for ongoing integrations.
- Set-based support from staging to target.
- Default value support.
- Number sequence support.
- External key mapping support.
  - Source to target in a single step
  - Multiple AOS support

AIF

This section describes the usage and description of AIF in context of data migration:

The Application Integration Framework is generally used in the following areas:

- For data from highly structured systems (XML Formatting)
- Has existing out-of-the-box data inputs

The framework is not recommended in the following situations:

- Large data sets
- Complex integration

The features of AIF

This section describes the out-of-the-box features of Dynamics AX:

- AIF can import many similar records, and repeat the same import at regular intervals, or it can be used for ongoing integrations
- Value mapping and error handling features provided by AIF can be leveraged
- Document services must be customized if the underlying tables and entities have been customized
- AIF uses the Dynamics AX business logic and validation

Custom X++

Custom X++ is commonly used for customizations or customized actions. For example, applying cash discount schedules to specific accounts after migrating vendor invoices or applying custom payment schedules to break the due dates of Open AR records. It is also used for large datasets to be migrated from SQL—a need to release 10 million product variants as part of migration.

It is not useful for entities that are supported by DIXF and can handle the large amount of volume.

 DIXF can help you avoid building a custom code for migration.

Describing custom X++

As the name suggests, you need to write a custom code to import it from a file and apply business rules for the import. In some cases, writing custom code/jobs to import SQL tables and CSV/Flat files for custom processes may be an easier and a faster way to approach data migration.

As this is a custom code, you have more control (and responsibility) over the number of validations you want to add or bypass depending on the pre-validation of source data; standard Dynamics AX business logic does not apply to your data.

In projects that need millions of records to be migrated, you may not be able to afford going through the Dynamics AX business logic. Hence, you need to pick a custom route. You can use the power of SQL to speed up the performance, directly load data into Dynamics AX, and use custom code in Dynamics AX to further process the data. For example, importing data in the staging table using direct SQL statements (you can work around *RecId* assignment by reserving *RecId* for the custom staging table through X++ and writing the X++ class, which can be multi-threaded for further processing of data).

To use such an approach, you need a deep understanding of the Dynamics AX processes, its data structure, and how data flows across tables.

Excel add-in

It is commonly used for the following purposes:

- Spreadsheet-based data, mostly setup tables (for example, payment terms and dimensions)
- Available document services for AIF

- It is useful for a small or medium number of records, where performance is not a concern (it is useful for a few hundred records; for more records, the process would be very slow)

An Excel add-in is not useful for larger datasets.

Describing an Excel add-in

Data is validated using the business logic in Dynamics AX. End users can use this method, and it is an opportunity to engage them in the system setup. The following screenshot shows the payment terms set up by uploading data (publishing) through the Excel add-in:

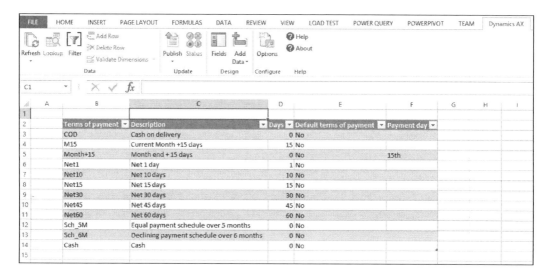

Data migration execution tips

This section includes the tips and tricks based on data migration experiences.

Initial templates for business

Define template spreadsheets for common data migration scenarios and collect sample data from the business early on. Use this data for CRP. This will help to identify problems sooner and eliminate surprises later.

Extracting source data into SQL tables

If possible, extract the source data into SQL tables. It is easier to clean and transform data using SQL queries rather than manipulating data in flat files. Data validation can be done directly on the source staging table to avoid repeated failure due to loading bad data and wasting time.

Never rename/repurpose fields

Even if you may never need a particular field, the future versions of AX may eliminate or add extra functionality to that field. Creating new fields in AX is easy.

Considering premigration steps

Come up with an approach to convert the bulky data pieces ahead of time. For example, in a project where we had to migrate 10 million products, we migrated most of them a week earlier and ran them concurrently for the one week period for product maintenance. This reduced our downtime over the release weekend.

Considering postmigration steps

You may have data elements that are not required at go-live (fixed assets migration); try to push them to the following weekend.

Changing SQL to simple recovery mode

Set SQL to the Simple Recovery mode for faster performance. Make sure to set it back when completed.

Multithreading and max DOP

Multithreading can help you speed up the process by executing it in multiple threads. However, it can degrade the performance if you add more threads than what your SQL or AOS can handle. Many times, the **Max DOP** (**Maximum Degree of Parallelism**) setting on SQL needs to be changed to allow multiple CPUs per thread in order to get an optimal number of threads that can be executed in parallel.

Index and statistics maintenance

Consider index and statistics maintenance after a bulk load of master data to speed up the dependent processes. If you have indexes that are slowing down your inserts, you will want to disable them during bulk load of data.

Disabling the AX logging

Turn off all database logging in AX; it will significantly slow down the process.

Considering SQL updates on migrated data

Sometimes, it is easier to perform a basic data migration of standard data in AX and then use SQL to update the values. Ensure that your scripts and steps are well documented.

The SQL import – through caution and expertise

Sometimes, it is faster to import high-volume data directly into SQL. You can save your time by bypassing the Dynamics AX business logic, so you only need to run validations on data quality. Generation of *RecID* in Dynamics AX can be tricky. However, it can be done with resources that are well versed with the Dynamics AX architecture (a number sequence is maintained in the *system sequences* table for each table ID), and which can draw boundaries between importing through SQL and running through the X++ business logic.

Managing configurations

This is another important area that can easily go out of control if not managed well. You need to have a good change-tracking mechanism for configuring the changes and the resources responsible for a specific area that are making changes in your golden (stage) environment.

Once you have the golden environment set up, take a backup of your database with all the configuration (premigration) data that can be simply restored every time you start a new migration run. If you have the liberty to set up a production environment ahead of time, all the configurations can be made in production. Bring the production data into the migration environment and run migration tests on it. If you cannot set it up and use the production environment for configurations, create the golden box and use it.

Configuration management simplified with DIXF

You can create a template legal entity and use it for setting up new legal entities. You can also copy configurations from one environment to another:

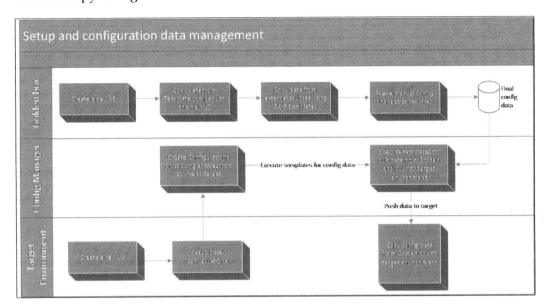

Copy company functionality from AX 2009, and prior versions are no longer available in AX 2012.

Reviewing and deciding on the configuration

There are certain configurations that you need to review carefully on the project, and make decisions for these configurations considering the cross-functional requirements. These are configurations where there is no going back, like the product dimension group, storage dimension group, tracking dimensions, inventory model group, and so on. Each checkbox is going to have a great impact on the outcome, and once you have transactions that take place, you can't change these selections easily. These configurations impact the financials and supply chain aspects, and that is why you need cross-functional reviews.

Data validation

With every iteration of data migration, you need to get progressively better. To achieve this, data validation needs to be a well-documented repeatable process and needs to start early on. Do not wait until the deployment stage to engage the business. Here are a few tips to make this process smoother:

Define validation test cases for both the business and IT validation.

- **IT validation**: This generally includes verifying record counts, totals, and referential integrity by running tools such as Consistency check (Consistency check is a tool available in Dynamics AX. It validates and fixes referential integrity issues. It can be found in System Administration module, periodic section). You need to acquire different types of validation scripts; it is a good idea to have scripts for validating extracts, if there was an issue in extraction, you can catch it sooner in the process.

- **Business validation**: The business owns the data, and it is critical to have the business involved to start data validation early on.

    ◦ Run the reports that the business is going to use. For example, comparing the AR aging reports between the old and the new system, verifying financial statements, and so on.

    ◦ Review the data on screen and use it in the processes for which the data is migrated. For example, running a check-run to verify whether you can pay your vendors and print correct information on payment advices.

    ◦ **Usability of data for future transactions and reporting**: validate your business processes that use the migrated data. Use migrated data in consequent rounds of CRP.

A classic example of a data migration issue in projects

Here's background. The project required migrating over 7 years' worth of transactional data (sales order, returns, and so on) over 7 years. The CFO was adamant about migrating the data and wanted it to report, provide year-on-year analysis, and undertake returns processing (they sometimes allowed returns up to 7 years).

The following were the challenges:

- The data quality in the legacy was bad (it always is due to bugs in the past and so on. This is the reason the company was moving to the new system).

- Another challenge was selling the solution. Even though the CFO was pushing for a high volume of data migration, nobody was pushing back with the facts of the legacy data, the impact of doing such a migration, and the ways to meet his requirements. Just refusing to migrate so much data is not enough; you need to convince your leaders. I would rather spend more time on this part to get it right than spending the humongous amount of effort required on data migration (and still come up with a messy outcome).

The impact on the project was as follows:

- Many rounds of data migration had to be done (more than ten). Each time the team discovered more issues in the legacy data; it was a painful, iterative process.

- The overall impact on the schedule and budget was that the data migration stream consumed most of the key resources on the project. It also had an impact on the overall schedule/budget as the data migration was on a critical path.

- A lot of data migration bugs were discovered during testing, and this slowed down the process. (In some cases, they had to redo the entire migration before moving further with the testing).

- After the release, new issues surfaced in many cases while processing the returns. It created a lot of noise in the returns process and impacted customer satisfaction. Moreover, it resulted in additional work for the accounting team, which had to analyze and post journal entries for the errors in the returns processing (accountants can fix anything through journal entries, but they shouldn't have to).

The customer decided to go on to the next version after a painful and expensive lesson learned.

- This time, only open orders, and no history from the legacy data, were migrated.

- Reports from the previous system, the data warehouse, were used to report on the legacy data.

- We also came up with a manual process to review the initial order in legacy prior to processing any returns as the volume of returns was not very high, and it went down significantly as time went by.

- Unfortunately, the customer had to spend money to do it all over again; rework can be avoided by keeping it simple the first time.

Summary

In this chapter, you learned the process of effectively scoping data migration, the planning process, data validation, and the tools available for effective data migration.

In the next chapter, you will learn about reporting and BI.

6
Reporting and BI

Usually, BI/Reporting is considered as an afterthought in ERP implementations. However, this is one of the most important outcomes of the project. Executives will be looking for reports to run their business.

Oftentimes, the business asks, "Where is my report"? And the answer that they get is, "Data is there…". That's not enough; you need to deliver reports or information in a form that the business can use. It's not uncommon to hear business leaders complain, "We are flying blind" due to the lack of reports or accuracy of reports. With cut-throat competition against low-margin businesses, it's important to have real-time visibility of the business for the respective business owners to react quickly in the changing business environment.

In this chapter, we will cover the following topics:

- Gathering BI and reporting requirements
- The many reporting tools available
- Mapping reports and identifying gaps
- Custom report development

Gathering BI and reporting requirements

It is important to start working on reports and the BI stream early on, along with the rest of the functional areas. Most of the time, reporting is not addressed as part of the analysis state. However, one of the most important goals of a new ERP implementation is to get better and real-time visibility into the business.

To start this process, work with the business to compile a list of reports—dashboards, kpis, operational reports—that are currently used to run the business. Document their use and the actions that are driven by those reports. Also, spend time to learn about the vision of the business leaders and the information that they would like to see, which they don't have currently. A combination of the current and future states would help you define the BI/reporting road map.

When gathering and documenting reporting requirements, make sure you ask the business users the following questions so that you can evaluate the need and be prepared to offer alternate solutions. Most of the time in projects, business users want to see all the reports that they have in their old system in the same format:

- Who's using the report?
    - Be mindful of your customer's needs.
    - Focus on the end-user experience. The audience would drive your delivery methods.

- What information is needed?
    - Avoid information overload
    - Find the right balance

- What actions are driven by this report?
    - Engage them with interactive solutions
    - Use reports to help drive navigation

- Is this report even necessary in the new system?
- Can we consolidate the multiple reports?

As part of requirement gathering, collect report samples that are used in the current system as well as manually generated reports. This will help in mapping standard AX reports and in identifying the gaps.

All the reports identified should be documented and categorized with the report name, the type of report, whether the report is internal or an externally used report, and how the report will be supported in AX. Remember, "No longer needed with the new system" is viable and, often, the preferred solution! The Sure Step Gap/Fit spreadsheet can be used to help document the reports just as with the other requirements.

Pay extra attention to mapping each column and formatting external-facing reports, such as invoice templates, customer statement, extracts going to banks, and so on. Invoice templates may show different information based on the product lines, customers, and so on.

The following table shows the categorization of sample reports based on their use and importance:

Type of report	Sub type	Examples
Operational	External	Purchase order
		Sales packing slip
		Sales invoice
		AP check printing
	Internal	GL trial balance
		Segment P&L
		Open purchase orders
		Purchase receiving log
		Vendor payment history
		Shipped not invoiced
		Accrued Purchases
Statutory and financial reports		Balance sheet
		P&L
		Tax payable
		1099
Financial consolidation		Consolidated financial statements
Analytics	Internal/ Management Reporting	Financial KPIs
		Sales by Region
		Spend by legal entity
		Budget versus actual
		P&L customer, product line
		Trend analysis

The top three customer issues in reporting

When working on report requirements, it is important to understand the common complaints or issues that business users face. Collect information early on to address these pain points.

Inaccurate data and calculation

Work with the business users on the calculations and logic needed on the reports and document them. Come up with scenarios and examples to explain the business logic and formulas in the requirement document. Many times, these issues would help in identifying the gaps in the overall design. For example, say the users want to see the financial values/costs by batch number in a manufacturing environment. However, if you are not set up to track financial postings by the batch number dimension, you won't have the data to build the report.

Performance

Understand how frequently the reports will be used and the acceptable runtime. Gather information regarding the common filter parameters that need to be added to the report. This also ties back to the volume of data that would have to be processed to generate the report. For example, if you are building a monthly commission report, it needs to consider the volume of sales orders during that month, including returns and the calculations involved in calculating the commissions.

Layout and formatting

Gather the layout and formatting information needed for the reports. Collect sample reports and document mock screens, if required, to explain the field positioning and formatting. As mentioned earlier, this aspect is extremely critical for external-facing reports.

Knowing about reporting tools

Microsoft Dynamics AX provides various tools for reporting. It is important to get familiar with all these tools in your Dynamics AX toolbox so that you can use them appropriately.

The following diagram shows the various reporting tools available for reporting in Dynamics AX.

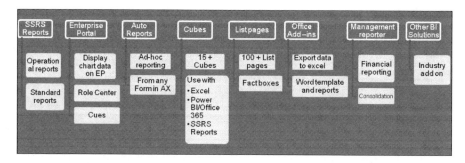

SQL Server Reporting Services

The Microsoft SQL Server Reporting server is the Server report platform for Dynamics AX. Dynamics AX delivers hundreds of reports out of the box, which can be deployed on the SQL Server reporting services. The following diagram shows the basic architecture and the data flow between the **Dynamics AX Client, Report server**, and the **Application Object Server (AOS)**:

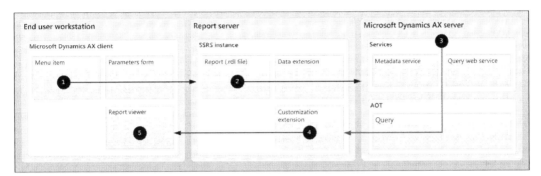

As shown in the preceding diagram, when a report is accessed via the AX Client, the following events happen:

1. The **AX client** first opens the parameter form to gather the input criteria for the report and makes a request to the report server for report definition (an RDL file).

2. The **Report server** retrieves the report request and retrieves the metadata and data from the AOS server.

3. AOS examines the request, validates the security, and retrieves data for the query and returns the metadata and data to reporting services.

4. The **Report server** customization extension renders and formats the report and sends a visual representation to the Dynamics AX client.

5. The AX client displays the report on the report viewer control.

Out-of-the-box SSRS reports

Dynamics AX ships with thousands of prebuilt SSRS reports, ranging from simple master data reports to complex reports with chart controls and graphs. There are more than a thousand out-of-the-box SSRS reports delivered with the Dynamics AX installation. There are several hundred country-specific reports available as well for local government and legal compliance.

The following screenshot displays a few sample SSRS reports in Dynamics AX:

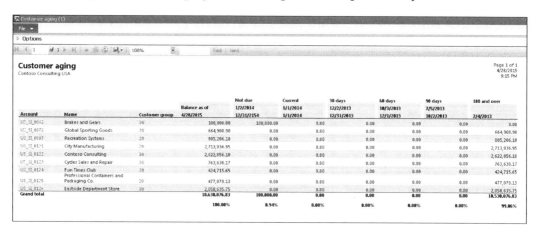

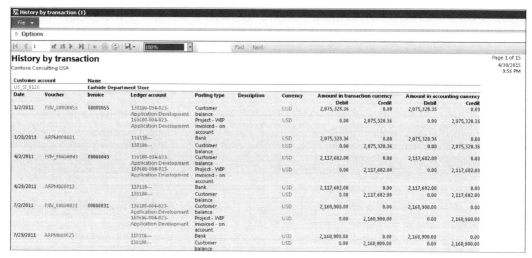

The key features of SSRS reports are as follows:

- 1000-plus out-of-the-box reports
- The Dynamics AX batch framework can be utilized to schedule reports and save the output
- Export to the Excel, PDF, CSV, and e-mail attachments

SSRS reports are useful for predefined purposes/layouts and ongoing operational reporting, such as customer aging, vendor aging, ledger account statement, customer statement, Subledger/GL reconciliation reports, shipped not invoiced, accrued purchases, and inventory value reporting.

SSRS reports are not useful for very large datasets and ad hoc needs, such as adding columns and grouping by different fields. In some cases, export to Excel while using SSRS reports may not be very user friendly.

You can refer to `https://technet.microsoft.com/en-us/library/hh334471.aspx` for more details about the out-of-the-box delivered reports in Dynamics AX.

EP chart controls

EP chart controls can be used to display chart data on the Dynamics AX **Enterprise Portal (EP)**. Chart controls provide better performance than SSRS reports for reporting on EP. Chart controls can display data using the report data provider class or analysis server cubes.

EP is deployed with many predefined charts that are associated with user profiles. In addition to this, new charts can be developed. The following chart shows an example chart control on an EP page:

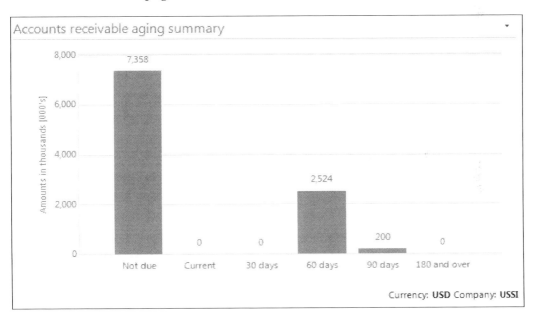

EP chart controls are useful for the light-reporting option on the enterprise portal and Role Center pages to build dashboards for executive users.

EP chart controls are useful to perform operational reporting.

Cues in Role Center

Cues allow users to see their work queue and continue to execute tasks rather than run and review reports to search for transactions that require action. It is a powerful tool that should be leveraged to avoid the expense of creating custom-reporting solutions.

Cues can be created by the users based on the filters that they use to filter the transactions that need their attention in List Pages. This is the best way to work on exceptions that the business needs to manage, such as purchase orders due but not received (buyers in purchasing need to stay on top of such POs and get new ETA from vendors), customer invoices past their due dates, project activities assigned to me, and back orders past due.

The following screenshot shows how simple it is to create a new queue and how the cue information is displayed on the Role Center page:

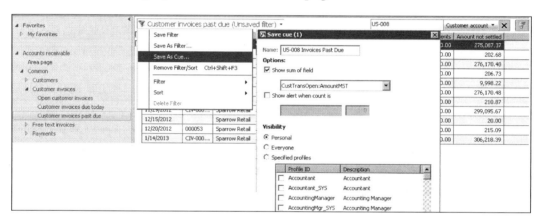

Cues are good for building and managing work cues, adding all the cues to the home page rather than the users going to multiple forms to track them.

Data on the cues are loaded every time the user opens the Role Center page. Cues with complex calculations can cause performance issues on loading the page.

The AX auto-report wizard

The AX auto-report wizard is an ad hoc reporting option that can be used by business users to print the data displayed on the form. Using this option, the user can generate an auto-report for one-time use, or you can create and save a custom auto-report that can be reused later.

The following screenshot illustrates how to generate an auto-report from the Vendor list page:

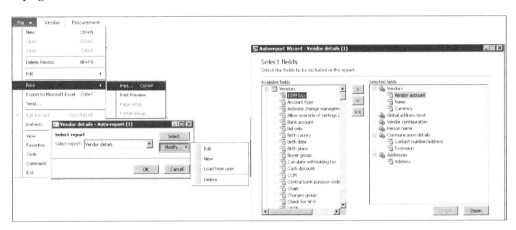

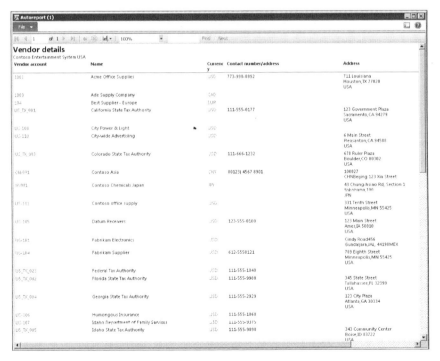

This is useful to perform ad hoc reporting from the AX client and printing the data available on the form for analysis. For example, printing vendor details in a report format.

Complex report layouts and calculations are not possible using AX auto-reports. You can just print data in a basic, tabular report layout.

The TechNet article at `https://technet.microsoft.com/en-us/library/gg213177.aspx` explains the step-by-step instructions to use the AX Auto report wizard to generate custom ad hoc reports.

Exporting to Excel from forms

Dynamics AX allows you to apply filters and sort rows based on specific criteria. Users can add more fields to form the layout through personalization.

Once you have all the data points on the form, export to Excel (*Ctrl + T*) can be used to get the data in Excel for further review. The following screenshot shows this:

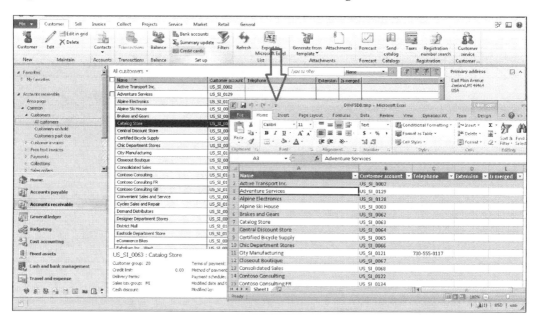

This is useful when reviewing data such as ledger account transactions, customer transactions, and so on for ad hoc purposes.

This is not useful for large datasets and data with complex calculations—you do not want to start using Excel to build complex macros and formulae to get the results you are looking for.

Business intelligence/analytics – cubes

Microsoft Dynamics AX uses the SQL Server Analysis Services (SSAS) platform for business intelligence and analytics reporting. The Dynamics AX database has been highly normalized with the release of Dynamics AX 2012. This helps with the performance and scaling of OLTP databases. However, it creates challenges for reporting. Hence, cubes are the best way to put together data in flat table formats, making it easy for reporting.

Dynamics AX provides several default cubes out of the box, which can be used as they are or customized as per your specific reporting needs.

The following diagram shows the high-level architecture of Dynamics AX analytics and components to access cube data:

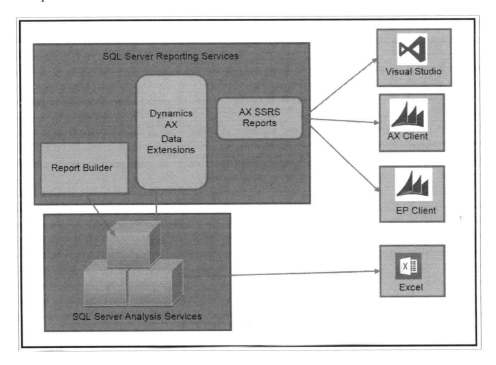

Here are a few considerations to note while building your cubes:

1. **Full refresh versus incremental updates**: Consider the frequency of updates and the volume/projected growth of data. You don't want cube refresh taking an exponentially longer amount of time as the data grows in volume.

2. **Building new versus modifying the existing cubes provided by Microsoft**: Every business has their unique requirements of reporting. You can use Standard Dynamics AX as a starting point and build on top of that.

3. **Performance considerations**: You may need a completely different set of indexes based on the searches that would be performed by the end users.

4. **Consider using 64-bit Excel for power users**: Super users may end up analyzing large volumes of data in Excel. Plan to make 64-bit Excel versions available to them locally or through a terminal server to support high resource utilization of Excel.

5. **Cubes to reference data sources outside Dynamics AX**: For example, the CRM system, or the legacy data warehouse (and it would save the efforts for data migration).

6. **Data Security**: Exposure to sensitive information stored in Cubes.

This is useful to perform analytical reporting, such as Sales by region, Sales by quarters, Spend Analysis, and so on. This supports ad hoc reporting and the analysis needs of marketing, sales users, and controllers especially. This is not useful for reports that require real-time data.

For more information about the default cubes that are included with Dynamics AX, refer to `https://technet.microsoft.com/en-us/library/jj710378.aspx`.

Accessing data from cubes

There are a number of ways in which you can use cubes provided with Dynamics AX. The following are some common ways to access cube data:

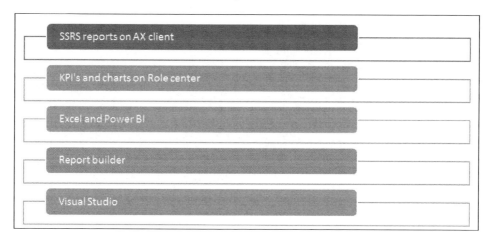

SSRS reports on AX client

There are several existing standard AX SSRS reports utilizing the existing cube data to display reports within the Dynamics AX client.

KPIs and chart on AX Role Center

You can add Cubes KPIs on the AX Role Center pages. The following screenshot shows KPIs on AX Role Center:

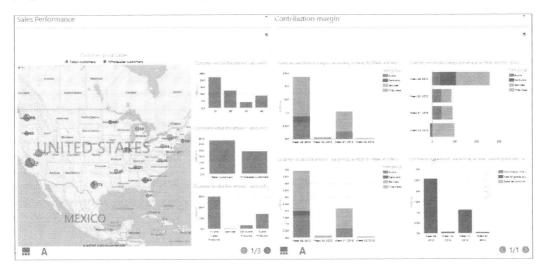

Excel and Power BI

Business users can use Excel to import cube data and create pivot tables. They can also use Power BI for Office 365 to build interactive reports and embed in role center pages as shown in the following screenshot:

The Report Builder tool

The Report Builder is a tool within the SQL server reporting services and can be used to build ad hoc reporting using the Dynamics AX analysis cube data.

Visual Studio

The Microsoft Visual Studio tools can be used to create SSRS reports that use cubes as a data source.

The Management Reporter tool

Management Reporter is an embedded Financial reporting tool provided by Microsoft Dynamics AX. Microsoft has made significant investments in Management Reporter in recent years, and it has paid off with this enterprise-ready tool meant to replace the Financial Statement setup in the General Ledger module.

The following are the key features of Management Reporter:

- Flexible report design
    - Saves dimension combinations, and reuses the dimension for multiple reports
    - Controls dimension descriptions and formatting
    - The *Missing account analysis* feature to identify accounts or dimensions that have been omitted from the report building blocks
    - Format headers to roll forecasts
    - Default report definitions that offer predefined reports for the balance sheet, income statement, and cash flow statement, as well as other financial reports that can be modified to meet customer requirements

- Interactive reporting
    - Creates a chart based on selected report rows and columns
    - Drills down to the original transaction in Dynamics AX
    - Views or shares reports in a web browser
    - **End user tool**: Finance team can make report designs and changes as needed

- Tight integration with Microsoft Dynamics AX
    - Defines rollups (reporting tree) across financial dimensions or legal entities. You can use organizational hierarchies defined in Dynamics AX.
    - Supports multicurrency, multi-company reporting along with eliminations and consolidations.

- Has its own data warehouse and does not impact the OLTP database for reporting. Very useful for organizations with high volume transactions.

- Financial report collaboration

  - Schedules reports to automatically generate on a daily, weekly, monthly, or yearly basis

  - Generates a report in multiple formats, such as XPS, Excel, and so on

  - Publishes reports to SharePoint or a network drive

  - Shares reports using e-mail with a link to report

The following diagram shows the high-level flow of financial information data in the management reporter:

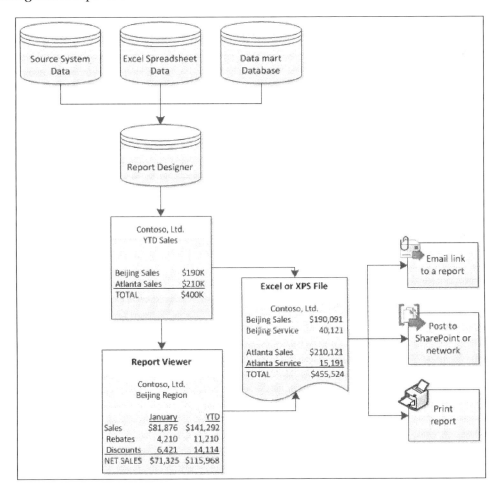

This is useful when performing financial reporting, such as generating the balance sheet, profit and loss statement, cash flow statement, budget versus actual analysis, and others.

This is also used to perform consolidated financial reporting (soft consolidation and eliminations in management reporter).

This is useful when performing management reporting based on segments and posting layers (operations and tax layers in Dynamics AX allow maintaining multiple sets of books for management and tax reporting).

This is not useful if you want to perform sub-ledger and operational reporting.

List pages

List pages provide a quick and easy way to view a group of similar records. There are two types of list pages—primary and secondary. Primary list pages display a set of records and the secondary list pages display a subset of those records. List pages also contain fact boxes that typically display information related to the selected records.

List pages are a great alternative to operational reports as they display the relevant data on a single screen and provide the quick-filter ability.

The following screenshot shows list pages in the **Account Receivable** module of the AX client. As you can see, All sales orders is a primary list page that displays all the sales orders in the selected legal entity. There are several secondary list pages, as shown in the image to display the subsets of the sales orders:

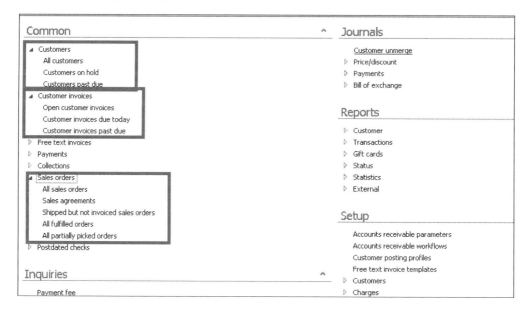

This is useful for day-to-day operational reporting, such as list of open sales orders, delivered sales orders/not yet invoiced, and so on.

Office Add-ins

Office Add-ins for AX 2012 is a great tool to work with Dynamics AX data. Office add-ins provide the ability to generate documents based on the AX data and can be used to perform ad hoc reporting by business users. Excel add-ins also provides the ability to manipulate and import data back into Dynamics AX. The following diagram shows the high-level architecture of Office Add-Ins with Dynamics AX:

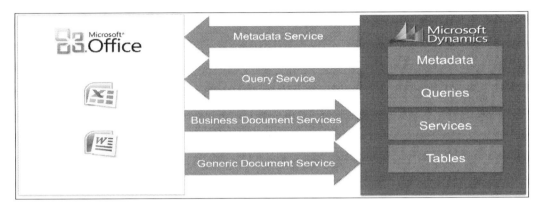

Word add-ins

Word add-ins can be used to create a document template and can be used for light reporting based on the templates personalized for the customer.

The following screenshot shows the use of Word add-ins to generate a personalized sales quotation using the AX data:

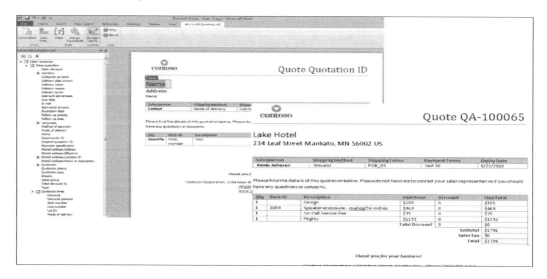

This is useful for performing light manual reporting based on custom templates.

This is not useful if you want to perform high-volume reporting.

Refer to the TechNet article for a step-by-step guide to using Word Add-ins at `https://technet.microsoft.com/en-us/library/hh781090.aspx`.

Excel add-ins

Excel add-ins can be used as another powerful, ad hoc reporting tool with Dynamics AX. A user can export data from any Dynamics AX form with just a click of a single button. AX 2012 Excel add-ins enables users to add additional columns, formatting, and to refresh data within Excel. The following screenshot shows the use of Excel add-ins to export the AX form data into Excel, adding additional fields, and formatting in the design mode:

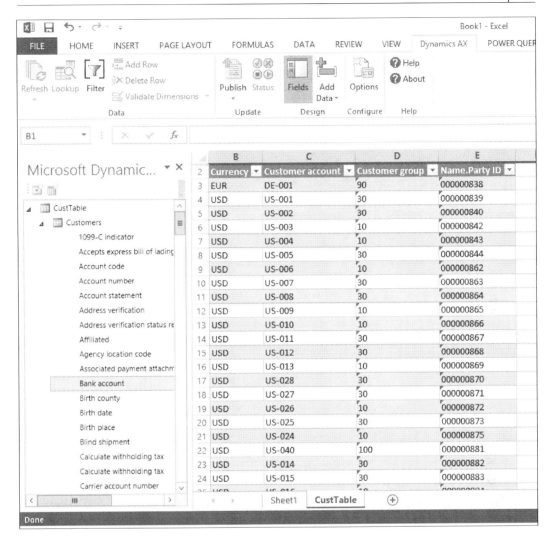

Using Excel Add-in, a user can also create an Excel template and share it with a coworker. This is also useful when performing ad hoc reporting and data analysis. This is not useful for high-volume data, complex design, and calculations.

For complete information on what the users can do using the Excel add-ins, refer to the TechNet article at `https://technet.microsoft.com/en-us/library/hh781099.aspx`.

Other add-on BI solutions

There are several independent and partner software vendors providing specialized BI solutions for Dynamics AX. The following table shows vendors providing add-on BI solutions for Dynamics AX:

Vendor Name	Solution	References
Microsoft	Power BI	`https://powerbi.microsoft.com/`
ZAP BI	ZAP for Microsoft Dynamics AX	`http://www.zapbi.com/DiscoverZAP/BYAPPLICATION/MicrosoftDynamicsAX.aspx`
TargIT	TARGIT Accelerators	`http://www.targit.com/en/software/accelerator/dynamics-ax`
BI4Dynamics	BI for Dynamics AX	`http://www.bi4dynamics.com/`
Solver BI360	BI 360	`http://www.solverusa.com/products/`
Globe Software	Atlas-Desktop	`http://www.globesoftware.com/Atlas-Solution`

These are useful for when you want to perform advanced and specialized BI reporting.

Mapping reports and identifying gaps

As described in an earlier section, there are hundreds of out-of-the-box SSRS reports, more than 15 cubes, and hundreds of list pages and inquiry forms that come with the Dynamics AX application. You would be surprised to know how many reports can be delivered using just the information on the forms and the AX standard reports. For analytical reporting, you can leverage the default cubes to deliver reporting requirements for your project.

Work with business users to evaluate out-of-the-box reports, cubes, list pages, and EP Role Center pages, and identify reports that can be directly replaced, reports that need modifications, or which need to be built. For reports that need to be built, select the correct tool set. The following table shows how to collect the required information:

Report name	Standard AX report	Fit/Gap	Additional comments
Sales invoice report	Sales invoice	Gap	There is a need to change the layout. The following additional fields need to be added to the report. Country-specific versions need to be created.

Report name	Standard AX report	Fit/Gap	Additional comments
Customer statement	Customer statement	Gap	Layout changes are required.
Purchase order	Purchase order	Gap	There is a need to minimize the header information. There is a need to print ship to, bill to, and vendor address in different columns.
Customer details	Excel Add-ins Customer list page	Fit	
Ad hoc margin analysis	Sales Cube	Fit	The controller wants to review the margin by different dimensions, such as product categories, product lines, customer segments, sales divisions, and so on
Customer P&L	Management Reporter	Fit	The customer is also configured as financial dimension (costs are tracked and allocated in GL by customers). Build a reporting tree in MR to combine related accounts for reporting.

The custom report development

It's very common for any ERP implementation project that standard, out-of-the-box reports do not meet all the reporting requirements, and that implementation will require either modification of the existing reports or the creation of new reports from scratch. Under this topic, we will learn the basic process of report design and development in Dynamics AX.

Report design is one of the most challenging parts of a project. You need business analysts who understand the business and how data is stored in the system. You also need good collaboration with business analysts and developers. To facilitate this process, a report specification document template should be developed and filled out for each report modification or new report identified. This specification should include the following information:

- Business purpose for change/addition of report
- Description of the report along with its data elements
- High-level description or picture of the layout

- Filters required (for example, select data set by date range, customer group, and so on)
- Test plan (the scenarios to test for and the expected results)
- Report placement and security requirements
- Output medium (laser printer/PDF/Excel)
- Scheduling requirements (weekly/daily/ad hoc)

The following diagram shows the process of report development:

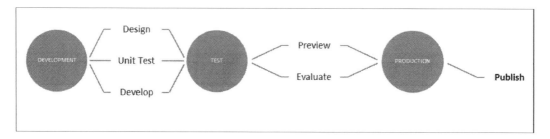

Development

Dynamics AX provides an extensive framework to develop custom reports as per customer needs. A developer uses Visual Studio to create report designs. Dynamics AX reporting extension provides easy access to the AX data source, labels (language support), and business logic. The following are some key considerations that a developer has to keep in mind when developing custom reports:

- **Picking the right tool**: Picking the right tool for report development based on the requirement is an urgent need. Do you need an SSRS report or an EP chart control report? If you decide to use Management Reporter and need to design financial reports, then, definitely, you need to select the management reporter tool to design your new report. Choice of the proper tool is very obvious when report requirements are clearly defined.

- **Deciding the source**: There can be multiple places in AX from where the data can be retrieved. Does your report need to be based on detailed transactional data or cube data? Do you want real-time data or can it come from an aggregate cube? Based on the requirement, the developer selects the datasets appropriate for the report. The following types of data sets are supported on AX 2012 SSRS reports—Query based, Report data provider, Data methods, and AX Enum provider.

- For more details on how to create an SSRS report for Dynamics AX, follow the TechNet article at `https://technet.microsoft.com/EN-US/library/cc557922.aspx`.

- **Design to perform**: It is important for the developer to understand the performance requirement of the report. Design appropriate filters on the reports to filter the data in the report. Consider some of the newest enhancements in AX 2012 to use the TempDB table and preprocessing classes to generate the required data for the report. Consider general best practices and design principles to create reports that need complex calculations and high-volume data.

- **Selecting appropriate report templates**: There are several predefined report layouts and style templates available for creating a Dynamics AX report. Layout and style templates provide consistent layout and formatting behavior for your new custom report layout.

- **Define data security**: That's another important consideration while designing reporting solutions. For example, you don't want a Sales Associate to see the commissions of other Sales Associates. Design appropriate security privileges and duties to secure data.

Testing

The testing process for a report is similar to any other custom development. As noted earlier, test scripts should be a part of the report specifications so that the developer can confirm that the report is doing what is expected before it is released to the test environment. This will reduce rework and multiple deployments for the developer.

- **Test data**: Generate sample data in the development environment to verify results. Evaluate the performance of report execution by testing it on larger data sets.

- **Verify layout and formatting**: In most of the project reports, development takes more time than anticipated most of which is spent on the layout and formatting of data in the reports. Pay special attention to external reports, such as customer invoices, customer statements, and purchase order reports, and verify the layout carefully to avoid multiple iterations or rework.

- **Test print medium**: It does happen that the report looks great onscreen, but looks different once printed on the printer or a PDF. Test the report by printing it on paper and other mediums to make sure that the layout and formatting is consistent and acceptable to the business user.

Deployment

Finally, the reports developed need to be deployed in order to be used by the business users. For report deployment, consider the following:

- **Security**: Determine appropriate roles and duties that need to be assigned to use the custom report. For analytics reports and cubes, you need to define the appropriate role at the cube level to enable users to access the cube data.

- **Scheduling and delivery**: Certain reports may need to be scheduled. You can set up batch processes in AX or configure the delivery schedule in SSRS to deliver the reports to the users directly.

Summary

In this chapter, you started with understanding how important reporting is to run any business. We reviewed a set of questions that need to be asked when gathering reporting requirements. You also learned about the different tools available in Dynamics AX for reporting and BI and how they can be used to fulfil the reporting requirements in the project. In the end, we discussed how, in typical implementation projects, we have to either modify or develop new reports from scratch. We also discussed the typical process of custom report development in Dynamics AX.

In the next chapter, we will learn about the functional and technical architecture of Dynamics AX. We will understand key design patterns and how to extend these features when needed.

7
Functional and Technical Design

The functional and technical design process begins once the analysis phase has been completed. By now, the project plan is ready, the requirements document has been signed off, **Conference Room Pilot (CRP)** has been completed, and the Fit/Gap exercise has been completed and documented as part of the analysis phase. Now, it is time for the implementation team to document the overall solution and produce the functional and technical design documents.

The following diagram shows the deliverables and activities in the design phase of the implementation project:

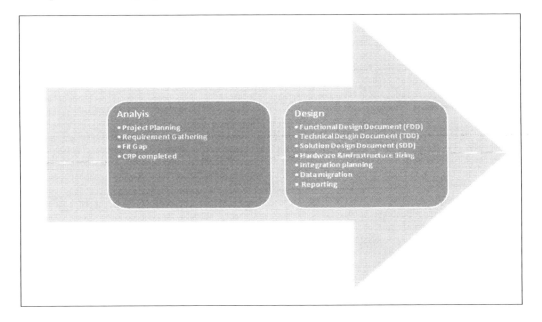

In this chapter, we will learn about the following:

- **Functional Design Document (FDD)**
    - ° Overview and objectives
    - ° Guidelines for FDD
    - ° Understanding product features and limitations
    - ° Common customization requests in Dynamics AX
- **Solution Design Document (SDD)**
- Evaluating ISV solutions
- **Technical Design Document (TDD)**
    - ° Overview
    - ° Guidelines for writing technical design

The functional design document

The functional design documentation is created after the requirements document has been signed off and the Fit/Gap analysis is completed in conjunction with the CRP. This documentation describes the features of the desired customizations. The document can include things such as flowcharts, screenshots, wire frames, and so on. At a minimum, an FDD will contain an organized list of requirements that can be used for development, testing, and client signoff.

Why write FDD?

Functional design documents help developers, testers, and customers to understand customizations in detail. The following are the key benefits of functional design documents:

- FDDs help the development team to understand the feature and provide a clear scope and definition of what to develop. Function design documents streamline the development process. The development team working on the feature has a clear understanding and answers to all their questions to start development. Since this document is approved by the customer, the developers are developing customizations which are approved.

- FDDs help the testing team to understand the feature under development and to develop a test plan around it.

- FDDs provide the customer with a clear vision and definition of the feature being developed.

- FDDs provide the baseline of the training documentation for the application support team and business users.

Fit/Gap review session

The Fit/Gap document is the primary input document to write the FDD. It is very important to review the Fit/Gap document in detail before starting with the FDD. The following are a few pointers to take note of when conducting a successful Fit/Gap review session:

- The Fit/Gap review session should involve the functional and technical solution architect, project manager, and customer subject matter experts (SMEs).

- It is important to remember that this is a Fit/Gap session, so Fit should also be analyzed. Any degree of customization identified in Fit should be recorded.

- Oftentimes, you find gaps listed that aren't really gaps as the solution can handle the requirement. The review session should discuss each requirement in detail and discuss all possible alternate solutions.

- All gaps should be recorded and assigned a unique number. The Microsoft LCS Business Modeler tool provides the ability to document your business process and record gaps.

- Take a detailed look at how the gaps are going to be addressed. Outline the testing/review process for customizations and how the testing will be administered.

- By focusing on these topics, you will soon learn where the team stands with regard to the appropriate documentation and its approach to the customization process.

Project management aspects of design

The following are a few pointer for project managers, to consider during design phase of the project:

- Fit/Gap, requirements, and the project plan need to be signed off to start the functional design phase. You can break them up into areas and start early if you have specific areas signed off.

- Make the team put together the overall functional architecture and the flow-across applications; review with the respective stakeholders.

- Start with the functional design for areas on which the rest of the solution has a dependency. For example, customer, product masters, and so on are important for the downstream supply chain, invoicing processes, and others.

- Dedicate resources for large, complex functional areas early on.

- Divide responsibilities by area and try to have smaller FDDs created for each area. This would help manage them better.

- Assign developers and a QA team to each area at this stage. Engage them in reviewing the functional design and in supporting the respective business analysts early on (do not start the coding).

- You need to plan for multiple iterations and reviews. Functional designs are very crucial. Upfront reviews can save a lot of development hours and rework and will also increase the overall quality of the deliverables.

- Identify all cross-functional requirements; the solution architect should lead them to suitable designs.

- Cross-functional reviews are very important in larger projects. Have recurrent meetings every week/twice a week (as needed) to review the functional designs with all the functional team members together. Prioritize reviews for foundational items (such as customer master and product master changes) that would impact other functional areas.

- Cross-functional reviews will help to improve solutions (the rest of the team may have inputs on doing the same thing in a better way or with less customization). Also, more importantly, you will be forcing the team to review each other's designs by pulling them together into a room.

- Engage business SMEs early on for reviews (set up a design walkthrough, provide deadlines for getting feedback, and seek a signoff for each of the functional designs).

- Depending upon the complexity, involve SMEs ,external to project, for an independent review and recommendations. Their presence itself will fix more than 50 percent of the issues. For example, when you start auditing the financial results of the company, your accounting practices will automatically improve as people know that they are going to get audited.

Things to know before writing FDD

FDDs speak the application language and terminology, so business analysts writing functional design documents must understand the Dynamics AX application and functionality. Lack of product knowledge and understanding can keep the documents at a high level, pushing the design aspects to the developers, which deviates from the purpose of the documents.

Microsoft Dynamics Sure Step provides good templates to write FDDs. Create your own version with the sections relevant to your project and have the team follow the template.

Always have one or many requirements in the **Requirements Traceability Matrix** (**RTM**) corresponding to the functional design document. RTM is a foundational element in ERP implementations as it ensures consistent delivery against the contract and business requirements.

The following sections discuss topics of common features and frameworks that business analysts need to be familiar with, while designing the solutions.

The party model

Party relations are one of the most normalized tables, and it's important to understand relationships with the customers, vendors, and other entities. This impacts the modelling of solutions for important business entities. The following diagram shows this:

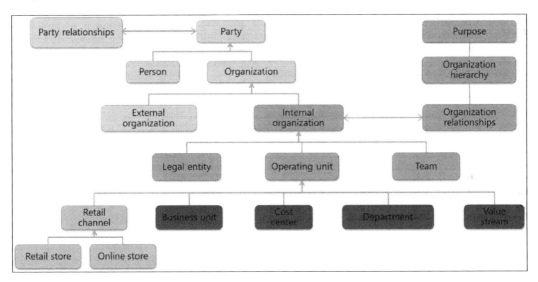

The global address book

This is the repository of people and organizations and their relationships with each other — whether they are internal or external to the enterprise.

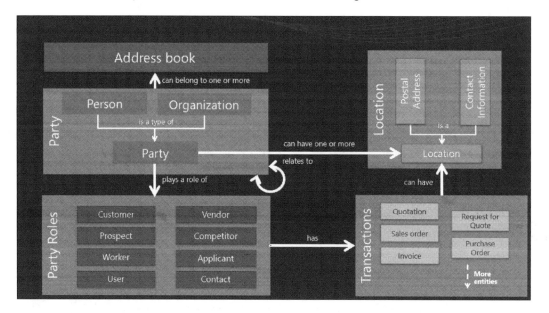

The financial data

The relationship between legal entities, COA, financial dimensions, and journal entries is shown in the following diagram:

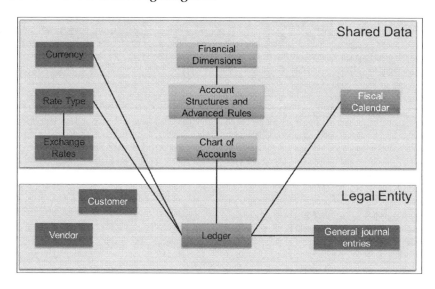

The reverse engineering tool

With AX 2012, Microsoft has normalized tables to a large extent. Understanding data models is important to designing the solutions. Reverse engineering tool in AOT is a good resource to visualize data and classes in Microsoft Dynamics AX by creating UML data models, UML object models, and ERX ER data models. More information on the Reverse engineering tool can be found on MSDN at `https://msdn.microsoft.com/en-us/library/aa499193.aspx`.

Key global features

In this section, we will discuss the key features that can be used across modules and are important to understand as you work through the design phase.

- Database logging
    - The database log is a feature that helps in auditing.
    - It keeps track of the changes made by users. You can enable *track* on specific actions, such as insert, delete, and update. For updates, you can turn on tracking for specific fields.
    - It keeps track of who created or modified the record and when. In case of updates, you can see the previous value and the new value.
    - This is typically used in areas where audit tracking is required, such as credit limit updates.
    - Standard Dynamics AX Reports are useful to review any changes made. Reporting on this data outside Dynamics AX can be challenging.
    - If changes are made directly in SQL through updates, these will not be visible to Dynamics AX AOS and will not be available in the Database log. It is one of the many reasons why Dynamics AX data should not be directly modified in the SQL database.

- Document management
    - The document management feature (also known as document handling) enables users to attach documents to a particular transaction or a master data record in Dynamics AX. It can be used to attach supporting documents, such as the invoice copy received from the vendor, purchase order quotes, contracts, and so on.
    - Different document types can be created and configured to be used across solution areas. Normally, separate document types are created for use by departments as you can limit who can see notes by document type.

- You can save notes and print them on output documents, such as packing slip and invoices.

- The files that are attached can be viewed using the **Attachment** option on the Dynamics AX screens.

- There are multiple ways of implementing this feature for storage, such as database, file share, and SharePoint are commonly used.

- If you have sophisticated needs, such as workflows to save documents, additional security or virus scans prior to saving documents, or **Optical Character Recognition (OCR)**, you can integrate with an external document management system; there are also several ISV solutions available in this area. These are especially useful for AP invoice automation.

- The files can also be controlled for maximum size or file types.

- Cues

  - Cues are visual representations of select information on transactions and are typically displayed on the user's dashboard/Role Center.

  - There are many purposes to use them and managing exceptions is amongst the top ones.

  - The foundations of cues are filtered queries that give the statistical input to be displayed graphically.

  - Cues can be created for different types, and some commonly used ones are count and sum.

  - Examples of cues include showing the sum of pending invoices that are due as of today, count of overdue invoices, count of delayed orders, count of POs past due that can be used by buyers, and so on. Users can drill into individual transactions and use this as a task list to address them.

- Alerts

  - Alerts are one of the most popular notification features in Microsoft Dynamics AX.

  - They can be set up to trigger notifications delivered on the Dynamics AX client and/or an e-mail.

  - The alerts work on a trigger concept and are set up in the select table.

  - They can be used for entire record-level change notifications, including create, edit, and delete and can also be used for field-level change notifications.

- Alerts are not meant for broadcast use; hence, the notification is sent to one user only. If you want a specific team to be notified, team e-mail (e-mail distribution list in exchange) can be used.

- A batch job in the system administration module delivers the alerts (usually, it is set to run every minute). Alerts tables can get very huge; clean up batch jobs should be scheduled as well.

- Alerts need to be carefully set only for actionable events. Otherwise, users often run into too many alert situations and get ignored. Alerts set up to generate huge numbers of notifications may also impact system performance.

- Personalization
  - Personalization is the feature to tailor-make the screen per user or group of users.
  - While the user can make the screens morph the way it suits them and helps their productivity, these personalization changes do not impact other users or the underlying code base.
  - Typical usage lies in rearranging the information on the Dynamics AX screen to best suit the purpose of the user.
  - Do not use this feature when you want to make screen changes across the board for all users.
  - While personalization is a powerful tool for users to use, personalization is lost when you clear usage data for the user (it is one of the first troubleshooting steps and may have to be performed).

- Batch jobs
  - Batch jobs is an automated work that Dynamics AX is capable of.
  - Any transaction that needs to be executed on the AOS server, and in a scheduled way, can be set up in a batch job. You can set up the frequency in terms of days, minutes, and hours. Batch jobs can have an end date or can be scheduled for only one occurrence.
  - If you want to run batch jobs in a specific window, for example. every 15 minutes from 7 A.M. to 6 P.M., you may want to put such jobs on AOS Servers, which are batch servers, during a specific time window. These AOS Servers need to be defined as batch servers; set up 0 batch threads between 6 P.M. through 7 A.M. for the AOS server and the batch job will be set to run every 15 minutes during the window that you defined.

- Consider the deployment window while defining the batch job frequency. Make all the batch servers have zero threads between 9 P.M. and 10 P.M., and don't schedule long-running batch jobs just before 9 P.M. This will ensure that you easily put all the jobs on hold for the deployment.

- Performance scaling of volume-intensive transactions or actions to be performed periodically are typical uses of batch jobs, for example, invoicing shipped orders every 15 minutes, daily export of positive pay file, and inventory recalculation or close process.

- In batch jobs, tasks are created to perform the necessary actions, and these tasks can be multi-threaded to fully utilize the available resources.

- You can also create dependencies using batch groups. For example, when you want products to be imported, the pricing information is received from the Product Management system before you start importing.

- Other usage of batch jobs include workflow execution, alerts trigger checking, scheduling reports execution, and so on.

- Partitions

  - Considerations for partitions to be used are important for global projects with multiple legal entities. The decision for partitions to be created needs to be made in the early part of the design phase.

  - In the glossary for Microsoft Dynamics AX, the formal definition of a partition is given as a division of an application's processing into logical or functional parts.

  - Partitions divide and isolate the business data of an installation using special processing that the AOS applies to data queries. This special processing occurs immediately before the queries are sent to the underlying Microsoft SQL Server database when a system field named *Partition* is present in a queried table.

  - The purpose of a partition is to logically separate the data within its boundaries from the data in other partitions. A partition enables AOS to isolate the data in the partition from users who are not authorized to access the data. For example, a holding corporation might have several subsidiaries or other legal entities. An installation of Microsoft Dynamics AX for the corporation can have several partitions, perhaps one for each subsidiary.

- Each partition contains at least one company or legal entity. A legal entity occurs in only one partition. When you create a legal entity, the system assigns it to the current partition. The legal entity can never be moved to another partition.

- With the installation of AX, a default partition is created and the system administrators and developers can create more as per their need. Partitions were introduced in Dynamics AX 2012 R2. While migrating from the previous versions, partitions need to be assigned to legal entities as part of the upgrade process. Do not create multiple partitions when data needs to be shared across companies, for example, in the chart of accounts, vendors, customers, and products.

- Virtual company
  - A virtual company allows you to specify a group of tables (table collection) that need to be shared among a group of companies. When users save information in one of those tables, the data is available to the other company accounts.

  - A virtual company is a good functional feature. However, it is difficult to implement and can cause data inconsistencies. It should be avoided if at all possible.

  - Ideally, you should make decisions to define virtual companies upfront in the design process. Defining a virtual company after you have input data in multiple companies is tricky and may cause data integrity issues.

  - Virtual companies play a key role in implementations involving a high number of legal entities.

  - Only use virtual companies to share setup and master data across companies. Do not use virtual companies for transactional data. Here is a practical example of virtual companies — an implementation that has 70-80 legal entities, that is, tables for maintaining payment terms, fixed asset groups, fixed asset posting profiles, value models, depreciation books, and journal names can be created in a virtual company to make creating and maintaining new legal entities much easier.

  - Use a number sequence of the type *shared* if number sequences are needed for the shared data.

- Workflows
    - ○ Workflows are the mechanism by which business rules and approval processes are implemented in the solution. You can direct certain transactions for approvals using workflows. Some examples of documents for which built-in workflows can be set up are AP invoice journals, purchase requisitions, expense reports, budget planning processes, general journals, customer payments, free text invoices, and so on.
    - ○ Always keep the workflow implementation as simple as possible. Many organizations move from paper or manual approval processes into systematic workflows and come up with complex rules. It becomes difficult to build and maintain such workflows as organizational changes occur and eventually these workflows are abandoned.
    - ○ While implementing workflows, show delegation functions to the larger user community as part of training. It needs to become a part of their out-of-office/vacation checklist to define delegates for time-sensitive workflows.
    - ○ The usage of workflows includes:

        Assigning a transaction for review

        Assigning a transaction for approval

        Automation of a business step

        Conditional decisions on business data, which the next steps are dependent upon

        Multiple level of approvals

        Approval type selection, such as based on role, based on position and managerial hierarchy, and so on

        Workflows can be delegated and/or escalated after a certain timeframe

Big picture diagrams

Big picture diagrams convey the entire solution map and flow in a way that is difficult to express in words. The following are the suggested and sample big picture diagrams that should be built and maintained for Dynamics AX and all other applications that are a part of the solution. It also helps get new resources up to speed with the overall functional architecture of the solution.

The functional architecture

Put together the functional architecture of all the systems involved in their business functions. Try to minimize the number of systems any specific group has to use for their day-to-day work:

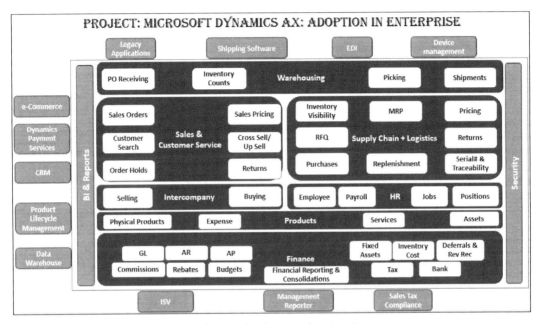

A big picture for complete business functions in one page

Integrations

Put together the technical architecture for the solution with all the integrations and their directions, as shown in the following diagram:

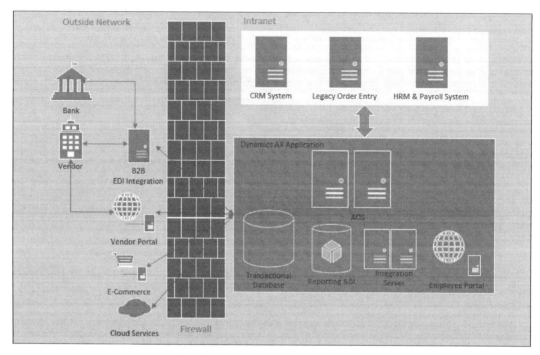

A bird's-eye view of the entire integration

The flow of data

Provide the *to-be* process references in the functional design documents. Use a business process modeler in the **Lifecycle Services (LCS)** portal to define the business processes in a swimlane fashion:

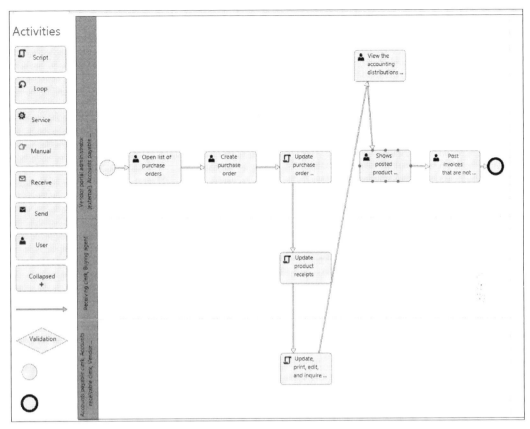

A process-oriented solution flow diagram (reference: LCS)

Do's and Don'ts

- Do not repurpose fields to avoid customization. You will end up causing unforeseen issues down the road or block future use of the functionality related to the field.

- Do not use smart numbering: You will be limiting functionality and developing a lot of dependency on reporting, and the like, based on smart numbering. If you have used a smart number in the past, this is the perfect opportunity to fix it. For example, say you have product numbers such as XXX-YYY-ZZZ, where XXX represents the category, YYY is for the Manufacturer, and ZZZ represents the product number. You will be better off having the product number as just a number rather than building logic into the number itself. Instead, use three separate fields on the item master, which will help drive business processes and reporting based on these fields.

- Keep the architecture simple and easy to follow. The more complexity you add to the solution, the more difficult it will be to implement and support.

- Try to reduce duplication of data in multiple places; avoid unnecessary/ complex integrations.

- Design solutions around standard functionality, without touching the core system. For example, say the customer wants to automate the creation of allocation journals based on the allocation rules defined in the general ledger module. As a functional consultant, I will design a separate customization that will extend the functionality of the core Dynamics AX allocation process rather than changing the standard AX forms and features.

The solution design document

A **Solution Design Document (SDD)** includes information about the working elements of the overall solution, including Dynamics AX standard features (Fits), Gaps, and integrations. It is important to get the entire solution depicted in a pictorial representation. The business process modeler in LCS is a great tool with which to put together the solution design document.

Overview and objectives

Solution design documents are primarily referred to by core team members of the implementation team. The following are the key objectives of solution design documentation:

- The details of the business flow in the future solution based on Microsoft Dynamics AX

- Solution validation

- The single point of reference for future value additions, issues, and troubleshooting

- Documenting the high level

- Business and solution flow diagrams

Guidelines for Solution Design Documents

Solution design is a solution binder and puts together all the aspects of the solution. The following are the suggested coverage areas that the solution design should comprise:

- There should be an end-to-end pictorial flow for the entire business process by organization function. For example, one end-to-end flow diagram for the supply chain, one end-to-end flow diagram for financials, and likewise for other business functions.
- The end-to-end flow must have starting/entry points, ending/closure points, and handover to other process diagrams.
- There should be all the decision points that can bring in additional business scenarios.
- There should be steps that are manual or automated.
- Roles expected to perform the function in Microsoft Dynamics in a swimlane view should be there.
- Key security and integrations solution components should be included.
- All artifacts and configurations that would be needed to deploy the solution in production should be included.

The key takeaway from SDD is that the implementation core team (especially customer members) is on board with the overall solution flow and design.

Engaging ISV partners

There are a lot of great ISV solutions available in the Dynamics AX ecosystem that can help you bridge the gap between the standard product and the required industry-specific functionality. Usually, if someone already has a solution that has been used by multiple customers, and has experience in that specific domain, it will be less risky than developing your own solution—you don't want to reinvent the wheel.

Project managers and solution architects need to act as the customer's advocate in choosing ISV solutions. Getting the right ISV solutions and holding them accountable within their areas is important for your success.

Before choosing ISV solutions

Before choosing ISV solutions, consider the following points:

- **Build versus buy analysis**: Sometimes, going with an ISV solution may look like a quick win. However, it may have a great cost associated with it. You need to make sure that the team has done a good build versus buy analysis.

- **Benefits and percentage of fit**: Understand all the benefits that the ISV product has to offer and identify the percentage of fit that you have with the requirements. If you still have to customize for more than 20-30 percent of the scenarios, you may be better off building the whole solution by yourself.

- **Readiness on current version**: It is very important to see a demo on the current version of the product (that is, the version you are planning to use) or understand how close the ISV is to delivering the solution for the version that you will implement. Try to defer the decision to buy an ISV solution until the product is functional for the version you need.

- **Product roadmap**: Understand their roadmap and features, if any, promised as a part of the roadmap. Make sure that those deadlines are mentioned as part of the contract. For example, ISV currently provides tax calculation only for the U.S. However, Canada is on the roadmap. Make sure that you understand the deadlines for Canada and have those documented as part of the contract to ensure that your project doesn't suffer due to delays from ISV. Also, review their roadmap for upcoming cumulative updates.

- **AX roadmap**: Be aware of any new functionality that Microsoft is working on for new releases. Will these features supplant the ISV solution? And how easy would it be to upgrade AX and take advantage of the new features? Would it be more cost-effective? How will it affect the business if you wait for new features versus doing a temporary customization or implementing the ISV solution?

- **Architectural review**: Have high-level architectural reviews done by the Solution architect/technical architect on the team as part of the evaluation (to ensure that there are no architectural gaps and the solution is scalable).

- **References**: If you don't have an existing relationship with the ISV, ask for customer references and have a discussion with the references prior to making a decision.

- **Company size and support**: Yes, it does matter! You don't want a multibillion-dollar organization to be dependent on the small ISV solution provider (that will be part of the tier 1 ERP system) that has only two employees. The solution may be great, but you need to evaluate the risk to the business if you are going to be fully dependent on an ISV partner to support you.

If there are a lot more features that are included in the ISV solution than the customer may ever need, and if these features touch any of the core features of Dynamics AX, you may have to reconsider the solution (more features would inject more bugs in the overall Dynamics AX environment and may cause issues for other standard AX features).

After selecting the partner

Consider the following after partner selection:

- Get the budget approved and have all the invoices billed through the partner. This way, the customer doesn't have to deal with multiple parties.

- Share your project plan with the ISV partner and align their delivery dates according to your schedule. Update your project plan to include key ISV deliverables.

- Have them attend weekly meetings for status updates (if they are working in parallel on building the solution).

- Install all the ISV Solutions in a specific layer other than the VAR layer. Usually, ISV solutions are imported in the ISV layer.

- Plan the code and configuration changes from ISV that must be incorporated into your development and other environments.

Common pitfalls

Consider the following to avoid common pitfalls during ISV selection:

- You don't want to involve too many ISV solutions as part of the overall solution. It would increase dependencies for upgrades, and there may be conflicts in their solutions, which would cause pain.

- Each ISV solution being envisioned in the overall solution design should have a minimum overlap of functionality and objects.

- Upgrades (or even hotfixes) provided by Microsoft may become challenging. You will have dependencies on an ISV solution if the hotfix provided by Microsoft touches the areas modified by the ISV partner.

- Access to the code base and any proprietary solution components: You must avoid any ISVs that have proprietary solution components that are not available for you to modify (for example, DLLs for which you don't have code. You are now dependent on the ISV Partner for every change that needs to be made).

The Technical Design Document

A **Technical Design Document** (TDD) includes information about the programmatic approach of how a particular requirement will be implemented.

Overview and objectives

TDDs are prepared primarily by the developer for the final development. They are also used by the testing team to write detailed test cases. The following are the key objectives of technical design documentation:

- Details of application architecture and design goals
- Data validation
- Documentation of the code (high level)
- Data flow diagrams

Guidelines for the Technical Design Document

We will discuss the design patterns and things to be cognizant of while putting together a technical design. A technical design is about the solution planning and putting together a skeleton of the technical solution. Putting together good design documentation will help you save development rework and improve the quality of code by allowing you to think through several facets of the solution before you start coding.

Preparation

Consider the following before starting to write TDDs:

- The technical design typically starts after the signoff of the functional design. It can also, start early for a functional area where the requirements are clear.
- Engage the technical lead early on during functional designing to understand the functional requirements and the functional flow.
- Plan brainstorming sessions amongst the team to discuss different solution ideas.
- Plan separate technical specs for integrations and data migration.
- Plan communication among the team to handle cross-functional designs.

Execution

Consider the following when writing TDDs:

- **Process flow**: Depict the overall process flow for the functional area so that it's clear to the developer what the final outcome is and how to reach it.

- **UI and usability**: Keep in mind the users and processes that will be using the new forms: is it workers on the floor or a person in the accounting department? Is it a repetitive function, such as shipping sales orders or invoicing POs, or is it a batch process, such as invoicing sales orders? Use familiar UI patterns considering the users of the functionality.

- **Scalability of solution**: Think about how the solution can be scalable, such as more controlled by parameters and data rather than code. Having it controlled by parameters will help you in global environments. For example, you can turn off the functionality for companies that don't want to use it. Also, should you have an issue in production with the recently released functionality, you might have the option to turn it off using parameters, rather than a full rollback during business hours.

- **Apply generic design patterns**: Utilize solution ideas and frameworks offered within the product. The goal is not to rewrite the Dynamics AX product; you are just extending its capability for business use. For example, if you have a bulk integration requirement, try to evaluate whether you can expand the DIXF framework for this rather than building a new framework from scratch. Follow the design patterns of the standard Dynamics AX Forms for custom forms.

- **Performance**: Identify the volume of transactions in the current production and anticipated growth in the next few years. The solution should consider the performance requirement early on. Design a prototype and generate sample data to test performance.

- **Exception handling**: Identify exceptional scenarios and document them. Build enough controls to avoid mistakes by users (you don't want to leave flaws that would let users hurt themselves). On the other hand, you don't want to spend too much time on building an extremely idiot-proof system.

- **Security**: Consider security aspects as part of the technical design.

- **Review**: Review the technical design solution ideas with the solution architect and functional leads for their input on a periodic basis to incorporate feedback.

- **Brainstorm**: There are multiple ways to solve a problem — discussions and brainstorming lead to the identification of the best possible one.

Outcome

Expect the following as outcomes of TDDs:

- Technical designs have been signed off by the technical solution architect. Track signoff e-mails or scanned copies of written signoffs on SharePoint.

- The development team has a good understanding of what needs to be built and how to build it.

Summary

In this chapter, we reviewed the key considerations for a functional design, including global features that you need to know in order to develop a good solution design. In addition to that, we walked through the evaluation, selection criteria, and engagement of ISVs on the project. We concluded with the technical aspects of the design, primarily around the generation of Technical design documents. In the next chapter we will learn another key aspect of design process, that is configuration management.

8
Configuration Management

In this chapter, we will learn about configuration planning, collecting configuration data, the tools available to facilitate configuration, and the various approaches towards configuration management and promoting configurations from one environment to another.

The configuration of an ERP system is one of the most important parts of the process. Configuration means setting up the base data and parameters to enable your product features such as financial, shipping, sales tax, and so on.

Dynamics AX has been developed based on the generic requirements of various organizations and contains the business processes belonging to diverse business segments. It is a very configurable product that allows the implementation team to configure features based on specific business needs. During the project, the implementation team identifies the relevant components of the system and sets up and aligns these components to meet the specific business requirements. This process starts in the analysis phase of the project carrying on through the design, development, and deployment phases.

Configuration management is different from data migration. Data migration broadly covers the transactional data of the legacy system and core master data, such as opening balances, Open AR, Open AP, customers, vendors, and so on. When we talk about configuration management, we are referring to items like general ledger, fiscal years and periods, chart of accounts, segments, and defining applicable rules, journal types, customer groups, terms of payments, module-based parameters, workflows, number sequences, and the like. In a broader sense, configuration covers the basic parameters, master data, and reference data that you configure for the different modules in Dynamics AX.

The following diagram shows the different phases of configuration management:

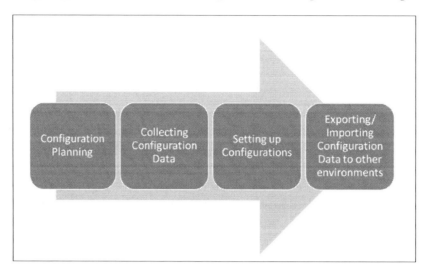

Configuration planning

Configuration planning is, basically, identifying all the configurations required for your implementation project. Most configuration requirements are known from the solution design phase and finalized with the sign-off of the functional and technical design specifications.

The first step towards configuration planning is to identify the modules and functional areas which need be to be configured. The following are some pointers for getting started with the planning:

- Create a list of configurations that are needed for the project, and identify and assign the resources responsible for configuration. As a part of this list, identify the cross-functional module configuration and add secondary responsible resources. Microsoft Sure Step provides a fairly comprehensive list of parameters and configuration data, based on the module and functional role, in the Data Migration Requirements checklist spreadsheet. You can use this spreadsheet as a starting point to identify all the configurations and add the column for the resources responsible for them.

- Build a list of environment-specific configurations. Some of the configurations, such as links between applications talking to each other, need to have different values in different environments. For example, you need to ensure that the test instance of Dynamics AX is pointing to the test instance of the shipping solutions and that the payment gateways are configured in the test mode.

- Identifying such lists early on helps in reviewing these configurations specifically in every environment, prior to, and after, going live (especially with data restores).

- Ideally, you should automate the changes to such configurations while moving the data across environments to avoid the risk of human errors.

- The following table represents a sample list of environment-specific configurations:

Configuration	Environment	Value
Web service URL for sales tax software	Development	`http://DEV.TAXServices.svc`
	Testing	`http://TEST.TAXServices.svc`
	Production	`https://Prod.TAXServices.svc`
Payment gateway setting	Development	`http://DEV.Paymentgateway.aspx`
	Testing	`http://DEV.Paymentgateway.aspx`
	Production	`https://Prod.Paymentgateway.aspx`
File-share path (document management)	Development	`\\DEVBATCHAOS001\DocumentShare`
	Testing	`\\TESTBATCHAOS001\DocumentShare`
	Production	`\\PRODDocumentShare001\DocumentShare`

- Maintain a list of company-specific configurations. When you are planning global roll outs, define a global template and maintain a list of configurations that needs to be revisited for every company.

  - As far as possible, you should try and keep the same reference tables (for example, same codes for customer groups). Of course, different companies may require different parameters or configurations to meet specific country or business unit requirements, but those should be specifically evaluated to ensure that these differences do not hamper intercompany transactions or future consolidation efforts.

  - There may be customizations that are company-specific which you may want to turn on or off in case of the other companies. Keep track of such parameters in your configurations list while you are building the functional/technical designs.

    ○   The number sequences and base currencies may be different.

    ○   Specific GL accounts would have to be added/suspended in a specific company.

- Maintain a list of batch jobs. Periodic processes can be scheduled using batch jobs in Dynamics AX. Even though scheduling a batch job is also a kind of configuration, you should have a list of all the batch jobs that you plan to have, along with their frequencies, parameters, and so on. Maintain a separate list of batch jobs to configured in each environment. The following table represents a sample list of batch jobs:

Columns	Description	Example 1	Example 2
Batch job name	Name of the batch job	Auto-invoicing domestic orders	Product creation batch
Functional area	AP, AR, Inventory, and so on.	AR	Product information management
Business owner	Who, from business, should be contacted for testing, errors (If batch job fails, once you go to Production)	AR manager	PIM manager
Consulting owner	Person responsible from the consulting team	Yogesh Kasat	JJ Yadav
IT owner	Person responsible from the internal IT team	Finance BSA	PIM BSA
Frequency	How often does the batch job need to run (for example, every 15 minutes, every day at 6 P.M.)	Every 15 minutes; from 6 a.m. through 7 p.m. (timings are driven by batch group and active AOS as batch)	Everyday at 6 p.m
Parameters	Any filters or parameters to be defined while scheduling the batch job	Sales origin = 'Domestic'	Record status = "Ready"
Dependencies	Scheduling dependencies between batch jobs		
Path or class name	Path from where to access the menu or class to be used for scheduling the batch job	AR\periodic\update\invoice	PIM\periodic\832 item creation (custom)
Batch group	Name of the batch group	DayTime*	NightTime
Comments	Additional comments		

*The DayTime batch group has AOS defined as a batch AOS only during business hours (6 a.m. through 7 p.m.).

Collecting the configuration data

ERP configuration requires coordination between the implementation and business teams to collect master data for the key modules.

These are some key pointers to keep in mind while collecting data and configuring the base functionality:

- Create a configuration template to collect data for the setup data of each module
- Describe the purpose of the configuration and its use
- Provide a description for the fields and applicable values

The following screenshot shows a sample data-collection template for a vendor group in the account-payable module:

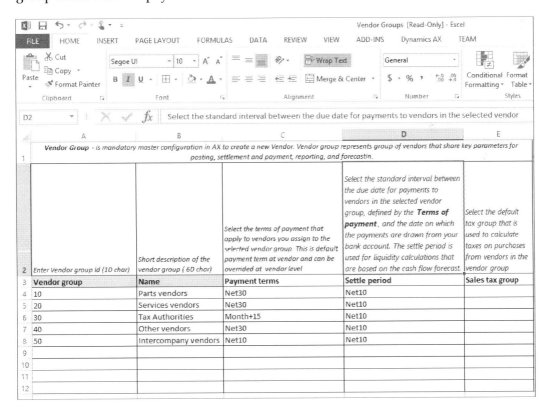

Configuration tools

Microsoft continues to add features and functionalities in every new release of Dynamics AX. With such a broad set of functionalities and features, the implementation projects become bigger and more complex, and thus, project teams require tools and technologies to support configuration management.

There are several tools available with Dynamics AX for the initial configuration and configuration management. The following sections describe some commonly used tools for configuration management.

The Data Import/Export Framework

DIXF is a powerful tool available in Dynamics AX 2012 for data migration and configuration. The chapter on data migration in this book has covered the basics of the DIXF tool. DIXF provides several out-of-the-box master data and parameter entities that can be used for configuration management directly.

The following sections define the key features of DIXF, which are useful for initial configuration and management.

Importing and exporting data using various formats

DIXF supports importing of data using various formats such as files and ODBC. Several file types such as CSV, Excel, and XML are supported for import and export. DIXF can also be used for exporting entity data in any of these supported file types.

Copying and comparing data between legal entities

Using DIXF, a user can compare and copy the data between different legal entities. The copy entity data between the company's wizard, under the Data Import/Export Framework module, can be used for this purpose.

The following diagram shows the high-level data flow that occurs while copying the entity data from one company to another:

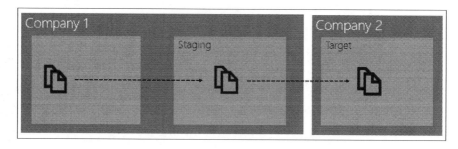

Copying data between Microsoft Dynamics AX instances

You can use DIXF to copy data from one Dynamics AX instance to another. The following diagram shows the data flow that occurs when copying the entity data from one instance to another:

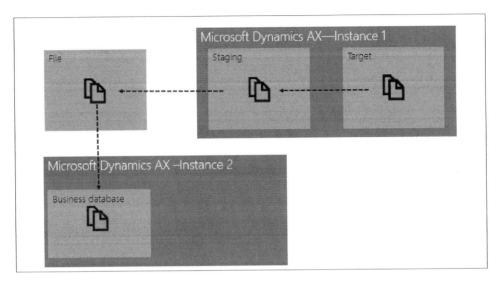

As shown in the preceding diagram, the entity data gets copied from the **Target** entity to a staging table and is then exported to a file in **Instance 1**. Now, that file can simply be imported into **Instance 2** using the typical DIXF import process.

Creating a custom entity

There are more than 150 entities available out of the box in AX 2012 R3, which can be used for the configuration. However, these entities are far from the complete set of configurations, which are required in typical implementation projects. DIXF allows the developers to create new entities if they do not exist. The developers can use the custom entity wizard to create new entities for the data export and import processes.

The following are some additional key features of the Export/Import Framework:

- Provides error handling support such as skipping error rows and so on.
- Set-based support from staging to target
- Default value support
- Number sequence support

The Microsoft Dynamics ERP RapidStart Services

The Microsoft Dynamics ERP RapidStart Services is a cloud-based service provided by Microsoft for its partners and customers for configuring a Dynamics AX 2012 installation using an interview-style questionnaire. After the questionnaire is completed, the responses and information can be imported into the specific Dynamics AX 2012 environments.

The RapidStart Services provide a framework which the partners and customers can use to create additional questions and question groups and map them to specific AX functionalities. They can also create a configuration template and then reuse the configuration for other customers who in the same industry.

The following image shows the architecture of the RapidStart Services for Dynamics AX:

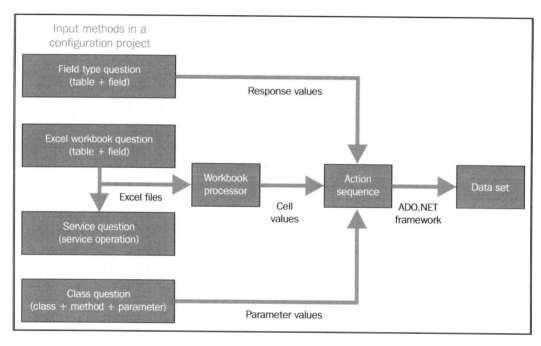

RapidStart services is available in the Microsoft Lifecycle Services tool set. However, a separate agreement is required in order to use the tool in your project.

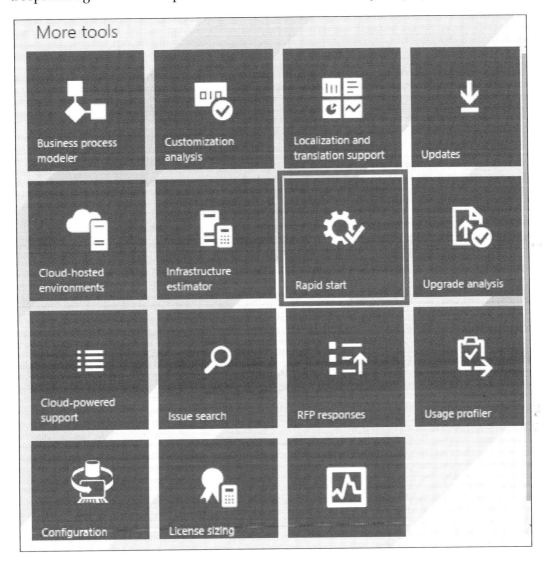

The key features of The Microsoft Dynamics ERP RapidStart Services are as follows:

- **Interview-style questions**: RapidStart Services asks interview-style questions for collecting the business configuration data.
- **Configuration library**: Microsoft provides a set of basic, ready-to-use templates. The customer or partner can build additional templates for specific processes and save them in the configuration library.

- **Cloud-based tool**: This is a subscription-based tool in the cloud and can be accessed via the Microsoft LCS portal.

- **Extensible framework**: Partners and ISVs can create additional templates to support their extensions and custom solutions.

- **Reusable templates**: Partners can create templates and reuse them for another customer, implementing Dynamics AX in the same business area.

 It is still an early version; you may run into limitations during practical use.

The Excel add-in

An Excel add-in is a very powerful tool available in Dynamics AX 2012, which can reduce significant amounts of manual configuration effort. Using the Excel add-in, implementation teams can design an Excel template by selecting the appropriate tables or data elements, and create or update the configuration data directly via the Excel spreadsheet.

The following screenshot shows the Excel add-in for the addition of the `CustGroup` table to create a customer group in the design mode:

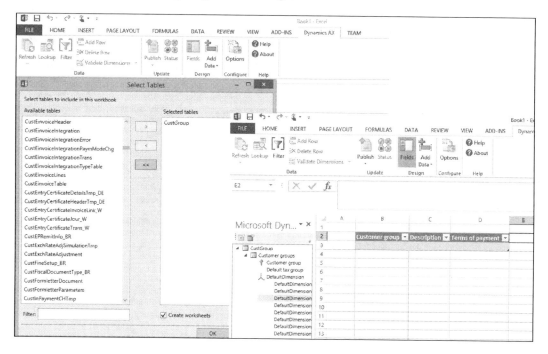

The key features of an Excel add-in as are follows:

- It is a very useful tool for initial data configuration
- It supports, creates, or updates data by adding tables, queries, or services
- It handles the financial dimensions and reference data

The limitations of an Excel add-in as are follows:

- An Excel add-in is not useful for importing large sets of data
- Not all tables and services for inserting or updating data are supported
- It is not the best tool to migrate data between companies or to another environment. The data on the linked fields is refreshed as soon as you change the company or connect to another server

Export/Import – DAT/DEF file

The Export/Import tool is a legacy data export/import tool in Dynamics AX. This is not a configuration tool but rather a tool to move the data from one AX environment to another or between legal entities. To use this tool, you should know the list of tables which contains the setup data.

The following sections define the key concepts of the Export/Import tool.

The definition group

The definition group is a mechanism to define a list of tables that need to be exported from a specific legal entity. To export data from one environment to another, you need to identify the underlying tables where the data is stored and then create a definition group comprising those tables. You also have an option to select the tables based on the table type properties. For example, base data tables and reference tables contain configuration data primarily. By selecting the option of table types while creating definition groups, the system will add all the tables containing the selected table groups.

The following screenshot illustrates the various options available for including the different table groups:

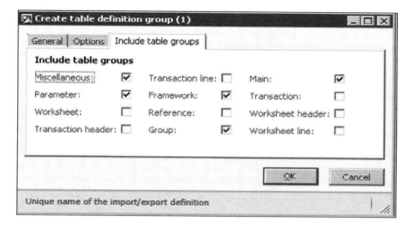

Defining the export criteria

A user can filter the data that needs to be exported from a table by defining the filter criteria. This can be useful when the user needs to export a subset of the data from a table:

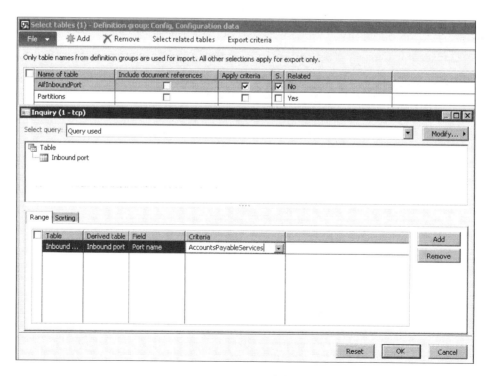

Finding related tables

Another option in the Export/Import tool is to find the related tables from a base table. This is useful when exporting multiple related tables such as `AifInboundPort` or `AifOutboundPort` records. You can start a definition group by adding one table and then finding all the related tables. The system will find all related tables which you can select to add into the definition group. Data from the related tables is exported only if the records are related to the primary table record.

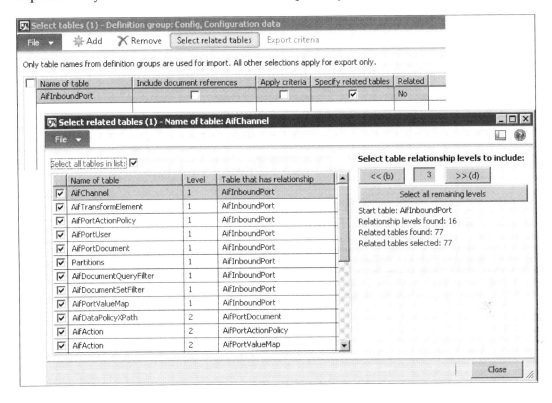

The key features of the Export/Import tool are as follows:

- Searching related tables is useful for copying data from one legal entity to another

- It is useful to export/import data from the master table and reference data, such as customer group, method of payments, and so on

The limitations of the Export/Import tool are as follows:

- This tool is not suitable for data involving default dimensions and ledger accounts

- This tool is not suitable for data with multiple tables and for complex data structures, such as customers and vendors
- This feature is deprecated in the future releases as Microsoft continues to invest in DIXF

The LCS configuration manager – the beta version

The LCS configuration manager is a tool that utilizes the DIXF entities and can export the configured entities' data from one environment to another. The following screenshot shows the configuration manager tool under the LCS project tools:

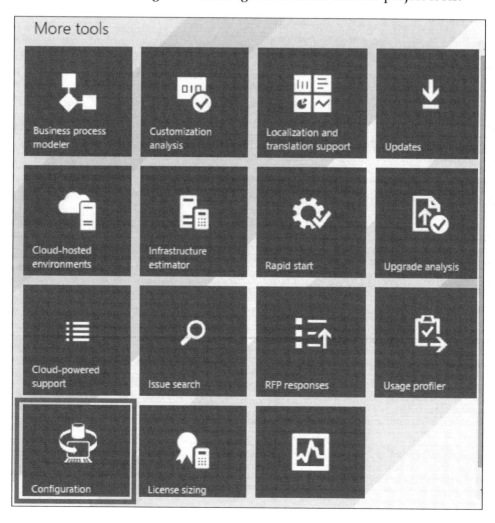

The key features of the LCS configuration manager are as follows:

- This is a cloud based tool for migrating the configuration data from one environment to another
- The user can select legal entities and partitions to export and import

Not supported for production use

This tool uses entities from the DIXF Framework. Since these entities do not include all the functionality in AX 2012 R3, the configuration data will not be migrated.

The Test Data Transfer Tool – the beta version

The Test Data Transfer Tool (dp.exe) is a command-line tool that exports and imports the data from one environment to another. It uses the SQL server bulk copy tool and directly exports and imports data using the Dynamics AX transactional database.

The following diagram illustrates the export and import processes using the Test Data Transfer Tool:

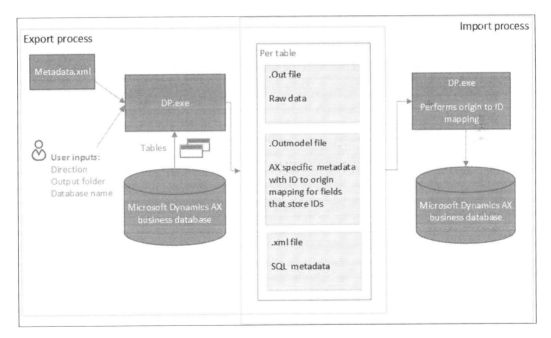

The key features of the Test Data Transfer Tool are as follows:

- This is useful for exporting or importing a large, multi-company dataset
- It can migrate data between different Microsoft Dynamics AX environments
- It can store data in a version control system
- It exports or imports data without running AOS
- It can filter data during export and import
- The Test Data Transfer Tool updates the data during the import process. This is useful for scrubbing sensitive and environment-specific data while migrating the production data to the test environment
- The **Test Data Transfer Tool (beta)** does not make sure that the data that you export is complete or coherent. It exports and imports whatever you ask it to export or import
- It truncates all the data in the table before importing it

It is not suitable for production use due to the preceding limitations.

> **Who should use this tool?**
>
> Only advanced users should use the Test Data Transfer Tool. You should be a database administrator or a developer who has an experience in using SQL Server.

Configuration data management

In any ERP implementation project, you deal with multiple environments. For example, you start with CRP; after the development you move to the test environment, and then training, UAT, and production, as shown in the following diagram:

One of the biggest challenges that an implementation team faces is moving the configuration from one environment to another. If configurations keep changing in every environment, it becomes more difficult to manage them. Similar to code promotion and release management across environments, configuration changes need to be tracked through a change-control process across environments to ensure that you are testing with a consistent set of configurations.

The objective is to keep track of all the configuration changes and make sure that they make it to the final cut in the production environment.

The following sections outline some approaches used for configuration data management in the Dynamics AX project.

The golden environment

An environment that is pristine without any transactions—the golden environment—is sometimes referred to as a stage or pre-prod environment. Create the configurations from scratch and/or use various tools to create and update the configuration data. Develop a process to update the configuration in the golden environment once it has been changed and approved in the test environments.

The golden environment can be turned into a production environment or the data can be copied over to the production environment using database restore.

The golden environment database can be used as a starting point for every run of data migration. For example, if you are preparing for UAT, use the golden environment database as a starting point. Copy to UAT and perform data migration in your UAT environment. This would ensure that you are testing with the golden configurations (if the configuration is missing in the golden environment, you would be able to catch it during testing and fix your UAT and the golden environment too).

The pros of the golden environment are given as follows:

* The golden environment is a single environment for controlling the configuration data
* You can use all the tools available for the initial configuration
* There is a lessened chance of the corruption of configuration data

The cons of the golden environment are given as follows:

* There is a risk of missing configuration updates due to not following the processes (as the configuration updates are made directly in the testing and UAT environments)
* There are chances of migrating the revision data into the production environment like workflow history, address revisions, and policies versions
* There is a risk of migrating environment-specific data from the golden environment to the production environment
* This is not useful for a project going live in multiple phases, as you will not be able to transfer the incremental configuration data using database restore
* You must keep the environment in sync with the latest code

Copying the template company

In this approach, the implementation team typically defines a template legal entity and configures the template company from scratch. Once completed, the template company's configuration data is copied over to the actual legal entity using the data export/import process.

This approach is useful for projects going live in multiple phases, where a global template is created and used across different legal entities. Whereas, in AX 2012, a lot of configuration data is shared, and it makes it almost impossible to copy the company data.

Building configuration templates

In this approach, the implementation team typically builds a repository of all the configurations done in a file, and then imports them in each subsequent environment, and finally, in the production environment.

The pros of building configuration templates are as follows:

- It is a clean approach
- You can version-control the configuration file
- This approach is very useful for projects going live in multiple phases, as you can import the incremental configuration data in the subsequent releases

This approach may need significant development efforts to create the X+ scripts or DIXF custom entities to import all the required configurations.

Summary

In this chapter, we started with understanding the importance of configuration management in a Dynamics AX implementation project. We learned about configuration planning and collecting configuration data. Then we analyzed the different tools available for the initial configuration and moving the configuration data from one environment to another environment. At the end, we learned the basic concepts behind configuration data management, the various techniques for configuration data management, and about promoting the configuration data from one environment to another.

In the next chapter, we will learn about building customization where a lot of time is spent in a typical AX implementation project. We will learn about the different approaches for customizing the Dynamics AX application and the best practices and recommendations.

Building Customizations

9

In most books that outline the ERP implementation best practices, customization is a bad word. However, in reality, one can't avoid it completely in the project. Hence, the ease of use in the development platform and the variety of tools available play a key role in the selection of an ERP system. One of the key reasons why Microsoft Dynamics AX is selected over the other ERP systems is the availability of the broad variety of technology toolsets for building additional solutions. The best practices need to be followed to ensure that the customizations are kept to a minimum, they avoid altering the core foundation of the product, and enough thought is put into making them 'temporary' and upgrade-friendly. I will explain the concept of temporary later in the chapter.

Dynamics AX provides a layered-development approach, where the partners, ISV Solutions, and the customers each have a layer where they can make the customizations without disrupting each other's work.

In this chapter, we will learn to get ready for the development phase of the project and understand the development environment, version control, and branching strategies. Then we will walk through the process of customization and the best practices. In the end, we will explore the **Application Lifecycle Management** (ALM) process for code promotion and release strategies, across environments.

Getting ready for development

Before the development phase of the project starts, the Project manager and the Technical solution architect need to set a few ground rules, such as defining the development environment, version control, the branching strategy and coding standards, the naming convention to be followed, and the code review process. In this section, we will walk through these topics in brief to understand what they mean.

The version control

Keeping track of the code is critical to good development practices. The following are the version control systems commonly used with Dynamics AX 2012:

- **Team Foundation Server (TFS)**: This is the most common version control system used with Dynamics AX. It provides source code management, reporting, requirements management, project management, automated builds, testing, and release management capabilities. It covers the entire application life cycle.

- **Visual Studio Online**: Visual studio online is a cloud-based service. It utilizes the TFS integration with Dynamics AX and provides various ALM capabilities.

- **MorphX VCS**: This is an inbuilt source code management capability within the Dynamics AX application. It is suitable for small projects as it can only be used within a shared development environment.

The development environment

The following are the two commonly-used development environment topologies for developing customization with Dynamics AX.

The shared AOS topology

In this model, a single Dynamics AX AOS and the database are shared among the developers. The shared AOS machine can either be configured to use the MorphX VCS, or the TFS version control with a public profile. This topology may be cost-effective as it requires a single development environment but it's NOT recommended for large projects as there are many known issues when using this topology(This model was popular prior to Dynamics AX 2012 when the project sizes were small, and the Dynamics AX architecture supported it with fewer issues):

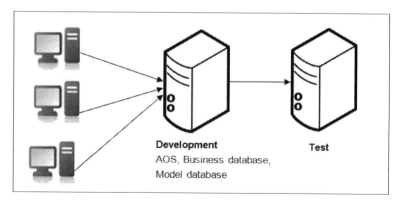

Following are few limitations why the shared AOS topology is not recommended:

- Stale metadata or unpredictable behavior on clients.
- Problems with installing new solutions or upgrading the existing ones, which may lead to corrupt data.
- Unresponsive AOS while another user is debugging the CIL code (The CIL process is used to compile the X++ code into the **Common Intermediate Language (CIL)** of the .NET Framework. Dynamics AX allows you to generate a Full CIL or an Incremental CIL).
- The need to frequently restart the AOS instance.

The private AOS topology

The private AOS topology is the recommended topology for a development environment. As shown in the following diagram, in this topology, each developer has his/her own Dynamics AX client, AOS, business database, and model database and is connected to the TFS. A separate build machine is also connected to the TFS, and is used for creating a build for deployment:

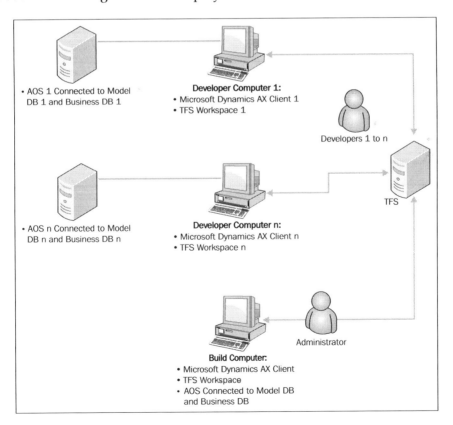

The TFS branching strategies

Microsoft's **Team Foundation Server** (**TFS**) is the preferred and the more widely-used version control system in the Dynamics AX development projects. One of the main features of TFS is Branching, which can be useful in the following scenarios:

- When a stable version is needed for testing while the development work continues in the other areas.

- When multiple development teams are working on a set of features that are independent, but each team also depends on the features developed by the other teams. You need to isolate the risk of the changes made by each team; and yet, you will finally need to merge all the features together into one product.

- When the implementation is being carried out in multiple phases, one phase that is in production may need continuous support but the team may be working on the next phase.

The main only strategy

This is the simplest and most basic branching methodology where one branch is created and all the developers check in the changes to the main branch. The build machine can be used to create a build out of the main branch to be released for testing and later, for the production environment:

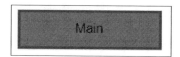

The development and main branching strategy

The development and main branching strategy introduces one or more development branches from the main, which enables the concurrent development of the next release, multiple projects running in parallel, experimentation, or bug fixes in an isolated development branch:

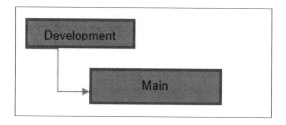

Development, main, and release

If you expect to be performing emergency break fixes outside of your normal release schedule, create a release branch. The release branch represents the code that exists in production:

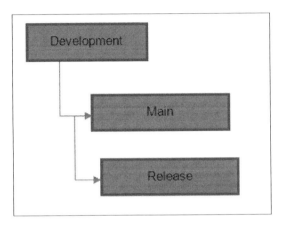

Ground rules for development

The next thing, after getting the development environment and the version control strategy finalized, is defining the ground rules for the development team. The following are some basic rules which need to be defined by the solution architect and the project manager for the development team.

Development layers and models

Dynamics AX provides a development approach of using layers and models. The team needs to make a decision regarding the layer (CUS and USR are, typically, the layers used by the customers) that will be used for customization. Models were introduced in Microsoft Dynamics AX 2012 to help develop and maintain multiple solutions side by side, in the same layer. By default, each layer has its default model. For example, the default model for the USR layer is USR-Model. Multiple models can be created for independent solutions. For instance, if a project involves customization for different business streams, and they are independent, you can create customizations in separate models for each business stream so that they can be installed and maintained separately.

For more information on the Dynamics AX Layers, you can read the TechNet article at `https://msdn.microsoft.com/en-us/library/aa851164.aspx`.

AOT objects' naming conventions

Naming conventions provide consistency and make the application easier to understand. The best practice is to use the following naming convention for the custom objects:

{client prefix} + {business area name} + {business area description} + {action performed (for classes) or type of contents (for tables)}

It is a good practice to add a client prefix at the beginning of the object name to get a unique name for each object and to avoid name collision with any other ISV solution or future upgrade.

For example, a new class created by the vendor ABC for the sales order import process should be named as `AbcSalesOrderImport`.

Label files and language

The labels in Dynamics AX are localizable text resources, and they are used throughout the product as messages to users, form captions, form controls, help text, and so on. When developing custom features in Dynamics AX, the developers should create new label files; they should also create labels and define the translation for each language to be used. The label file names which will be used during the development process should also be defined. Typically, the client prefix used for the AOT object name or the model name are used as the label file name. If your project involves development in multiple models, you should create label files for each model.

Establishing the code review process

Effective code review during the development phase helps identify issues earlier, and avoids rework and bug fixes during the later phases of the project. It is important for the project team to define the code review process and the guidelines for the project at the beginning of the development phase. The code review should not be limited to checking the naming conventions, indentation, and other best practices errors or warnings, which can be easily caught by the Dynamics AX best practices tools. The process should primarily be focused on achieving the following quality objectives:

- **Solution approach**: The code should be implemented in the correct way. If the existing business logic or processes are modified, they should be modified at the appropriate level. The code should be aligned as per the technical design documents.

- **Performance**: Code performance with a high volume of data and the production load.

- **Extendibility**: The solution should be extendible and appropriate.

- **Easy to read and follow**: The code should be easy to read and follow.

- **Error handling**: The code should be able to handle errors appropriately. It's easier to catch such issues during the code review process as compared to the testing phase.

- **Education for team**: The code review process helps in educating the development team members with review feedback from more senior resources. It needs to be used as a training exercise. Set up a culture where the code reviews and feedback sharing become a learning experience rather than a blame game.

One of the common issues that I have seen in the field is that the code reviews are ignored during the development phase, and are considered towards the end of the development cycle, or close to going live. Most of the time, the code review feedback at such later stages is just not feasible. It is difficult to make changes to the code that is already tested and stable. The best way is to embed the code reviews as part of the development cycle, and the learnings from the previous reviews can be used by the developers in further coding.

The development process

The key objective of the development process is to ensure a scalable, maintainable, and high-performing application. The following diagram shows the critical steps for the development process while developing customizations for Dynamics AX:

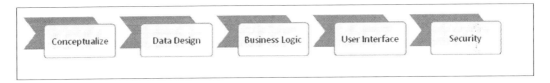

Conceptualization

The first step of the development process is conceptualizing the application. You must understand the problem that you are trying to solve. At this stage, you need to identify the where and the what—where in the standard flow do you need to add your code, and what code can be reused from the standard one.

Dynamics AX provides numerous application frameworks and patterns that can be reused when developing any new functionality or extending any existing functionalities. If you do not understand the existing application pattern and frameworks, you may create a functionality that was not necessary, or one that already exists in the application.

Data design

Data design is the process of analyzing and defining the data structures as per your requirement. In some cases, you may need to add additional columns to existing tables, or you may need to create one or more new tables from scratch. The following section describes the best practices to be followed when designing the data in Dynamics AX.

Adding fields to the existing tables

Dynamics AX has thousands of standard tables to store the master or transactional data. With the release of Dynamics AX 2012, the number of tables has gone higher than the previous releases because of database normalization. It was mainly done to reduce the redundancy of data across various tables, and also to improve the performance. Many times, the requirement is to store or process additional data in certain application functionalities, and so, you may need to add additional columns to the existing SYS layer tables. Consider the following points when adding additional columns to the existing tables:

- Do not add a large number of fields to the base tables. The guideline is to limit the maximum number of fields in a table to 50. Normalize the tables if it makes sense to do so.

- Database normalization is the process of organizing the attributes and tables of a relational database to minimize data redundancy. Normalization usually involves dividing the large tables into smaller (and less redundant) tables and defining the relationships between them. The objective is to isolate the data so that additions, deletions, and modifications on a field can be made in just one table and then propagated through the rest of the database, using the defined relationships.

- Consider adding the required fields to a new table, and add foreign keys to the base table. Adding fields directly to a base table has the following disadvantages:

  ○ New fields may not be required in all scenarios, so the query cost may increase with the new fields.

  ○ If the base layer table is modified or removed, upgrades can be complicated in the future versions of the table. If the fields are added to new tables, you may have to just change the foreign key to associate the customized table with the new table.

Table Types

All the tables in Dynamics AX 2012 have a **TableType** property, which supports three values:

- Regular
- In-memory
- TempDB

The value is shown in the following screenshot:

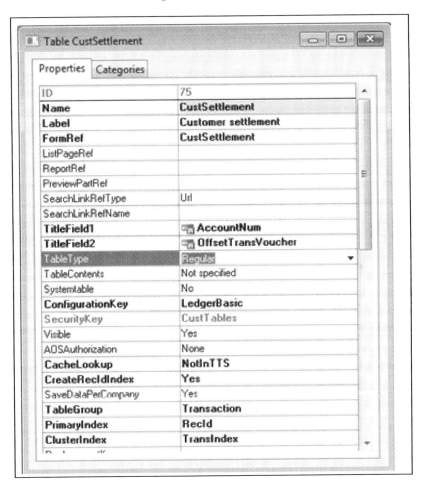

Regular

These are the regular and permanent tables created in the SQL server transaction database.

In-memory

The In-memory tables in AX 2012 are the same as the temporary tables in AX 2009 and earlier versions. The in-memory temporary tables are instantiated in the active memory of the tier that the process is running on. The process can run on the client tier or the server tier. The objects are held in the memory until the size reaches 128 KB. The dataset is then written to a disk file on the server tier. You can use the In-Memory temporary tables when the amount of data is small, and the Microsoft SQL Server round trips should be avoided.

The following example code shows how data can be inserted and retrieved using X++:

```
static void TableTmpInsertRecord(Args _args)
{
  TmpCustLedger custTmpLedger;
  ;
  custTmpLedger.Name = 'NameValue';
  custTmpLedger.Balance01 = 2345000;
  custTmpLedger.insert();

  while select * from custTmpLedger
  {
    Info(custTmpLedger.Name);
  }
}
```

TempDB

The TempDB tables are instantiated on the TempDB database of the SQL Server database. The TempDB tables utilize the power of the SQL tables and support joins, aggregation, and indexes with great performance. However, they have almost the same scoping mechanism as the in-memory temporary tables. The TempDB tables also provide the following capabilities which are available with the regular tables:

- These tables can be company-specific or global
- They support transaction processing

The following code example shows the use of a TempDB table in X++.

In the following example, all the customer accounts associated with the customer group Corp are filtered into the TempDB table CustTableTmpFilter, and then this table is used in join to filter CustTransOpen:

```
static void TableTmpDBExample(Args _args)
{

  CustTableTmpFilter custTableTmpFilter;
  CustTable custTable;
  CustTrans custTrans;
  CustTransOpen custTransOpen;

  Insert_ recordset custTableTmpFilter (CustAccount)
  Select AccountNum from CustTable
  Where custTable.CustGroup = "Corp";

  While select sum(AmountCur) from CustTransOpen
  Join AccountNum from CustTrans
  where custTransOpen.RefRecId == custTrans.RecId &&
  JOIN custTableTmpFilter
  where
  custTableTmpFilter.CustAccount == custTrans.AccountNum
  group by AccountNum
  {
    Info(strfmt("Customer:%1, Balance: %2",
    custTrans.CustAccount,
    custTransOpen.AmountCur));
  }

}
```

Table fields

Use the **Extended Data Types (EDTs)** and base enums to create fields for the tables. The use of EDTs and Base enums reduces work and promotes consistency.

Avoid changing the existing standard base enum values. Modifying the base enum values can have an upgrade impact in the future. In case you need to add new enum values to a standard enum, leave a gap between the existing and the new values. The gap can be useful in avoiding conflict if a new value is added to a standard enum in a future version.

For adding a field to a country-specific or region-specific functionality, add the country/region context on the EDTs and the table fields.

Extended data types (EDTs): An EDT is a primitive data type or container with a supplementary name and some additional properties. For example, you could create a new EDT called `Name` and base it on a `string`. Thereafter, you can use the new EDT in variable and field declarations in the development environment.

Base enums: X++ does not support constants but has an enumerable type (enum), which is a list of literals. There are hundreds of enumerable types that are built into the standard application. For example, the enum `NoYes` has two associated literals, where No has the value 0, and Yes has the value 1.

Date effectivity

Dynamics AX 2012 introduced the Date Effectivity Framework for handling the date-effective data. A simple example of date-effective data can be a discount table, where the discounts can be effective and/or expired at a certain date/time. To enable the Date effectivity on a table, you need to set `ValidTimeStateFieldType` to `Date` or `UTCDateTime`. This will automatically create date-effective fields in the table. The next thing that you need to do is add a unique index, and set the **Alternate key** property and the `ValidTimeStateKey` property to `Yes`. That's it! Your table now supports date effectivity:

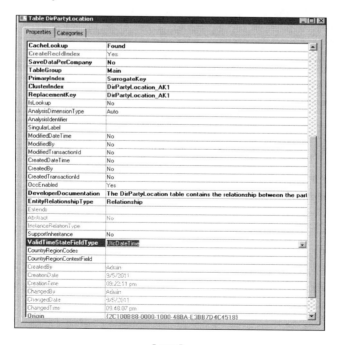

Table properties

When you create a new table, there are several table properties which need to be set for efficiency and maintenance. The following sections outline some of the key properties.

The table group

Use the following guidelines to set the table group property for the new tables:

Table Groups	Description	Examples
Parameters	This contains the parameter data for the module or features. Typically contains one record per company.	`CustParameters`, `VendParameters`
Group	This contains data to categorize the master data.	`CustGroup`, `VendGroup`
Main	This contains tables containing the key master data.	`CustTable`, `VendTable`
Transactions	Tables containing the transaction data.	`CustTrans`, `VendTrans`
Worksheet header	Tables containing the transaction entry data headers.	`SalesTable`, `PurchTable`
Worksheet lines	Tables containing the transaction entry lines.	`SalesLine`, `PurchLine`
Miscellaneous	Tables which do not fall into any of the other categories.	

The table caching

Set the appropriate table caching properties for the new tables. This is one of the most important properties of the tables. Not using caching properly can lead to significant performance problems:

Cache lookup property	Description	When to use	Suitable table groups
None	No data is cached.	Use table caching none for tables that are heavily updated.	Transactions
NotInTTS	All the successful key selects are cached. Select the inside transactions' result to database call for retrieving records.	CustTable is a perfect example for NotInTTS. Since the CustTable data can keep changing, it would be wise to use real-time data inside the transactions.	Main WorksheetHeader WorksheetLine Transactions
Found	All the successful caching key selects are cached. All the caching key selects are returned from the cache if the record exists there. Selecting forUpdate in a transaction forces reading from the database, and replaces the record in the cache.	Suitable for the main tables which do not change, or where the data is almost static such as Units, PaymTerm, and so on.	Main Group Parameters

Cache lookup property	Description	When to use	Suitable table groups
FoundAndEmpty	All the selects on the caching keys are cached, including the selects that do not return any data. Select forUpdate in a transaction forces reading from the database and replaces the record in the cache.	An example of the FoundAndEmpty record caching is in the Discount table in the Microsoft Dynamics AX standard application. By default, the Discount table has no records. By using a FoundAndEmpty cache on this table, the keys that are queried for but not found are stored in the cache. Subsequent queries for these same non-existent records can be answered from the cache without a round trip to the database.	Group Main
EntireTable	Creates a set-based cache on the server. The entire table is cached as soon as at least one record is selected from the table. An EntireTable cache is flushed whenever an insert, update, or delete is made to the table.	Small tables with few records.	Parameters Group

Index considerations

Indexes are the database objects in the table that provide the efficient retrieval of data. SQL Server provides two types of indexes:

- The clustered index
- The non-clustered index

The clustered index

Clustered indexes represent the way the data are physically stored in the tables. There can be only one cluster index per table. A clustered index is required in all the permanent Microsoft Dynamics AX tables. If you don't define a cluster index, `RecId` is used as one. The clustered indexes are often defined on the **primary key (PK)** of a table. You can define a cluster index for a table by setting the **Table Cluster Index** properties as follows:

The non-clustered index

All the other indexes in a table are non-cluster indexes. Non-cluster indexes have a structure that is separate from the data rows. These indexes contain the non-cluster index key values and a pointer to the data rows, called a row locator.

Both the cluster and non-cluster indexes can either be unique non-unique. In Dynamics AX, a unique index is defined when the index's `AllowDuplicates` property is set to **Yes**. When this property is set to **No**, a non-unique index is created.

Best practices for indexes

Consider the following best practices when designing the indexes in Dynamics AX:

- Assign a unique index to each table. Unique indexes are important for table caching. The `Found`, `NotInTTS`, and `FoundAndEmpty` caching will work only when a unique index exists.

- The clustered index is a critical property in a table. When you create a new table, the `RecId` is used as the default cluster index, but in many cases it is not optimal. Analyze the appropriate key and designate it as the cluster index. For example, for `CustTable`, most of the queries and searches will be based on the customer account number and not on `RecId`. Hence, the index on the `AccountNumber` field makes more sense as the cluster index rather than the `RecId` index.

- For cluster indexes, do not use the columns that are subject to updates. When a column in a clustered index is updated, the row may have to be moved to a new page, and all the non-clustered index entries for that row will have to be updated. This increases the I/O cost of updates.

- Clustered indexes do not necessarily have to be unique. When a clustered index is non-unique, the SQL Server adds a 4-byte uniquifier integer to the index entry. This happens only when a duplicate entry is detected; otherwise, the uniquifier is `NULL` and consumes no space. If there are a few duplicate entries in the clustered index, the incremental cost of a non-unique index is low. Do not add a column to a clustered index solely to make it unique.

- Consider the size of the clustered index key. Since the clustered index key is used as a row locator in non-clustered indexes in the same table, a long clustered index key can increase the size of the non-clustered index keys.

- Analyze the usage and queries, and create only the indexes that are necessary. Indexes which are not necessary add costs to the inserts and updates.

- When there are multiple keys in an index, define the fields in the same order as they will appear in the where clause of the query. If the order is different, the index may not be used during the query execution process.

- Design indexes to avoid index scans. An index scan requires the entire index to be read. A scan of the clustered index is equivalent to a table scan.

- Ax 2012 has the ability to use the included columns in non-clustered indexes for providing query coverage. Use the included columns as they may provide better I/O results as compared to adding columns in the key. A common example is seen in the case of date-effective tables, where the `ValidTo` column is defined as an included column.

Tables key considerations

Keys, as the name suggests, are a key part of a relational database and are used to enforce data integrity and table relations. In Dynamics AX, the keys are maintained at the application level and not in the SQL database. The following are the type of keys used in the Dynamics AX tables.

The alternate key

An index in Dynamics AX can be set as an alternate key by setting the **Alternate Key** property to **Yes**. An alternate key means that the other tables can create foreign key relations that reference this key as an alternative to referencing the primary key. A unique index with only one field can be defined as an alternate key. There can be multiple alternate keys in one table.

The primary key

The primary key is usually the type of key that the child tables refer to when a foreign key field in other tables need a relational identifier. There can be only one primary key in one table. In Dynamics AX, the primary key can be defined on the **Table Primary Index** property. Only a unique index with the property **Alternate Key** set to **Yes** can be defined as a primary key.

The replacement key

A replacement key is an alternate key that the system can display on forms instead of a meaningless numeric primary key value. Each table can have a maximum of one replacement key. In Dynamics AX, replacement keys can be selected on the table property as **ReplacementKey**.

The foreign key

In Dynamics AX, foreign keys are represented by table relations. In order to create a foreign key in a child table, you need to add a relation node to the parent table. Foreign keys are used to provide lookups and validation for the parent table record when used from the child record.

The natural key

The natural key is a term used to represent the keys which are meaningful to the users. Most of the replacement keys are natural keys.

Surrogate keys

The system fields as key fields such as `RecId` are not meaningful to the users, but are good to use as a primary key and a foreign key. Since surrogate keys are not attached to the business, even if the natural key changes, the references to the surrogate key do not need to be updated.

The delete actions

Define the delete actions on the tables to delete the related records from the child tables. Delete actions are better than writing a code to delete the records from the child tables.

Delete actions rely on table relations so if you create a delete action, make sure that there is a relationship defined between the relevant tables.

The business logic

The business logic is a part of a program or code that encodes the real-world business scenarios. In Dynamics AX, the business logic can be written at multiple levels, such as the form UI, enterprise portal ASP.Net code, table method, classes, SSRS reports, and so on.

While working with the customization requests for Dynamics AX, there are typically two kinds of scenarios presented to the developers. The first scenario is a standalone functionality, where new forms, tables, and business logic need to be developed and later integrated into the core modules. In the second scenario, the existing processes within the AX application need to be extended to support the requirement. In both cases, it's important for the developers to understand how the business logic for the core module and functionalities is implemented in the application layer. Understanding the implementation of the core functionalities and the framework is extremely important for the developers so that they can efficiently utilize, reuse, or extend these functionalities in their custom solution. In any case, customizations need to be added on a temporary basis. The customizations should be easy to isolate and remove when they are not needed anymore, or when the required functionality is added to the product in a later release. The following are some core technical application frameworks that a developer may need to know when creating custom features and functionalities.

The number sequence framework

Microsoft Dynamics AX contains a number sequence framework to generate alphanumeric number sequences. These sequences can be used for transaction documents, such as sales orders, purchase orders, invoices, and journals, or for master data entities such as customers, vendors, and employees. The primary purpose of the number sequence framework is to provide unique, user-friendly identifiers while maintaining a continuous or non-continuous alphanumeric sequence.

If your custom application needs to implement a number sequence, you can extend or utilize the number sequence framework to enable the number sequence code for your feature. The MSDN article at `https://msdn.microsoft.com/en-us/library/aa608474.aspx` provides a detailed description of number sequences.

The FormLetter framework

The FormLetter framework is used for posting business documents such as sales orders and purchase orders. This framework contains a number of class hierarchies and controls for document processing.

The key features of this framework are as follows:

- It interacts with the posting forms, such as SalesEditLines
- It creates and maintains the posting data, such as records in SalesParmTable
- It can create journal data, such as records in CustPackingSlipJour or CustPackingSlipTrans
- It enables validations
- This framework updates the sub ledgers such as ledger and inventory
- It controls the document outputs such as printing and XML export

The RunBase framework

The RunBase framework provides a standardized approach for creating processes and batch jobs in Microsoft Dynamics AX.

The key features of this framework are as follows:

- Query to define the filter criteria
- Dialog, with persistence of the last values entered by the user
- Validation of user input
- Batch execution for the users to schedule jobs
- Progress bar
- Client/server-optimization

Refer to `https://msdn.microsoft.com/en-us/library/aa863262.aspx` to understand the RunBase framework in more detail.

The SysOperation framework

Use the SysOperation framework for extending Microsoft Dynamics AX by adding a new functionality that may require batch processing. The SysOperation framework replaces the RunBase framework. It provides the infrastructure for creating user-interaction dialog boxes and integration with the batch server for batch processing.

The important features of the SysOperation framework include the following:

- It enables the menu-driven or batch execution of services.

- It calls the services in a synchronous or an asynchronous mode.

- It automatically creates a customizable UI based on the data contract.

- It encapsulates the code to operate on the appropriate tier (prompting on the client tier, and business logic on the server tier).

- Combining the SysOperation framework and services creates a good foundation for reusing the business processes for multiple user interfaces. For example, you can use the sales order invoice service for both, the rich client and the Enterprise Portal for Microsoft Dynamics AX, or for a custom C# application.

- The SysOperation framework supports a dynamic UI and different execution modes from X++, which makes the development very clean and reusable.

- For a comparison between the SysOperation and RunBase frameworks, and to view the sample code that illustrates interactive and batch execution, refer to the white paper, *Introduction to the SysOperation Framework* available at `https://technet.microsoft.com/EN-US/library/hh881828.aspx`.

Services and the Application Integration Framework (AIF)

Use services and AIF to code the business processes. The services can be used for normal business processes as well as for integration scenarios. Microsoft Dynamics AX 2012 supports the following three kinds of services:

- Document services are query-based services that can be used to exchange data with the external systems by sending and receiving XML documents. These documents represent business entities, such as customers, vendors, or sales orders.

- Custom services can be used by the developers to expose any X++ logic, such as X++ classes and their members, through a service interface. An example for custom services is a workflow approval via the e-mail service.

- System services provided by Microsoft Dynamics AX include the query service, the metadata service, and the user-session service. The system services are not customizable, and they are not mapped to any query or X++ code.

- Developers should use the existing services exposed in the Microsoft Dynamics AX base layer. Expose any new business processes through services.

- For additional details on Services and AIF and the scenarios in which the document services or custom services can be used, refer to *Chapter 3, Infrastructure Planning and Design*.

Other application and development frameworks

There are many such features and frameworks available in Dynamics AX. The following table lists a few of these frameworks and some useful links for additional details:

Framework	Description	Useful links

The global address book	This implements the party, association, and the address. The developers need to understand the global address book concept to implement any address or party-related functionality on custom objects.	`https://technet.`
		`microsoft.com/`
		`en-us/library/`
		`hh272867.aspx`

Financial account and dimensions	The financial account and dimension framework is core to the Shared financial accounting model and unlimited financial dimension architecture. The developers need to understand the underlying data model and the APIs available for integrating the custom modules to the financial module of AX.	`https://technet.`
		`microsoft.com/`
		`EN-US/library/`
		`hh272858.aspx`

The Source Document Framework	The Source Document Framework (accounting framework) will provide the functionality that is necessary for recording business events, and create accounting for the newly created documents, that is, accounting distributions and sub ledger journal entries.	`http://blogs.`
		`msdn.com/b/`
		`ax_gfm_framework_`
		`team_blog/`
		`archive/2012/04/26/`
		`extending-the-`
		`source-document-`
		`framework.aspx`

Framework	Description	Useful links
The Product Data Management Framework	This is a framework for managing the product attributes and for releasing the product to legal entities. It is very common to get customization requests in the Product management module and hence, the developers should understand the underlying data model and processes for customizations in this module.	https://technet.microsoft.com/EN-US/library/hh272877.aspx
The Budget Control Framework	The Budget control framework enables a budget control check on the processing of certain documents such as purchase requisitions, purchase orders, and projects. To extend the budget check functionality to a new module or to customize any process around it, the developers need to be aware of this framework.	https://technet.microsoft.com/EN-US/library/hh272864.aspx
The Reporting framework	The Reporting framework provides the ability to link the Dynamics AX application to the SQL Server reporting services. Using the reporting framework, the developers can define the business logic, datasets and user interfaces for providing report parameters and for calling the SSRS report execution process.	https://technet.microsoft.com/EN-US/library/hh500190.aspx
The Policy framework	The Policy framework provides the ability to define the organization policies such as purchasing policy, security policy, centralized payment policy, and so on. It enables the developers to define the rules for each policy, which can be evaluated during document processing. The developers can extend the existing policy by adding more rules, or they can implement a new policy if required.	https://technet.microsoft.com/en-us/library/hh272869.aspx
The Workflow framework	The Workflow framework provides the ability to define the business rules and approval process for document processing. This framework can be extended easily to any new custom document, or additional workflow controls can be implemented using the workflow framework.	https://technet.microsoft.com/en-us/library/gg731908.aspx

Framework	Description	Useful links

The Data Export Import Framework (DIXF)	The Data export and import framework provides the ability to export and import the configuration or initial transactional data for data migration and configuration purposes. This framework can be utilized to build typical file import scenarios or asynchronous file-based integration scenarios.	`https://technet.`
		`microsoft.com/`
		`EN-US/library/`
		`jj933277.aspx`

Best practices to customize business processes

The following sections describe the best practices when you customize the business logic in Dynamics AX.

Reusing the code

As explained earlier, Dynamics AX provides numerous application frameworks. When developing the custom features, you should be able to extend the existing frameworks or reuse the code for your customization. The suggestion is to try not to reinvent the wheel, but investigate and utilize what is already available in the system.

Using eventing

The use of events was a new concept that was introduced in the Dynamics AX 2012 release. Using events, you can create pre- and post-events to implement custom behavior.

Using events, you can add custom behavior to the standard business logic, without over- layering the base layer code to your custom layer. Events has the potential to lower the cost of upgrades to the later versions.

Events can be useful in supporting the following programming models:

- **Observation**: Events can be used to look for exceptional behavior, and to generate alerts when such behavior occurs. An example of this event is to alert the customer contact in case the customer credit limit has reached a certain threshold.

- **Information dissemination**: Events can deliver the right information to the right consumers at the right time. Information dissemination is supported by publishing an event for anyone wishing to react to it.

- **Decoupling**: Events produced by one part of the application can be consumed by a completely different part of the application. There is no need for the producer to be aware of the consumers, nor do the consumers need to know the details about the producer. One producer's event can be acted upon by any number of consumers. Conversely, the consumers can act upon any number of events from many different producers.

TechNet provides detailed information on Eventing in AX 2012 at `https://technet.microsoft.com/en-us/library/hh272875.aspx`.

Customizing the code

When the base layer code needs to be replicated or used in other places, it is always better to extend the existing classes and modify the derived class for the change in behavior, rather than creating completely new classes and then copying the entire code from the base class.

Extending the standard business logic by extending the class will makes it easier to upgrade the code. If you have created an extension, only the modified code must be restructured.

Create classes and methods so that the same piece of code can be reused in multiple places. Avoid creating long methods. They make the code difficult to read, hard to debug, and extremely difficult to upgrade and maintain.

Do not keep the commented code if you want to avoid the upgrade and maintenance costs. Keep the older version of the code in version control.

Where to add the custom code

Create the customizations in the appropriate location. Create the code for reuse as much as possible, but create it at the lowest appropriate location. For example, if something is required only in a form, do not put it at the table level.

The following examples describe the locations at which we recommend that you place the code:

- If it is related to the UI, place the code on the appropriate UI elements, or create classes to handle the scenarios specific to the UI. For example, you can create classes that handle controls, number sequences in forms, dialog boxes, and so on.
- If it is related to a business process, place the code in classes.
- If it is directly related to the tables and schemas, place the code in the tables.
- Consume the existing Microsoft Dynamics AX classes and table methods instead of writing direct X++ queries.

The user interface

When designing the user interface in Dynamics AX, follow the standard AX form templates and the UX guidelines to create familiar and consistent form patterns for the customized features.

Client user interface guidelines

The following sections define the different form types available in standard Dynamics AX and their usage scenarios.

The list pages

The list pages display a list of related data and provide the ability to quickly filter, take actions, and open the detail forms. They also display related information for the selected records as fact boxes. List pages are the starting point for performing the bulk of daily activities for the business users, such as creating and editing customers.

The following screenshot shows the standard customer list page:

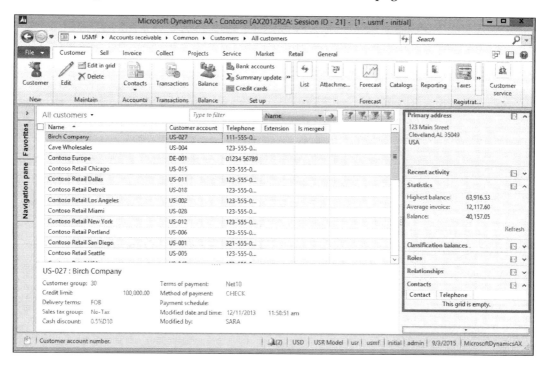

The details forms

The details forms are the primary methods for data entry. Using the details forms, the user can create, edit, and take action on data. The details forms also contain fact boxes on the right-hand side to display any related information. The following image shows a customer details form:

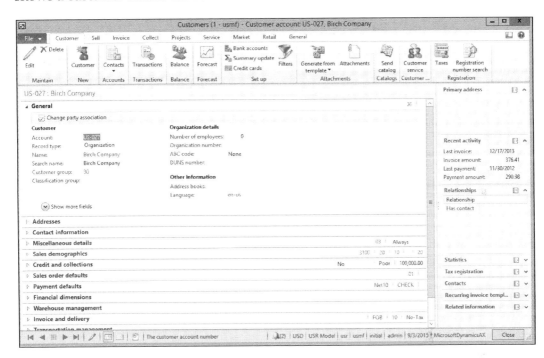

Details forms with lines

The details forms with lines have one form with a header and a line view which the user can toggle to switch between the views. An example of the sales order details form is seen in the following screenshot:

The simple list

The simple list form is typically used to display the reference data. For example, the customer group is shown in the following screenshot:

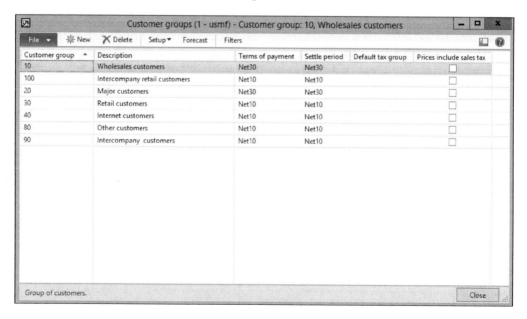

The simple details forms

The simple details forms are forms having a single page containing the details information. It is the recommended pattern for creating or viewing related or referenced data, as shown in the following screenshot:

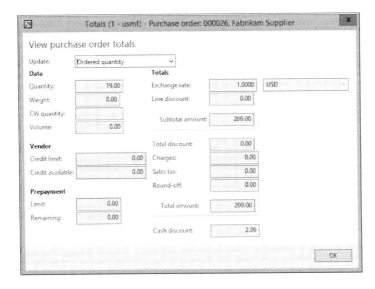

The simple list and details forms

The simple list and details forms contain the simple list and details page forms on a single page. These forms are useful for reference data with multiple fields. For example, payment terms, as shown in the following screenshot:

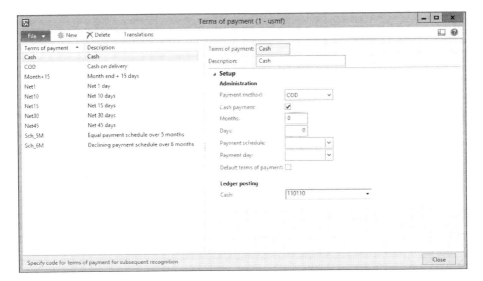

The table of content forms

The table of content forms use vertical buttons on the left to navigate and display the content on the right side of the page. The following screenshot displays the pattern that is recommended for the parameters forms:

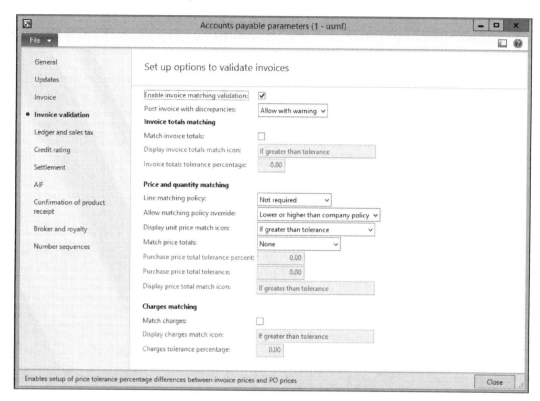

Enterprise portal user interface guidelines

Enterprise portal is the web interface for Dynamics AX. Enterprise portal UI guidelines follow patterns similar to the ones described in the AX client. The following sections define the three common page layouts in enterprise portal.

List pages

The list pages in Enterprise Portal are exactly the same as the rich client list pages and provide a similar functionality.

The details forms

The details forms in Enterprise Portal provides patterns similar to the details form in the AX client:

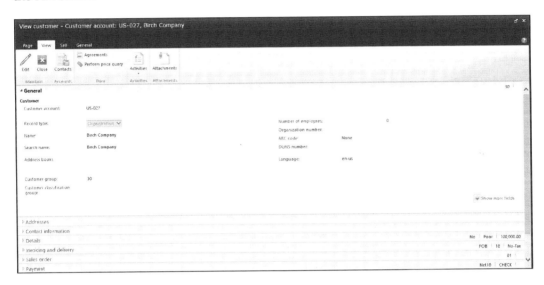

The two-phase create dialog

This is typically used to create a header record before creating a line record. The following screenshot is an example of a two-phase create header creation dialog:

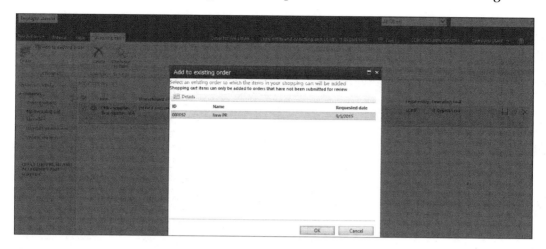

Report user interface guidelines

Typically, there are three types of report UI's in Dynamics AX: outgoing documents, simple lists, and grouped lists layouts.

The document type reports

The following screenshot displays the purchase order report layout in Dynamics AX. Most of the external facing reports, such as purchase order, sales order packing slip, sales order invoice and so on, use the same layout:

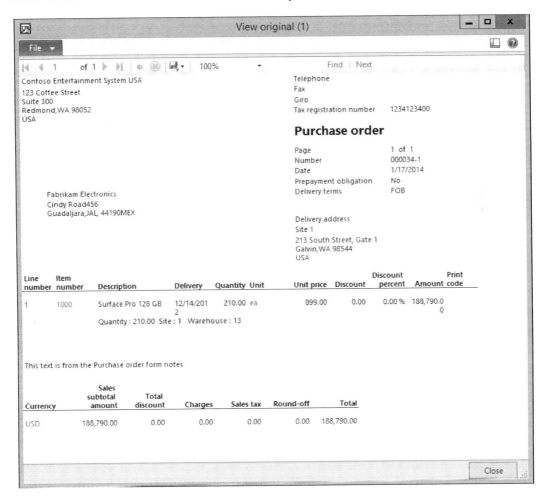

The simple list

The simple list reports are usually internal production reports used for data analysis. The following screenshot displays the **On-hand Inventory** reports, which display the on-hand information about the products:

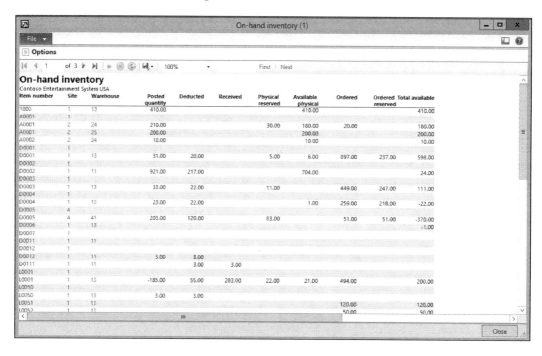

The group list type

The group list type reports are also used for internal production reporting. This report layout is used to display summarized transactional details and include sub totals and grand totals. The following screenshot displays **Customer transactions** grouped by customers:

Customer transactions
The Light Company

Voucher	Date	Text	Debit	Credit	Currency	Amount Currency
4000		**Light and Design**				
00003_042	01/16/02	Sales invoice 00000003_042	5,671.88		EUR	5,671.88
00005_CPA	01/31/02	Payment		5,671.88	EUR	-5,671.88
00029_PRJ	01/01/06	Test		100.00	EUR	-100.00
		Light and Design	**5,671.88**	**5,771.88**		
4002		**The Bright Idea**				
00005_042	02/01/02			1,512.45	DKK	-9,476.50
00005_042	02/01/02	Discount 00000005_042		30.25	DKK	-189.53
00005_042	02/01/02	Discount 00000005_042	30.25		DKK	189.53
00005_042	02/01/02	Sales Invoice 00000005_042	1,512.45		DKK	9,476.50
		The Bright Idea	**1,542.70**	**1,542.70**		
4004		**The Specialist**				
00006_42	02/04/02	Sales invoice 00000006_42	302.50		EUR	302.50
		The Specialist	**302.50**			
4006		**Furniture World**				
00004_42	01&31&02	Sales invoice 00000004?42		2,937.00	EUR	2,937.00
		Furniture World	**2,937.00**			
4007		**Office Design Inc.**				
00006_CPA	02/28/02			136.12	EUR	-136.12
00006_CPA	02/28/02	Discount 00000007_42		1.38	EUR	-1.38
00007_042	04/01/02	Sales invoice 00000007_42	137.50		EUR	137.50
		Office Design Inc.	**137.50**	**137.50**		
4008		**The Warehouse**				
00001_088	01/11/02	Project invoice 00000001_88	125.00		EUR	125.00
00002_086	01/31/02	Project Invoice 00000002_86	462.50		EUR	462.50
00003_088	02/11/02	Project invoice 00000003_88	125.00		EUR	125.00
00004_088	03/11/02	Project invoice 00000004_88	125.00		EUR	125.00
00007_CPA	02/28/02			125.00	EUR	-125.00
		The Warehouse	**837.50**	**125.00**		
4009		**Habitat**				
00001_086	01/31/02	Project invoice 00000001_86	743.75		EUR	743.75
00002_086	01/31/02	Sales invoice 00000002_042	240.63		EUR	240.63
00003_088	02/11/02	Project invoice 00000004_86	60,000.00		EUR	60,000.00
		Habitat	**60,984.38**			
4010		**The Lamp Shop**				
00001_042	01/16/02	Sales invoice 00000001_042	371.25		EUR	371.25
00006_0CPA	02/28/02			371.25	EUR	-371.25
		The Lamp Shop	**371.25**	**371.25**		

Security

Unlike the earlier versions of Dynamics AX, AX 2012 security definition is a development task, and the ground work for the supporting security definition of the custom objects should be done as part of the development process.

Key concepts

The Dynamics AX role-based security is based on the following key concepts:

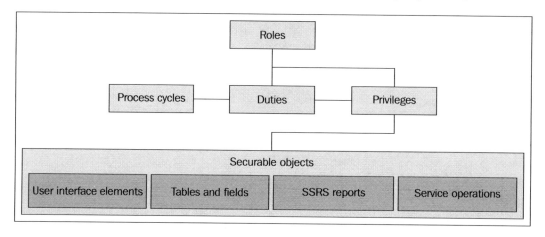

Security roles

The security roles that are assigned to a user determine the duties that the user can perform and the parts of the user interface that the user can view. All users must be assigned to at least one security role for accessing Microsoft Dynamics AX.

Duties

Duties correspond to the parts of a business process. The administrator assigns duties to security roles. A duty can be assigned to more than one role.

The process cycle

To help the administrator locate the duties that must be assigned to roles, duties are organized by the business processes that they are a part of. In the context of the security model, business processes are referred to as process cycles. For example, in the accounting process cycle, you may find the maintain ledgers and maintain bank transactions duties.

Privilege

In the security model of Microsoft Dynamics AX, a privilege specifies the level of access that is required to perform a job, solve a problem, or complete an assignment. Privileges can be assigned directly to roles. However, for easier maintenance, it is recommended that you assign the privileges to duties and duties to roles.

Permissions

Each function in Microsoft Dynamics AX, such as a form or a service, is accessed through an entry point. The menu items, web content items, and service operations are collectively referred to as entry points.

In the security model for Microsoft Dynamics AX, permissions group the securable objects and the access levels that are required to run a function. This includes any tables, fields, forms, or server-side methods that are accessed through the entry point.

Policies

These are used to restrict the data that a user can see in a form or a report. This is a new method in Dynamics AX 2012 to limit the data, similar to what you have with record level security. With this feature, you create a query with restrictions. Then, you create a security policy that can be applied to a security role. For example, if you wanted to limit your accounts-payable clerks from seeing the retail vendors, you could create a query on the vendor group table with a range that limits the retail vendors. You would then create a policy that includes this query and the security role.

Security for custom objects

While the administrators can maintain the security role assignment for individual users, most of the work for creating the security objects needs to be done by the developer in the AOT. The following security related tasks need to be created by the developers:

- Each user interface element in the AOT such as forms, menu items and reports has a security node. The developers must define appropriate security at the object level. In a normal scenario, the default security policy for the object is created automatically based on the properties defined at the form data source and control level. In advance scenarios, the developers can override the default security permission at the control level.

- The developers should create the appropriate privileges and add entry points (menu items and web page URL) to associate the functionality.

- Custom duties and roles should be created for custom functions, before they can be assigned to the users.

- The security policy nodes should be created by the developers to use the XDS security models in Dynamics AX.

Coding best practices

In this section, we will learn some best practices to be followed during development in Dynamics AX.

Best practice check

Run your code through the X++ best practices process, evaluate all the best practices errors and warnings, and take the appropriate action.

Naming variables and objects

Begin the variable and method names with lowercase letters like `custTable`, `validateFields`, and so on. Begin the names of the AOT elements with capital letters such as `CustTable`, `SalesFormLetters`, and so on.

Prefix the parameters names with an underscore (`Args _args`). Use meaningful and self-explanatory variable names. For example: `SalesTable salesTable` and not `SalesTable table1`

Commenting the code

Code comments enhance the readability of the code and are very useful for those involved in modifying or maintaining the code. Comments should be used to describe the intent, algorithmic overview, and the logical flow.

Add XML documentation for class, class methods, and table methods. You can generate an XML file from this documentation.

Labels and text

Use labels for all text such as labels, form caption, infolog, and so on and provide code comments.

Database

The following list provides the best practices guidelines related to the database:

- Avoid using direct SQL calls from the X++ code. Direct SQL statements do not respect application security.
- Consider specifying a field list in select statements to increase the performance.
- Avoid display methods whenever possible.
- Run the code on AOS whenever possible.
- Use the where clauses that align with the indexes in select statements and queries.
- Use `firstonly` where applicable to increase the performance.
- Use aggregates in the selection criteria instead of letting the code do the aggregation.
- Use table joins instead of while loops.
- Use `Update_Recordset` and `insert_recordset` wherever applicable.

Transactions

Keep the following best practices in mind when creating transactions:

- Keep the database transactions as short as possible
- Do not include user interaction inside the database transactions
- Use `throw` instead of `ttsAbort`
- On a server-side TTS block, do not call back to the client for displaying the dialog boxes

Exception handling

The following list provides the best practices guidelines related to exceptions:

- The `throw` statement an exception to stop processing. It will stop the transaction execution and rollback operations if inside the transactions.
- Use the info, warning, and error functions without a thrown exception in cases where the X++ call stack that is being executed should not be stopped.

The Application Lifecycle Management (ALM)

Every implementation project involves separate Dynamics AX environments for developing customizations, testing, and then finally releasing these customizations into the production environment. The **Application Lifecycle** is the process of governance, development, and maintenance of the customization process across these environments.

The following image shows an example application life cycle scenario for customization and code promotion across environments, using Dynamics AX:

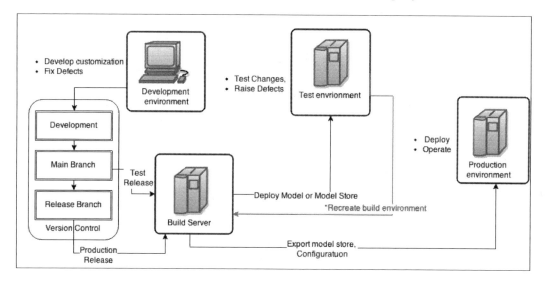

As shown in the preceding flowchart, this example ALM process goes through the phases described in the following sections.

Development

In this phase, the development team creates a customized solution, does unit testing, and when the code is ready for testing, the code is checked into the development branch of the version control system. When the changes are ready to go to the test environment, they are merged with the main branch. A build is created out of the main branch and released in the test environment. Any defect found during the testing cycle is fixed and is checked into the version control system. It then goes through the merge process and is released to the Test environment.

Creating the build

The build server collects the latest XPO (.xPO is an extension for the code files exported from Dynamics AX AOT) changes from the TFS version control main branch and creates build for the test environment. The output of a build would be a model store file.

> In Dynamics AX 2012, the application Ids are installation-specific, which means they can be different in different environments if they are not initialized from the same model store. To avoid conflict, you should initialize the build environment model from the test environment.

Testing/defect fixing

During this phase, custom solutions are tested end-to-end, ideally by a quality analyst. Defects are raised and assigned to the respective developers. The code changes made by the developer are checked in into TFS, and a new build is created and applied on the test environment. The quality analyst retests the process, and closes the defect when satisfied.

Release to production

When all the testing efforts have been completed, there are the following options to create the build for production:

- Export the model store for the QA environment and deploy to the production environment
- Create a release branch in TFS and create a build out of the release branch for production release

> The ALM process explained here is only an example. ALM processes can be different depending on the version control system, branching strategy, and the existing customer processes for release management.

Application Lifecycle guidelines and best practices

The following are some common guidelines and recommendations for the ALM process:

- Use version control and appropriate branching strategy for the development process.

- Implement a code review process to manage check-ins and control what needs to be released to the test environment.

- Implement comments during code checking, providing a brief description of the code, the linking feature, or defects to track the changes appropriately.

- Implement the formal release process (cadence of releases, manager approval, and so on) to avoid destabilizing the test environment due to frequent releases.

- Use the build server and build automation scripts to create an automated build creation and build deployment. There may be some initial investment to get the things in place, but it saves a lot of time during the testing phase of the project.

- Use the Microsoft guidelines for deployment in the test and production environments. Follow the Microsoft white paper, *Deploying Customizations Across Microsoft Dynamics AX 2012 Environments* at `https://www.microsoft.com/en-us/download/details.aspx?id=26571`.

- Avoid moving the code using XPO from the development to test or the production environment. Importing new objects using XPO can lead to object conflict during model store import.

- Do not modify the code directly in test or production environment; it's bad practice, and can create confusion and code loss. It is easy to miss merging the code back to version control properly and the next build deployment will override the changes.

- If not using build automation, keep a clean development environment, synced with the latest code, to create build manually and to promote the code to test and other environments.

Summary

In this chapter, we began with understanding the preparation needed before starting the development process such as setting up the development environment, version control, and setting up the process for a periodic code review. In the next section, we learned, in detail, about the development process in Dynamics AX, starting with conceptualizing the solution, understanding the importance of effective data design, implementing business logic, and building custom code considering long-term view/building for temporary use. We also learned about the different recommendations on the UI patterns for effective and consistent user interface design. We learned the common best practices and recommendations for coding in X++. In the end, we reviewed an example of an application life cycle process for Dynamics AX implementation and the common guidelines and best practices.

In the next chapter, we will learn about performance tuning and the various tools and techniques for identifying performance issues across the environment.

10
Performance Tuning

Performance tuning is a wide subject with far-reaching ramifications, and should not be limited to the performance testing and tuning exercise at the end of the project. Instead, careful consideration should be given to performance from the beginning of the project. We have talked about these considerations in the previous chapters. Let's review them once again at a higher level:

- **Infrastructure planning**: It's important to understand the underlying architecture and the peak workload as well as have the hardware sized appropriately; this planning should also consider the scenarios to scale for the expected future growth.
- **Requirement gathering**: Clarify and define the performance and peak-load requirements during the analysis phase.
- **Design and development**: Pay attention to scalability and the performance aspects during design. Follow the best practices and guidelines during the design and development phase for better performance.

In the end, we have to validate all the above considerations and make sure that the system is ready for production. Performance testing and tuning will help in defining a baseline and getting the system ready for the production workload.

In this chapter, we will cover the following topics:

- Planning performance testing and tuning
- Tools for performance monitoring
- Factors that impact performance
- Approaching performance issues

Performance testing and tuning

Performance tuning is a methodology of identifying performance issues and solving them. It is important to conduct performance and load testing and tuning before going live to eliminate the issues which can impact the business negatively. It does not matter whether you have high volumes or not; you still need performance testing. At this stage of the project, the infrastructure has been configured and reviewed to match the best practices. The development of custom features is complete and functional testing is in progress. This is the time to validate the overall performance of your Dynamics AX solution. The primary goal is to make sure that the solution will accept peak load without any major issue.

The key objective of this exercise is to establish a baseline for the key business scenarios and to test and execute performance tuning and optimization to achieve the following:

1. Create a baseline of your core business scenarios.

2. Simulate users and transactions in terms of concurrency and volume, and determine the load that the system can handle.

3. Execute performance tuning and optimization.

The following flowchart illustrates the performance and load testing and tuning process:

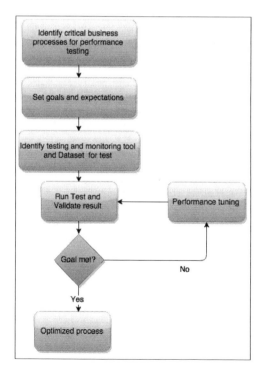

Preparing for the process

Preparation is the key to the beginning of any process. Consider the following scenario to prepare for performance testing and tuning:

- **Define scope**: Identify the potential bottlenecks and important business scenarios for which you want to run the performance and load testing on, such as product search, order placement, shipment posting, invoice posting, and so on.

- **Set goals**: Define the acceptable benchmarks for a combination of processes to be run in parallel.

- **Set expectations with the executives**: Performance testing is a process for finding the known unknowns and for finding the obvious bottlenecks in the solution. However, there may still be some unknown-unknowns that would surface after the go-live. Good performance testing is like a flu vaccine—it would address the most commonly expected flu for the season. However, it does not guarantee that you won't get the flu.

- **Identify the tools to be used**: There are several different toolsets for performance monitoring. The following section discusses the tools that will help you to prepare for this.

- **Identify the environment to be used**: You need to use an environment that is as close to the production in size and configuration as possible, so that you don't have to make assumptions. In my experience, it pays off if you procure the production hardware early on so that it can be used for performance testing.

- **Datasets**: You should consider a good mix of scenarios from a data perspective, such as shipments from various warehouses, different types of customers, and so on. Identify the critical scenarios from the business perspective and use these for testing. For example, one of my customers had a line of credit from GE, and most of their vendor invoices were paid by GE. It was obvious to use GE as a sample vendor for performance testing of the AP module. Many times, the developers running the performance testing make up their own sample data which may defeat the purpose of testing.

The execution stage

This is an iterative process, so use the tools selected and the scripts developed to run the performance testing to easily repeat the process. Capture and analyze the performance results, make appropriate changes, and repeat the process to evaluate the results.

1. Make sure that you are running performance testing on a set of completely migrated data so that your starting point is as **close to production as possible**.

2. Get all of your latest **customization** code in order to see the performance along with the custom code.

3. Run a performance test for individual areas. However, simulate multiple business processes together (that's the way the business will be using the system).

4. Try to find the **breaking point** by loading the transaction volume to know the bottlenecks (AOS/DB or something else), and the point at which the system would max out.

5. Analyze the *DynamicsPerf* (or the results of any other tools used for capturing the performance bottlenecks) results after every run, and make changes as necessary.

6. Document the results from every run, such as the time taken, number of records, resource consumption, bottlenecks, and any other observations and changes made.

7. Always make smaller changes at a time (like changing the trace flag on SQL, adding indexes, or any code changes) and get the results again. This way, you can see the impact of each individual change.

Outcome

Prepare and document a summary of the performance testing to be presented to the stakeholders of the project.

- Benchmark the performance numbers for each area, like time taken to process the sales order, number of invoices posted per minute, and the orders created per minute through integration. Document the performance bottlenecks identified and fixed during this process. Review the report on what was found and fixed with the key executive and the project sponsor. If you haven't found issues in testing, most likely, the quality of your testing is questionable.

- This review would be a good time to remind them about the expectations. Otherwise, with the first performance issue in production, you will hear about concerns regarding money invested into the solution.

- They should have a good understanding of what the system can handle, and the system behavior under peak business hours.

Tools for performance monitoring

There are several tools which can be used to monitor the performance of the Dynamics AX application. The following sections identify some useful tools, along with their brief descriptions and how they can be used. It is important for the technical architect on your project to be familiar with these tools to ensure that your performance monitoring plan is effective.

The trace parser

The trace parser is a useful tool for developers and system administrators to collect trace events produced by the Dynamics AX application. You can import the trace events into the trace parser and analyze the results to identify performance issues in the code. The trace parser tool comes with the Dynamics AX 2012 package, and can be installed using the installation options. The trace parser can be installed as a standalone tool for Dynamics AX 4.0 and AX 2009.

The trace parser is useful for the following reasons:

- The trace parser is useful in identifying the reason for a specific process being slow (you can run the process itself in isolation and find the performance bottleneck).
- More than 70-75 percent of the performance issues can be identified using this tool, prior to going live. Take the traces for all the important processes and identify the piece of code that may be running slow. Using the right set of data (product/customer with a high number of transactions), using an environment with the latest code, all the migrated data, and so on, would increase the chances of catching issues early.

The trace parser is not useful for the following reasons:

- The trace parser is not useful in the case of processes that are running slow under load
- It cannot be used for production issues that are not replicable in isolation from other processes

The performance monitor

The performance monitor is a basic tool provided with the Windows operating system to collect the important performance counters related to the CPU, disk, and the memory, and which can aid in finding the performance issues. The Dynamics AX application provides the performance objects with different performance counters related to the Dynamics AX application, which can be traced using the performance monitor.

The performance monitor can be used to create counters to collect information about the performance on each component of the Dynamics AX architecture, such as **Application Object Server (AOS)**, the database server, and the **Internet Information Services (IIS)**:

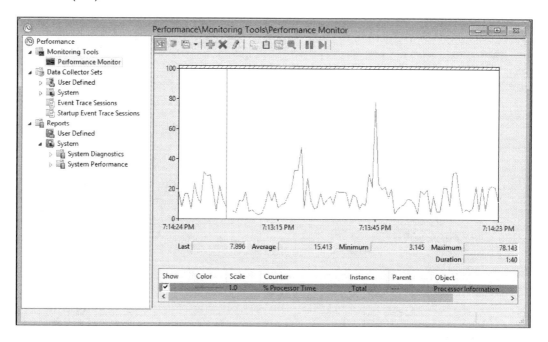

The performance monitor is useful for the following reasons:

- The performance monitor is useful for giving proactive alerts to the IT administrators when the system utilization is above the normal limits. These alerts are helpful in getting early notifications about the issues that may cause system-wide slowness; they may help in reducing the potential impact to the business users.

- These are used for discovering the potential bottlenecks in the hardware, such as the CPU, memory, and I/O by monitoring the counters during the performance testing phase.

These are also used for discovering the root cause of the issue reported, as an overall slowness of Dynamics AX in a specific environment.

The performance analyzer – DynamicsPerf

DynamicsPerf is a performance tool for the DBAs and system administrators to capture and analyze the performance data from SQL Server and the Dynamics AX application. DynamicsPerf is an SQL based tool and includes SQL jobs, X++ class, VB Script, and performance counters to collect the data. It also includes sample SQL scripts and SSRS reports to analyze the collected data in the DynamicsPerf database.

At a higher level, DynamicsPerf captures the following set of data to aid in the investigation of any performance problems:

- Performance data
- Database blocking
- Performance counter data

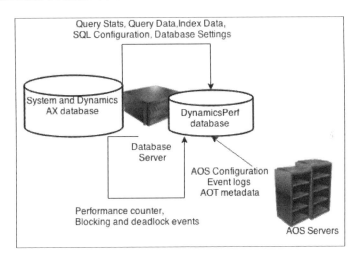

DynamicsPerf can be used in a production environment to collect and analyze the performance data. It has very little impact in a production environment, as it is simply collecting the **DMV (Dynamic Management Views)** — that the SQL server captures about execution, indexes, OS, I/O, and so on — data that the SQL Server already has in the memory and inserting that into the DynamicsPerf database. It captures additional configuration information from the Dynamics AX database, which can be scheduled to run during the non-business hours. On average, the first data capture of the daily capture stats job runs for 3-5 minutes with the subsequent captures taking 1-2 minutes. The hourly performance-capture job normally runs for about 5-6 seconds.

DynamicsPerf is a tool for identifying performance issues proactively, and hence, it is a good idea to use it in your Development, Test, or QA environments and fix the performance issues beforehand to prevent them from getting into production.

> The DynamicsPerf tool is available on the codeplex website and can be downloaded from `https://dynamicsperf.codeplex.com/`.
>
> For additional resources on installing, configuring, and using the DynamicsPerf tool, visit `http://blogs.msdn.com/b/axinthefield/`.

DynamicsPerf is useful for the following reasons:

- It is useful in discovering the performance issues related to environment, system setup, long running/expensive queries, missing indexes, and so on

- It is a tool for monitoring the performance proactively rather than reacting to the performance issues

- It collects the historical performance data to compare the performance issues over a period of time

- It provides SSRS reports for analyzing the performance issues

The LCS system diagnostics

System diagnostics is a cloud-based tool for the administrators to monitor and understand the health of one or more Dynamics AX environments. System diagnostics is basically a collection of rules defined by the Microsoft solution architecture team. The LCS tools collect the data from your environment and the basic setup data. It then runs these rules against the data collected and displays messages if there are any deviations from the best practices defined as part of the rules. The good thing is that Microsoft keeps adding new collectors and rules which can be used for your project as soon as they are available in the LCS.

The LCS System diagnostics helps the administrator monitor and manage one or more Dynamics AX environments. It provides a graphical dashboard which administrators can use to monitor the overall system health, discover errors, and flash warning messages. For errors and warning messages, the tool also provides additional resources and recommendations which can be used to further investigate and resolve the issues. The system administrators can also generate detailed reports for the issues and send these to the development team for further analysis and corrective actions to resolve them. The following diagram illustrates the LCS System diagnostic capabilities and processes:

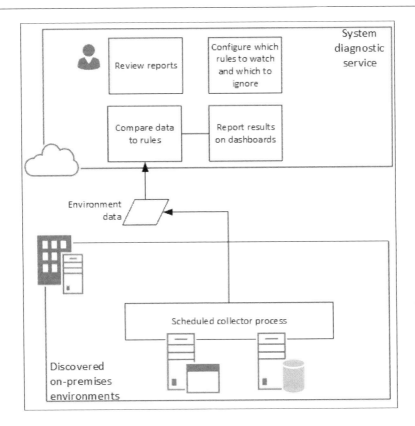

The LCS collector collects the following data from each environment, and runs several rules to check the health of the environment:

- **Microsoft Dynamics AX**: This is module-specific data, such as account payable parameters, workflow, vendor invoices, and vendor journals
- **The AOT data**: This is the Dynamics AX AOT data, such as table properties, table method, and query properties
- **Environment**: The environment data includes environment details from the AOS server and the database server

LCS is useful for the following reasons:

- The LCS collector is useful for discovering the common environment setup issues
- It helps in discovering the common best practice violations related to configuration
- It monitors the overall health of one or more of the Dynamics AX environments

The performance benchmark SDK

The performance benchmark SDK is a performance and load testing tool for Dynamics AX. It leverages the load test functionality of Visual Studio and provides the ability to develop, manage, and execute load testing by simulating multiple-user activity on Dynamics AX. The benchmark SDK comes with several prebuilt standard scenarios, and can be extended further by customers and partners for custom features.

It is useful for load and performance testing by simulating multiple users' activities simultaneously. The performance benchmark SDK can be downloaded from `http://www.microsoft.com/en-us/download/details.aspx?id=39082`.

The SQL Server Profiler

The SQL Profiler is a graphical tool that allows the database administrators to monitor the events in an instance of SQL Server. You can capture and save the data about each event and analyze it later.

The SQL Server Profiler lets you define a trace to capture all the T-SQL scripts that run simultaneously on the SQL Server. As you might expect, this data can be very large and is not easy to analyze. It is important to define the objective of the trace and define the appropriate filters and events to capture only what is needed.

Using the SQL Profiler in the production environment needs careful consideration, as tracing can enable an overhead to the overall performance of an SQL Server instance. To use the profiler in a production environment, you should define the appropriate filters and events and trace for a small duration.

The SQL Server profiler is useful for the following scenarios:

- Finding activities on an SQL Server instance when performance issues are observed
- Finding and diagnosing slow-running and blocking SQL queries

The SCOM pack for Microsoft Dynamics AX

SCOM stands for System Center for Operation Management. SCOM is a Windows Server tool to monitor and control the Windows servers. SCOM for Dynamics AX is a preconfigured package that you can import into SCOM to discover, monitor, and manage your Dynamics AX environment. The Management pack automatically discovers the entire AX environment, such as the databases, reporting servers, analysis servers, enterprise portal server, and the application frameworks, and monitors each component for configuration, availability, and performance.

In addition to the monitoring features, SCOM can also be used to perform maintenance tasks on the AOS instance directly, such as starting and stopping the AOS service and draining the clients from the server.

The SCOM pack is useful for the following:

- Monitoring the Dynamics AX production environment for availability and performance
- Monitoring the performance counters for the different server components
- Setting up alerts and warnings for the system administrators for early warnings

Factors that impact performance

Performance bottlenecks can occur at any level, so it's important to understand the different dimensions where things could be wrong and where to start. In a broad sense, there are three common factors that impact performance, as illustrated in the following image:

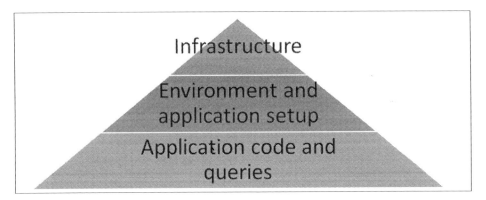

Infrastructure

As described in *Chapter 3, Infrastructure Planning and Design*, the infrastructure plays a vital role in system performance. It is very important to select appropriate hardware for the various components based on the usage profile of the system. We also recommend an infrastructure design review to evaluate the hardware and software requirements during the infrastructure planning stage.

Issues due to inadequate hardware

The following are the typical performance issues related to the hardware that are found in the customer AX projects:

- I/O contentions issues
- Low memory on the remote desktop servers
- Low memory on AOS

There are a few tools that help you monitor performance for the hardware, which are explained as follows:

- **The Windows Performance Monitor**: This monitors the performance counters for each of the component installed for memory, I/O, and the CPU to discover the overall hardware utilization and any potential bottleneck
- **DynamicsPerf**: The DynamicsPerf tool collects the SQL Server data from the **Data Management Views (DMV)** related to the memory, CPU, and I/O, which can be useful for identifying the hardware issues related to SQL Server

Virtualization

Hardware virtualization is the recommended option for Dynamics AX, as it reduces the cost of the initial setup and maintenance, in addition to providing high availability. The following are the common performance factors in a virtualized environment:

- Overprovisioning (thin provisioning) for AX production servers
- There are no dedicated resource pools for the CPU and memory
- The memory balloon driver is not disabled (ballooning equivalent to dynamic memory)
- The use of storage thin provisioning (on-demand allocation of blocks of data)
- **RSS (Receive Side Scaling)** is not enabled (network traffic handled by CPU 0)
- Outdated Synthetic Device Drivers (for disk, NICs, and so on)

The following tools can be useful for viewing virtualization:

- **Windows performance monitor**: This uses the performance counter to monitor and discover the hardware utilization on the various server components in the Dynamics AX environment
- **Third-party tools to monitor the virtual environments**: Sometimes, the problem could be in the virtualization layer, and hence specialized software provided by virtual solution vendors can be used to identify any such issue

The environment setup

There are several environment and application-recommended settings that, if not done appropriately, can cause performance issues. The following sections explain a few issues at the high level.

Network bandwidth and latency

Network bandwidth and latency plays an important role in the performance of the system. This becomes extremely critical when you have remote sites connecting to the Dynamics AX client. Make sure that the system requirements for network bandwidth and latency are followed as per the Dynamics AX system requirements recommendations.

It is highly recommended to use the Citrix or remote desktop/terminal services for WAN access. Enable compression by enabling the setting on the AOS configuration to minimize the size of the data packets between the AX client and AOS servers. Consider using other user-client performance options, such as disabling the fact boxes and the preview pane on the list pages, to improve performance.

Setting up Windows

Make sure to validate the following settings for Windows in the Dynamics AX environment:

- Verify that the SQL Server is configured to run as a background service in Windows. Ensure that the memory allocation is done correctly so that the OS has enough dedicated memory.
- Set the power plan to high performance (all AX servers).

Setting up SQL Server

SQL Server is the most important component of the Dynamics AX architecture. Most of the performance issues usually point to issues on SQL Server—setup or queries that are not optimized. Hence, proper configuration and recommendations need to be followed on SQL Server the optimal performance of the overall Dynamics AX application.

The following are some key considerations for SQL Server's optimum performance:

- Review the maximum degree of parallelism setting (ideally set to **1**).
- Enable only the required network protocols—AX requires only TCP/IP. Any protocol other than TCP/IP can significantly reduce the overall performance of the Dynamics AX application.

- Disable hyper-threading on the SQL Server services.

- The Dynamics AX application uses TempDB heavily; make sure that the Microsoft recommendations are followed on the TempDB storage and settings.

- Run performance tests and monitor the TempDB contentions using the **Wait Stats** technique.

- Make sure that the best practices and recommendations are followed for the Dynamics AX database, which is available on the Dynamics AX Performance Team blog at http://blogs.msdn.com/b/axperf/.

- Implement the appropriate database maintenance processes, like reindexing and defragmentation.

- Apply the latest service packs for SQL.

- Update the firmware.

- Download and install the DynamicsPerf tool to periodically collect and monitor the performance data and take corrective actions.

- Ideally, do not put other databases on the same SQL instance (it may compete with the Dynamics AX database for the server resources).

An outdated application, kernel, and missing hotfixes

It is important to maintain your Dynamics AX solution with the most current releases and fixes available. Microsoft continuously releases hotfixes and kernel updates for performance issues as the customers come across them. You would rather run into issues that have already been reported by other customers and where the fix is available from Microsoft. During the project life cycle, keep looking for the important hotfixes/cumulative updates and evaluate if they can be applied. At least the kernel-level hotfixes should be applied, as they do not have any code upgrade constraint.

Inappropriate AX configurations

There are a number of settings and application configurations within Dynamics AX which can cause performance issues if they are not used appropriately. The following sections outline a few key configurations that require attention:

Number sequences

In Dynamics AX, the number sequences are used to create automatic sequences for documents and master data, such as customer account, voucher numbers, invoice numbers, and so on. A number sequence can be set to continuous or non-continuous. When using a continuous number sequence, gaps are not allowed, so a trip to the database is needed to get the next number. When the number sequence is non-continuous, you can allow preallocation per ID, and therefore reduce database calls and improve performance. Avoid using continuous number sequences unless required by the application.

Database logging

Database logging is a feature in Dynamics AX that enables the logging of any data change when enabled for a table. This is a cool feature but needs to be used with caution, because it can cause a significant degradation in performance when used inappropriately. The following are some guidelines for using the database logging feature in Dynamics AX:

- Have a valid business reason for each database logging rule
- Only track what is needed (for example, track updates at the field level, insert/delete actions, and so on)
- For large transactions, do not use tables or the information that changes based on the transactions
- Purge or archive the `sysDatabaseLog` table regularly

Debugging in production

Debugging is a great tool for Dynamics AX developers to troubleshoot the ongoing issues. However, it should not be enabled in the production environment. Even though you are not using the debugger in the production environment and it's just enabled on the AX Server Configuration utility, it can cause around a 10 percent performance degradation.

Maintaining indexes

Database maintenance is important for any OLTP database. Having bad index maintenance or no index maintenance can severely degrade the performance of Dynamics AX. Many performance issues can be resolved if the appropriate database maintenance processes are put into place. The following are a few index maintenance guidelines:

- Reorganize the indexes that are larger than a thousand pages and are between 10 percent and 30 percent fragmented.

- Rebuild the indexes that are larger than a thousand pages and more than 30 percent fragmented using a fill factor between 85 percent and 95 percent, depending on the frequency of the job execution.

- It is also strongly recommended to run the update statistics regularly with a full scan, or with at least a 50 percent sample, as well as having `Auto_Create_Stats` and `Auto_Update_Stats` enabled. If you are running SQL 2008 R2 SP1 or greater, you can also enable the trace flag, **2371**.

- Run the database maintenance script weekly or more frequently.

Batch servers

We often find in customer environments that there is only one AOS instance for batch processing, and the setting on the AOS batch is the default setting with a maximum of eight batch threads. A good way to calculate the number of threads is to multiply the number of cores by two, but this depends on the processes running and should be validated in the testing phase. You can also set the user AOS to act as a batch server during the off-business hours when there are no user activities.

Code and queries

The code and queries used in the application logic can cause significant performance issues when the proper best practices and guidelines are not followed. The following are a few common areas where the code can cause performance issues.

Data caching

As explained in *Chapter 9, Building Customizations*, data caching is an important property in the table. When the `CacheLookup` property on the tables is not set correctly, it can cause performance issues due to an increase in the number of database calls. Just as an example, set the `CacheLookup` property of `CustParameters` to none and run a trace using the trace parser tool for the sales order invoicing process. You will notice a database call for `CustTable` thousands of times. However, when the `CacheLookup` property is set to `EntireTable`, there will be one or zero calls to the database. This is a small but really important setting for performance. Follow the development best practices, and set the appropriate `CacheLookup` property in the custom tables.

Too many RPC calls between the client and server tiers

A code running on the wrong tier can cause too many RPC calls between the client and the server tiers and can cause significant performance overhead. Refer to the following guidelines to evaluate whether the code is being run on the appropriate tier:

- The code related to database operations or heavy calculations should be run on the server tier
- Minimize the interaction between the client and server tier by grouping the appropriate tier code into a method
- Send the information between the client and the server in a serializable format
- Use the `TempDB` tables when you need to join them with the regular tables

Set-based operations

It has been discovered in code review or performance tuning that the business logic is often implemented using loops to manipulate the transaction data. When the number of records grows, the processes start slowing down due to the increased number of round trips between the database and AOS.

Dynamics AX provides the following set-based operations for data manipulation (`INSERT_RECORDSET`, `UPDATE_RECORDSET`, and `DELETE_FROM`), which could be used as an alternative to the loops to complete the data manipulation in a single round trip.

However, in a few scenarios, these set-based operations are converted into row-based operations. Examples for such scenarios are as follows:

- When joined with the `inMemory` temp tables
- When the database logging or alert is enabled for these tables and the `skip*` method is not used
- When the table has the delete actions defined; `delete_from` will turn into a row-based operation if `skipDatabaselog` is not used
- When the table methods insert/update/delete are overridden, and the `skip*` methods are not used

Batch parallelism

We often hear the complaint that batch processes take too much time to complete. Often, the issue is that parallel execution or the resources available are not used effectively. The result is less throughput, longer response time, and inefficient use of all the hardware resources.

Depending on the nature of the workload and work, you can use the following three techniques for parallel batch processing:

- **Batch bundling**: In this technique, a static number of tasks is created. The work is split among these tasks by grouping the work items together into bundles. Each worker thread will process a bundle of work items before picking up the next bundle. For example, suppose you need to invoice 1,000 sales order invoices. To do so, create 10 tasks, and allocate 100 sales orders to each task. So, 10 sales order invoices will be posted in parallel.

- **Individual task modeling**: In this technique, a batch task is created for each work item. Here, you have a 1:1 relation between the batch task and the work item, and hence a more consistent workload distribution. For example, if you need to push the AX retail transaction data to 10 different stores, create 10 different batch tasks; each batch task will process the data for one store.

- **Top picking**: In this technique, you create a static number of tasks similar to batch bundling, but do not preallocate the work items. A staging table is created and populated with a list of work items to be processed. Each batch thread will pick the next available task and update the current one with the status **In Progress**. Each task will read the staging record data with the **PESSIMISTICLOCK** hint along with the **READPAST HINT** to get the next available work item without any blocking.

Parallel processing can cause a deadlock and blocking in the system, but they can be taken care of by exception handling with the deadlock and retry mechanism.

The standard AX functionalities are a great source of information about how the batch framework can be best utilized in different parts of the system. The best example for this is the **Data Upgrade Cockpit** (read *Chapter 14, Upgrade* for more info on the Data Upgrade Cockpit), which uses multiple batch processing techniques for parallel execution.

Long-running queries – missing indexes

Long-running queries are a very common cause of performance issues reported in Dynamics AX. You can often see long-running queries in the standard business logic, SSRS reports, and customizations; most of the time, this is due to missing or inappropriate indexes. It's important to understand that every business has different data composition and usage patterns, and the index usage depends on these factors. Hence, indexes need to be designed and optimized for the usage pattern of the business.

There are various way to monitor long-running queries. For example, you can monitor long-running queries in Dynamics AX itself by setting the AOS configuration client tracing option and the SQL trace option for Dynamics AX user options. You can also use the SQL Server DMVs or the DynamicsPerf tool to monitor long-running queries.

Displaying methods on form grid

Using the display methods in Dynamics AX is a great way to show the calculated information on forms and reports. But using display methods can cause significant performance issues. Particularly when complex methods are used to calculate the values being shown on grids, a visible slow-down in form performance can be experienced. This is largely due to the fact that the methods are often run repeatedly with no apparent reason and the values are unchanged.

The performance issues reported by end users about a particular form taking a long time to open is quite common. Check if the form uses the display methods on the grid; this could be one of the reasons why the form is slow. Display method caching can be used to resolve this issue.

Approaching performance issues

Performance issues can be due to many factors, and to identify the root cause, you may need to involve multiple groups within the organization. This makes it challenging and, sometimes, even political. Also, performance issues are complex and hard to reproduce. Therefore, it's important to understand the issue clearly, set priorities, and get the appropriate people involved for the analysis.

Understanding the issue

The very first step is understanding the issue. "We are having performance issues!" is a very broad statement. You need to identify all the symptoms, and these symptoms may help you define the course of action. It's important to ask the right questions, such as:

- How many users are affected and in what areas of the business?
- Is this a general performance issue or related to specific processes?
- Is there a pattern for the issue like particular users and/or times of the day?
- Can it be recreated in a test environment? If not, can it consistently be recreated in the production environment?
- What are the expected results, such as duration, concurrent users, and so on?

Planning and defining the analysis strategy

When you have enough details and an understanding of the issue, it's time to formulate an action plan and an analysis strategy.

- It is more important to resolve performance issues affecting the end-user productivity earlier rather than with a nightly batch job that is taking longer than expected (unless the nightly job is impacting the business SLAs or making the business slow down).
- You may need resources from different teams, or you many need to source an external/contract resource. Coordinate and find the right people in the team.
- Identify appropriate performance monitoring tools and install and configure them in the affected environment to collect the data.

Based on the issues defined in the investigation strategy, the following diagram can be a good starting point on where to look:

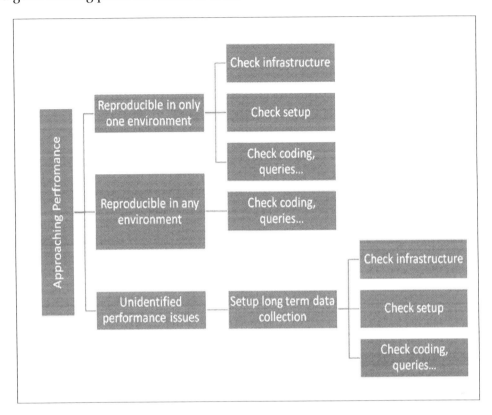

Corrective action and review

Solutions to performance issues could be as small as changing a parameter setting, or it could be so complex that it requires design or code changes. The following are a few tips on implementing the corrective actions:

- If the problem is not just limited to a specific process, a quick validation of the environment setup and configuration is a good place to start.

- Validate the SQL server and AOS configurations, as recommended. Some issues can be resolved by correcting the simple setup issues like rebuilding indexes, updating the statistics on the affected tables, or setting the MAXDOP setting in SQL Server to **1**.

- Performance tuning is an iterative process; try one tuning at a time and verify the result.

- *Minimum effort maximum result*: When analyzing a performance issue, you may discover many factors that could be adding to the performance issue. Start with the one that requires minimum effort and gives the maximum result.

- You should also know when to stop tuning a particular scenario and move on. Remember the law of diminishing returns; this means that in each iteration of performance tuning, the potential for improvement reduces exponentially.

General scenarios and investigation strategies

The following sections define a few scenarios from my experience to help in brainstorming the identification of the root cause for the performance issues.

Issue 1

The entire company reports slowness issues. The performance is getting worse day by day.

Investigation:

- Check the application for the following:
    - The number of concurrent users connected
    - The batch jobs running at the moment

- Check the AOS utilization of:
    - The CPU
    - Memory

- Check the DB for symptoms like:
    - CPU, memory, and IO
    - Any blockage
    - Long running queries
    - Index statistics not being up-to-date

Root cause: After investigation, it was found that index maintenance was not put into place. The DBA used the DynamicsPerf tool and observed bad execution plans and several long-running queries.

Solution: Reindexing and defragmentation of the indexes resolved the issue. Index maintenance was put into place to avoid such issues in the future.

Issue 2

Operations in all warehouses are slow.

Investigation:

- Check the network for connectivity, bandwidth, and latency issues
- Check SQL server for blocking, CPU, and memory utilization

Root cause: Testing the network connectivity revealed that the bandwidth between the warehouse locations and the headquarters was limited.

Solution: The AX AOS configuration was updated to enable the sending of smaller data packets. This option is available under Microsoft Dynamics AX 2012 Server configuration/performance/minimum packet size to compress (in KBs). For more details, visit the TechNet article at `https://technet.microsoft.com/en-us/library/aa569624.aspx`.

Issue 3

Operations at specific locations are slow.

Investigation:

- Check the network connectivity, bandwidth, and latency issues
- If RDP or the Citrix layer are used, check the resources on the RDP and Citrix Servers

Root cause: It was found that the RDP Server's CPU and memory utilization was very high. The RDP Server was over-provisioned.

Solution: Upgrading the resources on the RDP Server resolved the issue.

Issue 4

Printing in the warehouses is slow.

Investigation:

- Check the drivers on the printer
- Check the bandwidth and latency
- Check the resources on the print server

Root cause: An outdated driver on the printer.

Solution: Updating the printer driver resolved the issue.

Issue 5

The business users are experiencing performance issues when creating the PO invoices. The PO invoice form takes several minutes to open. The same behavior is observed in other environments with the same dataset.

Investigation: Since this is limited to one specific process, we used the trace parser tool to generate a trace for the invoice posting processes with specific datasets. It was observed that there are hundreds of receipts for each purchase order, and the system typically matches all the receipts against a new invoice. However, as per the business process, the customer usually gets an invoice only for a few receipts. The invoicing clerk was facing double issues: first, he was waiting for minutes to open the invoice form, and then he had to deselect all the receipts and then select an individual one.

Root cause: Code and business logic inappropriate as per the business process.

Solution: We created a new button on the purchase order to open the invoice form without matching any receipt. This enabled the opening of the invoice form within fractions of a second. Additional index was added for improving the query performance during the posting process.

Issue 6

Nightly jobs for generating the file output for the e-commerce solution (custom process) is taking several hours to finish when the data set is large.

Investigation:

- Check the memory and CPU utilization on the batch server
- Check the blocking processes when the batch process is running
- Check if there are enough batch threads available for all the batch tasks
- Check if we can we utilize the regular AOS during the night for extra threads

Root cause: We found that the process used multiple nested while loops to look for different information, such as product, product dimension, trade agreement, and inventory on-hand, and then combined them in staging to generate the final file. The issue was too many database calls.

Solution: A development resource was assigned for investigation and performance tuning at the code level. The nested while loops were replaced with joins and set-based operations. The updated code was tested with a large set of data. The performance improved from 6-7 hours to under 30 minutes.

Issue 7

Users are getting kicked out (AOS is restarting).

Investigation:

- Check if this is being caused by a specific user's action. (Every time the user tries to confirm the order, it causes the custom code to go into an infinite loop. The system reaches 100 percent memory utilization and the AOS restarts)
- Check the AOS server event log
- Utilize the windows AOS server memory dump if the crash happens frequently
- Check if your AOS has the latest binary updates

Root cause: After analysis, it was found that the installed AOS sever did not have the latest binary updates.

Solution: Installing the latest kernel version on the AOS server resolved the issue.

Issue 8

System is slow at 6 p.m. everyday.

Investigation:

- Check the scheduled backups or maintenance activities running at this time
- Check the CPU and memory utilization on the AOS and database servers
- Check blocking at the database server
- Check if you have any Dynamics AX batch processes running at 6 p.m.
- Check an anti-virus scan is running on the servers
- Check for any network issues caused by massive data transfer (unrelated to Dynamics AX)

Root cause: An antivirus scan was scheduled to run every day at 6 p.m. causing high utilization of the memory and the CPU.

Solution: The antivirus schedule was moved to a later time, after the business hours.

Summary

We are getting very close to go-live and making sure that we have all the ground covered before we turn the switch on. In this chapter, we learned about performance tuning. We started the chapter with performance testing, understanding the importance of performance testing and tuning exercises in an implementation project. We went through the preparation, execution, and outcome of a performance testing and tuning exercise. Then, we looked at the various tools available for performance monitoring, testing, and troubleshooting the performance issues. To appropriately investigate and solve performance issues, you need to know about the causes. We analyzed the various factors which can cause performance issues in Dynamics AX and reviewed the guidelines and recommendations to avoid them. In the end, we talked about approaching the performance issues by understanding the issue in detail, creating a plan, and taking corrective action. We also talked about some real-life examples of performance issues and the approach taken to investigate and identify the root cause.

In the next chapter, we will talk about conducting system and user acceptance testing, as well as preparing the users for the new system through training and the change management process.

11
Testing and Training

Quality, budget (schedule and resources), and scope are the fundamental constraints on every ERP project. Most of the time, when the scope is increased and the budget stays constant, the quality gets compromised. One of the biggest mistakes that people end up making, especially on fixed-bid contracts, is that they reduce the testing budget when there is budget pressure.

I have heard this several times and would like to call it out. In many post-release postmortem meetings, I would hear, "If I was to do this again, I would spend a hundred thousand dollars more on testing." You have the opportunity to do it right and not having to regret it later. Let's review the different phases of testing and their importance/execution:

- Test plan
- Unit testing and feature testing
- System integration testing
- User acceptance testing
- End-to-end testing

Similar to testing, training is another key aspect for the successful implementation of an ERP system. Ensuring that the users are comfortable with the new platform and understand the new business processes and their new role in the organization is essential for attaining a good working platform. For example, usually, the finance department is involved in journal entries for re-classing entry errors and playing a tactical role within the organization. In their new world, after the project implementation, they will be managing exceptions and reviewing key KPIs/trends. Training needs to be delivered to support this cultural shift.

The process of unlearning the old practices and learning new ways of doing things may take several iterations. Hence, training and an evaluation of adopting of that training are very essential. We will discuss the following important aspects of training in this chapter:

- Putting together a training plan
- Training preparation
- Change management
- Training tools

While discussing this topic on testing and training, our focus will *NOT* be on generic areas; we will talk about them at a higher level and focus on the Dynamics AX specific elements.

In this chapter we will learn the following:

- Key considerations for testing a Dynamics AX solution
- Training plan and execution

Testing

Testing is the process of validating the system and processes to meet the business requirements. It includes testing the custom as well as the standard features, along with the migrated data, integrations, reports, and security aspects of the solution. It is an area that is most often underestimated and, as a result, hampers the success of your project.

A very common misconception is that testing starts after the development phase is over. The primary goal of testing is to provide feedback on the product as soon as possible. Identifying any issues in the requirements phase prevents them from becoming a part of the design. Similarly, identifying any issues in the design phase prevents them from being coded. The cost of fixing a defect depends on the phase where it has been detected; the cost of fixing a defect in the early phases of **SDLC (Software Development Life Cycle)** is much lower than in the later phases. The farther you go with the backlog of testing/validation, the more debt you carry on the project. Mostly, such a debt gets unmanageable and it becomes hard to predict/commit to the schedule. Remember, you are not the government to carry high debts—the more you add to it or the longer you carry it, the worse it gets.

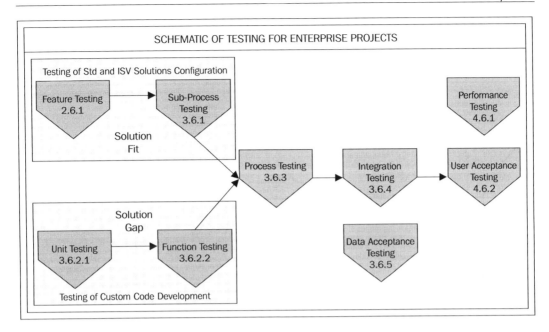

The test planning

The following are some guidelines to keep in mind when planning for the testing phase:

- During the planning phase, create a test plan to define the scope, resources, and tools to be used for the testing, and to identify how bugs will be tracked. Establish the criteria for defining S1/S2, P1/P2 bugs depending on the business criticality (severity and priorities).

- Dedicate QA resources for each area in the similar way we do for the functional analysts and developers. You need them to start on the project right from the beginning to understand the requirements and the design that is being put in place. Good QA resources will have very valuable inputs in the design phase, and they can watch out for design gaps.

- Identify the external resources that need to be engaged during testing. For example, testing with banks for checks/electronic payments, positive pay files, EDI trading partners (customers/vendors, and any other parties to whom you send/receive data like D&B (credit), third-party invoice printing, and so on. Start engaging them as early as possible, and align their schedule into the project plan.

- Plan for performance and load testing in addition to functional testing. performance and load testing is addressed in detail in *Chapter 10, Performance Tuning*.

- The automation of testing is used in very large Dynamics AX deployments that can afford to invest in the automation of testing scripts, and where you need to verify the generic processes repeatedly during the development and stabilization phases. Many such customers end up investing in test automation after going live and once they have stable processes defined to reduce the rework in test automation.

Test scenarios and test case development

Building test scenarios and cases are important for executing a good test plan. The following tips will help you in developing effective testing scenarios:

- Prepare test scenarios and test cases while the development is in progress. Review test cases with the business analysts and the business SMEs, as applicable.

- Align test scenarios to the business scenarios that are put together by the business team.

- The goal should to be identify and document each scenario in detail in the form of test cases rather than staying at a very high level. If you don't document the test cases, there is a high chance of missing them during execution. If you were to hire an army of temp staff to perform the testing, they would need enough details to execute all the test cases based on the documentation.

- Every test case must have the following sections:

    Test-case ID

    Test scenario

    Title

    Prerequisites

    Role(s)

    Steps

    Expected result

- Maintain a traceability matrix with the number of requirements, function specifications, technical specifications, test scenarios, and test-case ID.

- Identify the test data to be used and the specific deviations in data to maximize the coverage of your testing. Say, for example, if a company has four product lines and all are sold differently, you will need to have scenarios that address each product line.

Unit testing

Unit testing is the standalone testing of customizations, usually performed by the developers to ensure that an individual customization is working as expected. Although in software engineering terms, unit testing typically refers to automated testing, the developers can run and execute manual tests to ensure the completeness of the feature.

It is important for developers to perform unit testing to ensure that the feature developed is working correctly. Most of the time, it is seen that the development environment does not have the right data set, and this is often used as an excuse for not testing the feature in the development environment. Plan on having appropriate configuration and transaction data in the development environment to encourage early unit testing.

Unit testing provides many benefits that include finding bugs earlier, providing a safety net of tests for changes that are made later, and improving design. Over the long term, unit testing improves customer satisfaction and developer productivity.

Function testing

Function testing, also known as feature testing, is standalone testing performed during development by the QA resources or business analysts. As each feature is gets developed, engage the QA resources and business analysts to use test cases for testing it. Engage the business team members to review individual features that will help reduce surprises during the UAT phase.

Performing feature testing in the development phase will validate that the requirements are being met by that functionality. Testing at the features level enables a fast turnaround on defects, which improves the efficiency of the development process.

Start testing the security roles at this stage. Ensure that the roles defined can use the intended functionality. You can use the Security Development Tool for security role testing without using any additional test accounts. It allows you to test a newly created or modified security role, duty, or privilege from the development workspace using the security permissions associated with that security artifact. The security development tool can be downloaded from the Lifecycle Services portal.

System integration testing

Testing the integrations with other systems that have been developed is just as important as the features and functional testing of the product itself. The following are some points to think about when planning and executing system integration testing:

- System integration testing is performed across applications to verify the seamless flow of information. By this time, all individual features should have been tested by the QA and business analyst resources.

- You will uncover integration issues across the streams, like data migration and reporting, or across applications during this phase.

- The go-live plan should be used to migrate and verify the data in the system integration test environment.

- All individual applications must be tested independently and made ready for integration testing. You will need integrated environment across applications to perform this testing.

- Carry out a QA team exercise for going through the UAT test cases (including user roles) to validate readiness and a smoother UAT phase.

User acceptance testing

The goal of **User Acceptance Testing (UAT)** is to engage the users across business groups who will be using the new system to run the business. This is an opportunity to provide them with hands-on experience for learning the new system as well. The more testing that the users perform, the more comfortable they will be using the new system.

The UAT planning

There is quite a bit of planning required to perform a successful UAT. Just throwing the business users into a room with computers and test scripts is not going to get you the results of an effective UAT. The following details should be considered when planning for UAT:

- Plan multiple rounds of testing, scheduled a few weeks apart to fix issues. It is not uncommon to find a few pieces missing once the business starts looking at the solution. The goal should be to fix everything in between both the cycles so that the business does not experience the same issues or the test cases are not blocked due to those issues.

- Prepare a list of all the batch jobs, their frequency, business/IT owners, dependencies, the path in Dynamics AX, batch group, and so on. This needs to be well documented. All the batch jobs should be scheduled, results validated, and errors/execution should to be monitored.

- Engage the DBAs and the IT operations team to monitor UAT environment, like they do in production. Similar to the business getting ready to use their new system, DBAs and IT support teams need to get familiar with their new toy for troubleshooting.

- Set up and verify the security roles assignment, access to the UAT environment, and reports for all the users. Do not use the system administrator roles for testing during UAT.

- You need to have the full data migration completed in the UAT environment. Reconcile the migrated data as a first step in UAT, before you start making changes in the environment. The Go Live plan should be in place and be used for UAT data migration. Refer to *Chapter 5*, *Data Migration— Scoping through Delivery* for additional tricks on data migration testing.

- Fix the test cases and their sequencing to ensure the correct flow. For example, you start with the data migration validation and then move on to customer/product creation, to order processing, shipping, invoicing, processing returns, commission reports, financial postings and financial statements, tax reporting, inventory value reports, and so on.

- You need to have the environments locked down to a few folks from IT (only the operations team responsible for deployments and the business analysts directly supporting the business users during testing). No changes should be promoted without going through a change control/formal release process.

- The people who run the business should be engaged to verify the system; the team should have cross-functional knowledge and knowledge case scenarios. For example, your top performing, most brilliant sales talent pool needs to be involved in testing the order entry system. They will know all the different scenarios and *gotchas* from the current system, and they can help you break the system.

  ○ Avoid relying on the temporary staff for testing; you need FTEs to review your new world. Engage the temporary staff in backfilling the FTE jobs to run the day-to-day business tasks, not in reviewing the future of the company.

  ○ Encourage the business to bring in as many real examples as possible. For example, the AP can bring in a day's worth of a stack of invoices for processing, running a check run on the migrated Open AP and newly created AP invoices to review the results and real customer orders for order entry. This will help verify credit limits, customers/products, on-hand inventory migration, and the related scenarios.

- The key messages that should be put across during the UAT kickoff are as follows:

    ◦ Finding bugs is the goal of performing UAT. If you find them in UAT, that's a great thing. Don't get frustrated because you've find issues and thus, get stuck in testing.

    ◦ Focus on first verifying all the critical business scenarios before getting into exception scenarios that won't happen frequently. Follow the 80-20 rule to define focus. This is also a good time to remind everybody about the goals for the project.

    ◦ Review the reports from previous testing and communicate any open areas.

    ◦ Communicate the schedule for testing and re-testing.

    ◦ Cover the tools/process to be used for logging bugs, triage, and communication after fixing the bugs.

    ◦ Set the sign off and exit criteria (communicate upfront that they need to sign off at the end of it).

- Provide templates for logging the bugs (capture screenshots, provide a reference to the test case, the step that failed, description of the issue being reported, any input file used for uploads, business impact, and so on for every issue that is being submitted by the users). Users need to be educated on bug-tracking tools and the overall triage process. The more information you have, the less time will be required for the development team to analyze and fix the issues.

UAT execution and experiences

During the execution of UAT, consider the following points:

- Track the testing progress along with the test cases that passed/failed. Publish reports on progress, bugs reported, and resolved bugs (for re-testing).

- Actively manage blocking issues. You need to stay on top of the issues that are blocking testing of certain areas; try to be creative in finding workarounds to continue testing.

- Issue a triage and managing issue list. Have multiple reviews with the team every day for issue statuses and resolutions. Set daily meetings with the business leaders to discuss issues and provide updates on the progress made. You need to hear their firsthand feedback on the issues being experienced.

- Ensure that the formal release process is defined and validations are performed to verify that the release has not broken the environment. This will ensure that precious testing time is not lost due to the broken UAT environment, which is especially important when you have multiple applications integrated with Dynamics AX.

- Track dependencies between test cases. You may have a dependency between the test cases that will need coordination among the different business groups for testing. For example, when a sales order is created, you need to verify with the warehouse to ship it, and then the AR can see the invoice and collect against it.

- On larger projects with a multi-location roll out, it is a good idea to execute testing at a central location. However, you should also perform some testing locally. For example, we had the warehouse and all other users gathered inside the HQ for testing for one of our clients. They tested the shipping labels and the product labels, and it was all okay at the HQ. However, when testing was done in the warehouse, it was terribly slow. As the print was sent from the terminal server at the HQ to a network printer in the warehouse, the network latency was making the process very slow. Upon making some tweaks with the help of the network team and some code changes, we were able to get it working in the warehouse as well.

- Poor analysis and design for complex areas will get exposed in UAT and cause a lot of rework/continuous break-fix. Identify such critical areas and put in dedicated resources to get extra focus on such critical path items. In one of my large Dynamics AX implementations, a focus team was defined for testing and fixing the revenue recognition and deferral scenarios. It was one the most complex parts of the project, and was dependent on many other processes like correct product and customer setup, order entry with different combinations of products and the way billing frequency was chosen by the customer, order entry and CRM integrations, invoice distribution and rounding of totals, and so on. Every time one scenario was fixed, another was broken in deferrals; issues in the upstream processes like order entry impacted the testing of deferrals functionality. The focus group helped track this subproject with additional visibility and helped fix issues faster.

- If complex features and processes that are dependent on several other upstream features are not tested until the later part of UAT, it leaves you with very little time to test the complex areas. Creating focus groups early on, or having an additional round of testing focused on such features, can help reduce the exposure.

- Testing with the system admin role in UAT will force you to go live with a large number of users in a system admin role. This will cause issues post go-live and call for testing rework once you have the roles defined. One customer insisted on continuing testing with the system admin role and went live with many system admins. Someone accidently (I am sure it was unknowingly) unchecked two check boxes in Production (Post Physical inventory to GL and the Post Financial inventory GL on Inventory Model group). No inventory transactions were posted to the GL for two weeks until the issue was identified by the finance team. It was a project by itself to retroactively come up with GL entries, posting of accrual entries for several months until all the POs were invoiced, and so on. Would you like to be in a similar situation?

The UAT outcome

A successful UAT is one where the business can show that they are comfortable with the application features, and thorough testing has been done with good involvement of the business users across areas. The key deliverable of UAT is the business sign off on the **User Acceptance Testing (UAT)** and test results. There may be cases where items do fail, but the team agrees to a conditional sign off. Track any bugs that are critical for going live as a part of this conditional sign off. Most importantly, all areas should have been tested by now. There is a difference between knowing the open issues and being unable to test specific areas due to open issues.

End-to-end testing

In addition to UAT, you need another round of testing to verify the end-to-end execution of a business process. The key difference between UAT and end-to-end testing is that UAT is more focused on validating individual business processes, while end-to-end is focused on validating all of them together once each of them have been stabilized and tested.

End-to-end test planning

You need to have the testing of individual features completed and all the areas to be stable to truly start end-to-end testing. In reality, sometimes you end up making some exceptions, but this is not ideal.

Pick a selected core group for end-to-end testing. Everyone involved needs to know the end-to-end business flow. Usually, the finance team has a bigger role to play here as they have a visibility into all the parts of the organization.

Plan for at least two rounds of end-to-end testing with some time in between to fix the bugs.

Define the exit and success criteria prior to getting into end-to-end testing (such as 100 percent test execution, more than 95 percent pass rate, no more than five critical bugs open, and so on).

Execution and real-life examples

Similar to UAT, you need to publish reports on the test results and follow a triage process. Areas that are blocked during testing need to be unblocked and tested again. Assess whether you have met the exit criteria and review with the executives.

The following are few examples of areas that you should focus on during end-to-end testing:

- The goal of end-to-end testing is to simulate real business. Right from data migration to new product and customer creation, using this data for placing orders, fulfillment, invoicing, receiving cash, reverse logistics, transactions using migrated data, verify reporting, and so on. Come up with all the key business scenarios that should be tested:

    ◦ **Customer invoicing**: The timing and accuracy of invoicing customers is such a critical business function because it has a direct impact on the customer and on the cash flow of the company. On the other hand, invoicing is a downstream function—you have a dependency on products, customers, tax, fulfillment processes, and so on—which must work correctly before you can produce the invoices.

    ◦ **Commission reporting**: As commission reporting has an impact on the paychecks of the sales floor, you need to verify the accuracy of the commission reports with migrated orders and invoices. It should be a top priority, as you want the sales team to trust the system and focus on selling rather than tracking their orders on spreadsheets for an expected commission or worrying whether they'll be paid. Commission reporting could be even trickier for orders shipped in the previous system, and you might have to pay a commission upon receiving customer payments.

    ◦ **Inventory costing and valuation**: Each customer has a different way of using weighted average, FIFO, and other inventory costing methods. It impacts the P&L, their bottom line, how executives are compensated, the inventory value on the balance sheet, and so on. Efforts need to be put in during UAT and end-to-end testing to validate that inventory costing is done according to the needs of the company and understood by the financial controllers and the rest of the stakeholders.

       ° **General ledger postings**: You need to verify the posting for each type of transaction, and run month-end reconciliation reports (to verify that the general ledger and sub ledger are in balance).

       ° **Key reports**: Identify the key reports that are important to run the business, and validate the data based on the transactions that were processed in end-to-end testing.

- Engage domain experts during end-to-end testing like tax auditors for tax integration testing. They will be able to put together a great test plan and execute through unique scenarios to ensure that you have configured the system correctly. I have seen great examples of bugs that the tax auditors discovered (I don't think the internal team may have found them even after a few weeks of release).

Training

Training drives the successful adoption of the new system and processes. The learning capacity of the audience and the amount of changes being introduced to them dictate the amount of time you need to spend on training and re-training. The more people you have up to speed on the new processes and system, smaller the chances of them making mistakes, and the volume of support calls will be highly reduced. Ultimately, this results in a smoother adoption of the new system.

The ERP project is an opportunity for organizations to get people up to speed on end-to-end processes and training them on cross functional areas. If you have a great system designed but people are not able to use it, can you call it a success?

A training plan

Put together a training plan that covers the following points:

- **Understanding the audience**: How quickly are your users likely to catch up with the changes? The training plan needs to be defined accordingly to support their transition.

- **Trainers**: Consultants train the trainer - the business super users or internal business analysts. Hopefully, multiple rounds of CRP will help the business users and internal business analysts get up to speed on the system in order to be trainers.

- **Scope of training / areas to be trained**: You need to account for both the system and the process changes. There are three usual cycles of the training process — UAT training, end user training, and post go-live (training for areas that are struggling).

- **Logistics**: This includes factors like meeting rooms/travel, centralized versus location-specific, and so on.

- **Training schedule and timing**: Timing is key. In some areas, you may need to train the users multiple times to ensure that they are comfortable. On the other hand, areas that have not changed much may need light training, close to going live, to ensure that the users don't forget.

- **Training assessment**: This pertains to the ways and methods that you will use to get a feedback on the training process.

- **Retraining**: Build retraining into the plan, and modify it based on the feedback.

- **Training material and user manuals**: Reviewed this with the business SMEs. It may come in different forms. For example, checklists, Visio for business processes, documents with screen shots, recorded videos, mapping between the old versus new world, and/or a combination of multiple methods. The development of the training materials should be agreed to at the beginning of the project, in the planning phase, so that the appropriate time and resources needed are built into the plan.

- **Signing off**: Define the sign off process and the criteria for training sign off. It is one of the major considerations for go-live.

The change management

The usual human psychology is to resist change. In the earlier chapters, we talked about minimizing the process changes along with the major releases to focus on the system side of implementation. You will still be left with a good amount of change management due to the new system. Change management may shift jobs or workload from one department to another. The project managers of an ERP project often end up utilizing a lot of political power to fight such battles for getting the right decisions made. Even though you may have won the battle for driving the change, you may have lost a few partners that you needed to champion the project. Hence, leaving the major business process changes for the transformation phase of the project (post go-live) can be wiser and a better way to manage the scope.

Training is a good opportunity to help prepare people for the change. The more training you provide, the higher the confidence that the users will have in embracing the change, and you will receive less pushback.

Training preparation

A lot of preparation goes into executing a smooth and effective training. This preparation includes validating system readiness, verifying the roles, putting together multiple forms of training materials, creating and maintaining a stable training environment with valid data, and so on. We will discuss these aspects in the next section.

System and business readiness

Ensure that the system is ready and stable enough (testing complete) prior to training a larger audience. You also need to gauge the business readiness for training and help them prepare. The following are some tips to do so:

- If a smaller group is being trained prior to UAT, the expectation may be different, as the system has not been tested as yet, and you may want to communicate the known open issues. However, when training larger groups, try to do it post UAT when the system is stable enough and the processes have been finalized.

- Create a forum for the users to participate in and get more hands on experience from training through go-live. Arrange *Lunch n Learn* or other such team activities that will encourage more practice. From my experience, business leaders that encourage their teams for extra practice after training, and take the initiative to drive it, will have a lot less issues to deal with post release.

- Have a process to capture and respond to bugs/queries that are raised in the training. Most likely, you will find some critical items that were not known before.

Security roles

Let every user be configured with their *to be* production security role. Avoid the use of the system admin role during training. Of course, roles should have been tested prior to doing this.

Business process flows

Use the business process flows at the beginning of every session. Give a ten-thousand feet high walkthrough of the overall business process and of the piece that you plan to show before getting into application and details.

Engage the Business SMEs or internal business analysts to do the training or to assist in the delivery of the training:

- To train others, you need to get up to speed first; the person that learns the most is the trainer. The trainer approach will ensure that the business SMEs or internal business analysts have got up to speed well enough. It will reduce the dependency on the consulting team post go-live, and internal resources can be your tier 1 support.

- The internal SMEs can reference the current process/systems during training and will help in delivering the training.

- Once I had the controller of an organization deliver AP training; he was able to speak their language and relate to the screens of the existing system. It helped the users in mapping their old versus new world easily, and the training was very well received.

Training manuals and user guides

Training manuals and user guides are good references for the users to look at post training. An ideal team for developing the training manuals should include business super users, technical writers, and business analysts. Distribute them in a medium that the users are comfortable with—putting check lists at desks, posters in the building, or binders or electronic formats on shared drives are the commonly used methods.

In each cycle of training, use the training manuals, and make corrections based on the feedback. The training manuals will stay as living documents and can help on board the new employees, process documentation.

There are a few very powerful tools available to build training manuals for Dynamics AX, which are described in the following section:

The Task Recorder

Users can use the Task Recorder in Dynamics AX to quickly document a business process or task for training or other purposes. You can use the Task recorder to create videos or documents in Microsoft Word, Microsoft PowerPoint, and Microsoft Visio. If you are using the Task Recorder in advanced mode, you can also capture additional metadata that can be packaged and then uploaded to the business process modeler in Microsoft Dynamics Lifecycle Services. The file that you upload includes cross-functional flowcharts and activities that you can modify to identify the business requirements and generate implementation artifacts.

Be sure to have a script to follow for the process that you plan to document, so that you can avoid unnecessary clicks while the recording is on. Once you are done with the recording, generate a word document and clean up the extra steps that you do not want in the document.

The business process modeler

In Lifecycle Services, you can use the business process modeler to create, view, and modify the business-process libraries and flowcharts for Microsoft Dynamics AX. Business process modeler helps you align your Dynamics AX processes with industry-standard processes, as described by **American Productivity and Quality Center (APQC)**. There are more than a thousand business processes that are available, and you can tweak them as per your needs. As referenced in the earlier chapters, business process modeler can be used right from the Gap/Fit analysis phase of the project to track all customizations. You can convert the process flows in Microsoft Word or Visio for use in training.

The Help system

The Microsoft Dynamics AX Help enables you to add new documentation, update existing documentation, and add entries to the table of contents. To customize the documentation, you add one or more files to the Help server.

You can press *F1* to get the help from any form. Microsoft ships the product with the help documentation and the content can be added or modified according to your requirements.

Personalization

This is a good feature in Dynamics AX. Users can personalize their screens such as add/hide fields. However, while training the users, you need to remind them about the side-effects of personalization which are as follows:

- If you are on a support call with the helpdesk team, they may not be seeing the same information as you are seeing on your screen.

- It may vanish with the system updates or during troubleshooting. One of the first troubleshooting steps from Microsoft is to delete the personalization if the user is facing issues. Advise the users to document the screens that were personalized or save their personalization, so those can be added back quickly when lost.

The training environment

Having a stable training environment is important for successful training. A lot of time will be wasted in training if the training environment is not in a good working order. Look at the following tips to keep in mind when managing your training environment:

- You need to treat it like production; many people will be using it at the same time and you want it to be stable while the training is going on or when the users are practicing after training.

- Keep it updated with the latest code and data. Have a communication plan for any downtimes for deployments to ensure that the users are aware.

- Have it available for the users to practice after training.

- It should share an integrated environment with the other applications. For example, if you plan to use Dynamics CRM in Production for order entry and integrate it with Dynamics AX for fulfillment, ensure that you have the training instance of the CRM connected to the Dynamics AX training environment. This will ensure an end-to-end training experience for the users.

Example of issues from poor training

One of my customers on-boarded the temporary staff just before the go-live to help with the returns processing. They knew that the returns volume was going to be high for the first two weeks, as the returns were put on hold for a couple of weeks prior to go-live (to avoid any in-process returns that would have to be migrated). Also, the returns team had to go through two different systems for a period of time to verify the original purchase in the old system and enter the RMA in Dynamics AX. Due to lack of training, the temporary staff made a lot of mistakes. One of them input the per unit return cost instead of putting the extended amount on the RMA. This impacted the inventory cost, their pricing (was dependent on inventory cost), commissions, and so on for every product that had issues in RMA processing. The overall system-wide impact was negative, including commissions/paychecks for a lot of sales reps.

Summary

In this chapter, we reviewed test planning, types of testing, resources, and goals at each stage. We discussed the ways to make UAT and end-to-end testing most effective by uncovering issues prior to going live. We also discussed the training plan, preparation for an effective delivery of training, and the tools that can be used for change management and training.

12

Go-live Planning

Go-live planning is not like wedding planning, it is like planning a marriage. It is not just planning for a big day; it involves planning the events prior to the go-live phase and afterwards too. A huge amount of effort has been put into the project—teams have been working extremely hard designing, developing, and testing, and a lot of communication and dollars have been put into planning the release. A well-documented go-live plan can help ensure a smooth execution of the release and make the most of all that hard work and, of course, the dollars invested in the project.

As part of the release, you may be performing hundreds of tasks, so it is important to track their progress, dependencies, and corrective actions. Go-live planning involves the following:

- Putting together all the steps in the plan
- Defining the sequence and dependencies between the steps
- Determining the time needed for each step
- Defining the owners, and ensuring that all concerned parties have a clear understanding of what is required

Multiple reviews with the IT and business teams can ensure that you have identified every task that needs to be performed as part of the cutover, and that everyone involved understands the big picture of all the tasks involved in the release and not just their piece. Using such a plan for UAT, end-to-end testing, and pilot releases can help you identify any gaps in the plan as you practice the overall release execution process. This includes the communication required across groups such as turning off certain integrations of the legacy system, the setup of a new system, data migration, data validation, release testing, or a roll back process. All the steps need to be documented in the go-live plan.

In this chapter, we will cover the following topics:

- Key considerations prior to going live
- Putting together the go-live plan
- Execution of the plan
- References to a few real examples

Key considerations prior to going live

ERP implementation is like a heart surgery for the organization. A readiness check needs to be done carefully, prior to going live.

There is always a tremendous amount of pressure to make the go-live date, oftentimes somebody's job(s) is on the line, and so on. However, the readiness of the organization for the new system needs to be evaluated carefully prior to flipping the on switch. The following table enlists a few important considerations and criteria to evaluate if you are ready for going live:

Area	Description	Sign off criteria
Training sign off	• The business teams should be comfortable with the training that they've received and have access to the training documents. • People play a key role in your ERP success, and the end users, across all areas, need to be comfortable with using a new system and the business process changes.	• All business leaders should have signed off on the training for their teams. • The IT operations team should've signed off for their training.
User Acceptance Testing (UAT) sign off	• As mentioned in the chapter, business should have verified the business scenarios, and testing should be completed using real life business scenarios. • Testing of all items needed to run the business including functionality, integrations, reporting, data migration, and so on should be completed.	• All the business leaders should have signed off on the testing for their areas. • Document the open issues and their due dates. Review any critical issues that may be open and their impact/workarounds.

Area	Description	Sign off criteria
Go-live plan	• This is a step-by-step, hour-by-hour plan that is reviewed with all the IT/business teams involved in the release, including the roll back plan and an overall timing to fit within the downtime window. • Release the validation scenarios and processes defined by the business/IT.	• The plan that has been used in the previous iterations of the simulation of releases (including UAT and data validations). • It should've been signed off by the business and IT stakeholders.
Support plan	• The support plan includes the support resources per area, their location and schedule, the issue communication process, (templates for providing issue description, screen shots, business impact, severity, and so on; information and tools for tracking or logging issues), Triage, and loop back with the business teams. • You need to ensure that there is an adequate budget approved for support (prior to going live). You don't want to be in a situation where you have to discuss dollars with the customer/business leaders while the business is impacted due to system issues. Also, you need to have a budget to not lose the resources that would be required for fixing the issues.	• Review the support plan with all the stakeholders and users to ensure that the process for logging issues and communication is clear. • Set up business, IT war rooms at different locations; the handing over process between support teams can help with better communication.

Area	Description	Sign off criteria
Operations team readiness	• The IT operations team needs to have enough knowledge to own support for the new system. • Basic items like DB backup processes and high availability/DR testing need to be in place by this time. The team should be comfortable in the monitoring of services/processes, like batch jobs and failure alerts from AOS servers. • The production support team needs to be up to speed in code-push procedures and additional steps like data change requests, configuration changes, and so on. • Security reviews and sign off (PCI compliance, SOX compliance reviews as applicable) must be completed. • The infrastructure setup should be based on the Infrastructure architecture and reviewed. • Monitoring tools (dynamics perf, trace parser, and so on) must be deployed and ready for use when needed.	• Sign off from the IT operations team.
External sign offs and communication	• The external sign offs as applicable for the business. For example, sign off from the bank for check/electronic payments testing, EDI customers, vendors testing, and auditors.	• Sign offs from the respective parties.

Any exceptions need to be documented and presented to the business team and the management for making decisions. Discounting any of these areas could result in an unquiet environment post go-live and negatively impact the business.

The decision to go live

The decision to go live is very dependent on the quality of end-to-end testing and user/organizational readiness, as mentioned earlier. The following are some experiences that I would like share in this area:

- Once, I was in room full of executives, making the decision about pulling the trigger on a new system. Everyone was under pressure from the CEO to say, "We are ready". However, most of them were not ready. They did not have enough time to go through the testing due to a lack of staff, but everyone said, "yes". (There was a fear of getting fired; this was way back in 2009 when the economy wasn't doing well). I failed to push back as well. Any guess as to what happened next? The customer went live, and it was very painful to stabilize them. But, lesson learnt!

- A similar situation occurred again, a couple of years later. Of course, I was smarter this time. The CIO called for a meeting to check the readiness on the project. Everyone said they were ready (the CIO was driving the dates very hard, and again there a was fear of getting fired). It was my turn—I bravely stood up and said, "No", handing over a list of areas I wasn't comfortable with and which needed more testing. The CIO called for another meeting to understand better what was needed to finish those areas and decided not to go live. We ended up extending the schedule by six weeks based on what was on the list. The CIO thanked me (and still continues to) for standing up and challenging the decision to go live based on the bugs that were reported/fixed in those six weeks.

- On another project, I was involved in the executive reviewer capacity, where I challenged their readiness, but the CEO did not want to listen. I told them it was their call, and we would support the release if they signed a liability waiver, as my team was not comfortable (due to lack of testing from the business team) with them going live. When we gave them a piece of paper to sign, the CEO chose to reconsider his decision. The customer ended up delaying the release by four weeks. The CEO who was not very happy when he received the push back, but now he feels thankful to my team for "watching his back".

There are more instances like these that I can share. The point is that you need to think about the client and the impact on their business. As a consultant, you are their advocate, and you need to protect the customer from hurting themselves (even though it's not what they wanted to hear, you are doing it in their best interest). This is the time to utilize the relationships and the respect you have earned from the customer to protect them. Don't be shy.

It is even trickier when you have to stand up for someone else's deliverables. For example, say the customer owns certain deliverables internally, and those are not production ready. You need to request the delay due to their internal deliverables, as you don't want to project to fail due to specific areas.

Saying that you need more testing is easy. The tough part is to decide how much more time you need. You won't get such an opportunity again. Thorough planning needs to be done to identify all the pieces that are incomplete and to put together a plan to come up with a realistic date. Many project managers fail in this exercise; just hitting the snooze button and delaying this by a few weeks may cost you a job eventually.

Picking realistic dates that will work for the business is important. You don't want to perform an ERP go-live right before or during the peak period for the business. challenges from the go-live will have a severe impact on the business. There are many examples of companies going out of business due to an ERP go-live during or just before the busy holiday season.

Business contingency planning

Part of your go-live planning must address the business contingency planning. Conduct a pre-mortem session to brainstorm areas that may go wrong, and to find ways in which the team can reduce the likelihood or mitigate the business impact if the issue occurs. Review the critical business functions that are important for the organization, and develop contingency plans to run the business if you did not have the computer systems in place momentarily. The goal of this exercise is to plan for the unknowns that may come your way. The following are a few examples to help with the brainstorming process:

- **Third-party considerations**: You have SLAs for next-day deliveries to the customers; work with your shipping carriers, and have them stand by to schedule a delayed pick up, in case you need it.

- **Inventory levels**: You have a great dependency on planning and the stock levels; consider beefing up your inventory prior to go-live.

- **Additional workforce considerations**: Look at adding temporary staff or approve overtime for areas that have changed the most or processes that would need more hand holding. I quote one of my customers, "If I was to make a mistake on spending here, I would rather make it by spending more than less".

- **Additional technology resources to support the go-live**: You may have a lot of things uncovered during go-live. It is like having an insurance policy: it's good to have it but it's better if you do not have to use it.

- **Communication team**: Have them stand by in case you need to communicate with the outside parties (customers and vendors) or even internally. You may not want to let the customers know ahead of time about the ERP release, as they would consider it as an upcoming glitch and go somewhere else.

- **Cash flows**: It may take a little longer to get paid for a few weeks (or months) after go-live due to system or training issues. You need to have an additional line of credit available in case you need it.

- **Key processes and proactive planning**: Identify the key processes and their first occurrence to provide some hand holding and validation. For example, after processing the checks for the first time, ensure that you can validate them against the checks that passed testing. The first time you are ready to start invoicing, try a few orders first and verify the results before you open the flood gates of batching hundreds of orders. In case of files that are supposed to be sent out (like EDI or positive pay files for the bank), verify those that were sent and accepted/processed faultlessly at the receiving end.

- **Going back to the previous system after a few days or few hours into using the new system**: Once you move to new ERP system, it may not be possible to go back to the previous system. It is not easy to perform a reverse migration from new platform to legacy. Make sure everyone understands that once you are live, there is no going back. Everybody is in it together and issues need to be resolved on the new system. This helps in avoiding unproductive discussion of going back to the previous system after going live.

- **Running parallel**: It seems like an easy solution for business contingency planning. However, it may not be practical unless you are staffed high and the transaction volume is not high.

    ◦ Running parallel usually adds more burden and stress on your staff while they are trying to deal with new system. In general, it would cause more issues/noise (as users would make more mistakes under stress) than helping.

    ◦ If you had to go for running both the systems in parallel, the amount of time to run parallel should be kept to a minimum.

    ◦ Very often, running parallel is looked at as a replacement for inadequate testing; you think you are better off not doing testing in production (and hoping everything would be fine).

    ◦ There is sometimes a belief that running parallel helps validate the new processes against the old system processes. This is a fallacy, as part of the point of implementing a new system is to improve the processes that may fundamentally change the way you do business. So it is like trying to compare apples to oranges.

- **Release validation**: As mentioned earlier, going back to the previous system or running parallel is not easy. How can you verify that there are no critical issues as part of the release itself? The following are are some ideas:

    ○ Set aside a good amount of time in your release plan to allow for the release validation.

    ○ Once the business has signed off data migration in the production environment, they can start the release validation testing. You don't want to start creating new transactions until data validation is complete, else the numbers won't tie.

    ○ Identify the key end-to-end processes, and processes by functional areas to be verified; keep the step-by-step validation scripts ready.

    ○ It is ideal if you can hold certain transactions from the previous day. For example, let the AP team enter real vendor invoices, perform a check run based on what's due, orders that were received from the customers during system downtime, incoming EDI transactions, and so on. The goal is to have good samples and real transactions to verify the system behavior.

    ○ In one of my projects, performance was a concern. The customer involved a good part of their sales team to validate the order entry process after the initial validation was completed.

    ○ This process enables you to identify any remaining bugs (due to setup or code push issues) and resolve them or make a cautious decision to go-live or rollback.

    ○ Once you are live, there is no going back.

These are some ideas based on past experiences. You need to review these with the business leaders and determine what is applicable to your business to make appropriate arrangements.

Some technical tips

The following are some technical tips to keep in mind while planning for the go-live:

- Have tools like Dynamics Perf and Perf Monitor installed and configured in the production environment ahead of time. You can use them when needed.

- Set up an additional AOS server for troubleshooting. This is helpful when you want to troubleshoot a specific process by a developer with the business user. Provide an icon for connecting this AOS to the business user (an AXC file would connect to this AOS). That way, the developer can take traces and the like in an isolated fashion only for this user. You do not have to turn tracing on for all other users, which would slow down the environment and give you a lot of noise in the traces. This would reduce the effort needed to reproduce the issue in the non-production environment and help find a quicker resolution.

- It is not uncommon to see a high number of security requests come through in the first few days after the go-live (for example, changing user roles, giving them additional roles, setting up new users, allowing more access, and so on); dedicate resources to handle such requests. Once the initial security issues have been resolved, you may want to start looking at what you would need to pass a system audit and ways in which you can start taking away the privileges that may not be needed.

- Provide a heads up to the Microsoft Support team for large releases, more importantly if you are an early adopter of a specific feature or release. Try to get additional consulting support for the go-live. The onshore and offshore models are very helpful to keep the ball rolling round the clock on critical issues.

- Consider engaging the Microsoft Premier Support team to perform a proactive health check prior to the release, and to be available on standby during/and for a few days after release. This is especially important if you have a high transaction-volume environment.

- Another checkpoint is to ensure that backups are being taken and indexed and other SQL maintenance jobs are scheduled.

- Use the latest kernel version for AOS servers. Updating the latest Kernel version does not need much effort for deployment and testing. However, it would help you get to a more stable state.

- Check if there are any hotfixes that have been released recently and which should be considered. You can check the hotfixes in the Lifecycle Services portal or you can check if any cumulative update has been released recently. Review the list of hotfixes that are critical. This is very important if you are an early adopter of a new version/module.

- Refresh the data into the non-production environment for troubleshooting. This would help troubleshoot and fix issues quickly. You need to do this with caution though. Make sure that you have captured the steps (preferably automated) needed for scrubbing the environment specific connections. I have seen situations where these steps were missed during refresh and the test environment charged real credit cards or printed real shipping labels, connected to real instances of tax calculation software, and so on. The Test Data Transfer tool can be a better solution for this instead of a data restore. Using the Test Data Transfer tool, you can exclude specific tables containing the system configuration data. Refer to *Chapter 5, Data Migration – Scoping through Delivery* to learn more about the capabilities of the Test Data Transfer tool.

Putting together the go-live plan

Having a detailed plan put together, which can be used for multiple simulations prior to the go-live, is important. It gives you an opportunity to get the go-live plan validated and address any bugs/issues due to missed steps in the release plan. It also allows you to make changes to the plan, allows more time to review with multiple groups and identify the missing elements, and helps educate the team about dependencies and the big picture. The following are some guidelines for putting together your go-live plan:

- A smaller number of manual steps and more automation is ideal to ensure that you don't have too many steps to perform and track. As mentioned in *Chapter 5, Data Migration – Scoping through Delivery*, the validation of extraction, migration, and IT data should be automated as much as possible.

- Include a configuration checklist and any new configurations which need to be completed in the production environment prior to the go-live. Adopt automation or document in detail what needs to be done to complete the required configuration.

- Minimize dependencies; if activities can be completed in the production environment, mention that as a pre-release item. For example, if an integration solution requires creation of a new database, and if it can be done prior to the release, mention it as a pre-release item.

- You may be implementing ISV solutions or integrations with third-party systems, or integrating with an application managed by a different team in the same organization. Coordinate with different teams to understand the dependencies and activities needed to deploy or enable their solution. There should be one single deployment plan for all the components which need to be deployed as part of the release.

- Keep the overall deployment plan simple. Add additional attachments or links for the detailed steps which need to be performed.

- Create a repository to collect the artifacts and documentation required for completing individual tasks including release notes, validation plan document, configuration checklist, code artifacts, and so on.

- Put together a visual summary of the detailed plan (as referenced in *Chapter 5, Data Migration – Scoping through Delivery*). It helps in communicating with the stakeholders.

- Every step, including logistics like booking hotel rooms and ordering pizza, should be put on the plan with their owners.

- Ensure that you have not burnt your key resources with the release. Spread out tasks in a way that allows for downtime for the key resources. The real journey starts after putting the system into production, and you need everyone to stay energized for those first few weeks of transition.

- Try to keep the plan simple and easy to follow for the team. I have used the following table to put together a plan:

Column	Description
Sr. No	This is the task number
Dependency	These are the task numbers that needs to be completed prior to starting. Used to define the dependencies between tasks.

Column	Description
Type	• **Pre-release**: Identify all the tasks that can be completed prior to getting into the system's downtime window for release. For example, communication for the upcoming changes, installation and preparation of the future production environments, and tasks for tracking all the necessary sign offs. • **Release**: Tasks to be completed during the system's downtime window for release, such as taking the systems down, ensuring all transactions are complete and your source for data migration has the latest information, running extraction and migration tasks, communication at specific intervals during the release, taking SQL backups during the release, and identifying good checkpoints when backups should be taken (in case you have to go back to previous state). For example, before starting the posting of transactions, as you can't un-post them easily if you found an issue. • **Validation**: Tasks for validation, such as IT validation and business validation (verify the vendors and addresses, open balances, the validation of processes/functionality that were identified in the release validation, and so on). • **Decisions (Go/No go)**: Identify the multiple check points when you need to make Go/No go decisions with the executive/project team. • **Post release**: Tasks to be performed after the final decision has been made to go-live. These tasks may go on for multiple days into using the new system. For example, pushing icons on user desktops/enabling users, communication for release, turning on automated processes, verifying acceptance of the outgoing EDI files by customers, verifying acceptance of positive pay files by each of the banks, and so on. • **Roll back:** You may have to roll back to state prior to the release in unfortunate events like when something goes wrong during the release, critical issues that are identified, or external, uncontrolled dependencies that caused the issues. In any case, you need to have rollback steps defined and practiced in the release simulation phase in order to have an uninterrupted availability of the systems to the business. The time needed for the rollback procedure needs to be considered in the release process the go/no go decisions need to be made in a timely manner to allow completion of the rollback procedure.

Column	Description
Description	This is the task description.
Owner(s)	This defines the owners to perform the tasks.
Start date/ time	This is planned start time for the task. It is important to keep track of the timing on tasks that are on a critical path. Any delays in critical path items would impact the overall schedule of the release.
Time needed	This is the time needed to execute the task.
Comments	These are the comments and/or additional information.
Detail steps	These are the detailed steps to execute the overall task, if applicable. Attach or link to the detailed document if required.
Status tracking: Status, actual start time, finish time	Keep track of the actuals in release simulation cycles to adjust your plan, and work with the technical teams to reduce the time taken by critical path items. During production release, keep track of the actual timings for each of the task.

Executing a release

More simulations, prior to going live, will make the final execution easy. It also helps prepare the recipe for the no panic pill.

No matter how much preparation goes into planning a release, there may still be a few last-minute new discoveries. It is important how you react to them and maintain a *no panic* environment.

- Track the tasks as per the go-live plan and their dependencies.
- Send communications a multiple number of times (on track/ahead or behind, and the like) during the release window (communicate the frequency to all the stakeholders).

- The following diagram shows a visual form of communication that you can use to show the status of the release:

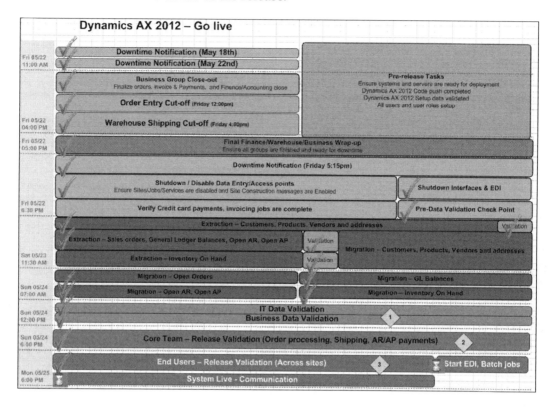

- Schedule conference calls with the leadership team to provide updates (you need to be giving them proactive updates rather than having them at your back, chasing for updates) as well as the go/no go decisions at specific intervals.

- Engage the IT SMEs and business SMEs for data validation. You need to record these tests (reports from the previous system and the new system), and save the test results. You will need them for your audit.

- Run through the release validation tests to verify that a functionality is working as expected. If you can hold a good sample of transactions from the previous working day, try to process them in the system and take them end-to-end. (You can hold half a day worth of orders from a day prior to go-live, enter them manually in the new system, and try to take them all the way through invoicing. Verify the reverse logistics as well.)

- Verify access to reports and integrations across multiple systems.

- Stay alert for upcoming surprises, and handle them sooner.

The importance of communication

Communication is a crucial part of go-live planning. The following is one of the references I would like to provide on why communication is so important when avoiding turning smaller issues into bigger challenges:

- In one of the upgrades, we had a very small downtime window to perform the upgrade. It was shortened further as updates in the data warehouse were going to take time, and we had to keep aside some time for roll back as well. However, with multiple iterations (thanks to the great technical team that was on the project) we were able to squeeze time to meet our requirements. Most of the core technical team was up the whole night to perform the upgrade and went to bed after the hand over to the team in the morning. It was almost bug free until the users showed up at the warehouse and started shipping. The requested delivery date printed on the shipping labels was the same day, the warehouse couldn't start shipping.

- Multiple e-mails, phone calls were received with messages like 'Warehouse can't ship.", "Warehouse is down.", "Need to call FedEx for delayed pickup.", "Should we stop picking?", and so on. This noise went on for two hours. It was hard to get a clear understanding of the real issue, until we reduced the audience and got on to call.

- In AX 2009, Microsoft added multiple dates on the sales orders that is, estimated ship date, requested shipping date, confirmed ship date, and so on. One of these custom date fields to be printed on the shipping label was mapped incorrectly to the default value (that is, the system date). This date was the delivery date given to the Japan post which, obviously, couldn't be the same date. It was just one line of code change for the developer once the real issue was explained.

- Out of the many learnings from this experience, I would say that managing communication after the go-live is most critical.

Summary

In this chapter, you learned how to prepare for release by making sure that all the the prerequisites have been addressed. We discussed how to prepare for **Business Contingency Planning** (BCP), how you can put together a plan, and mitigate the risks through multiple simulations and multiple reviews. This was followed by tips for execution of the go-live plan and the importance of managing communication.

You are now live and the business has a stable system to use. Going live is an important milestone. Now you have a solid ERP platform in place. It opens up the door for business transformation opportunities through the power of the new modern ERP.

13
Post Go-live

The journey post go-live starts with the goal of keeping the system up, but you ultimately need to lead it through to business transformation. While the initial focus is to keep the lights on, eventually, the focus needs to shift on taking the business to the next level, with the new ERP platform as its foundation. The organization needs to start taking ownership of the new platform in this phase, and start scaling back on consulting resources.

It is not uncommon to see firefighting situations as you fly into the storm at go-live. The amount of preparation and testing that was done ahead of the release will minimize the impact of the storm. Moreover, the way you react and keep control of the situation can magnify or reduce the impact.

In this chapter, we will talk about the different phases post go-live, what to expect, and the preparation required for these phases, along with a few real life examples.

In this chapter, we will learn about handling the key components of post go-live, which are as follows:

- Initial stabilization
- Proactive preparation – what's coming
- Post-implementation review

Initial stabilization

Now that you are live, the first few weeks — usually until the first month-end close — are going to be long weeks. During the initial stabilization period, it is important to ensure that the business is not hurting due to system issues. Communication is most critical, and investments in your support plan will pay off now by handling the communication to all stakeholders effectively.

As part of the initial stabilization process, you should be prepared to handle the prioritization of issues, management of bug fixes (along with their deployment into production), as well as transitioning support to the business by building a repository of FAQ's that they can begin to manage. The following sections walk through these key components of stabilization.

Triage and prioritization

Regularly triage the open issues with the business and IT. Prioritize issues and provide due dates. Communication is a very important part of this process:

- **Limiting the noise**: Very often, there is more noise than real issues. You need to set up a process to control any miscommunication and handle the noise. Direct reviews with the business teams and triage can help reduce the noise and get first-hand information.

- **Don't forget about your support plan**: As noted in *Chapter 12, Go-live Planning*, you should develop a support plan that includes a process for the business users to document, report, and, ultimately, track issues. It is very important that the entire organization understands this process and abides by it to aid in issue prioritization. This also provides another tool to help limit the noise.

- **Confidence and body language**: Things may be messy initially. However, it is important for the leaders to demonstrate that things are in control. ERP projects are complex by nature, and you are not the first one going through such issues. Higher stress and reduced confidence can only add to the issues.

Bug fixes and their business impact

Now that you are in production, there are multiple aspects of bugs that need to be fixed. The business impact of each bug needs to be evaluated carefully:

- **Stop the bleeding**: How do you stop more damage because of an issue? Say, for example, you know that the invoices for XYZ customers are not showing freight. Put a hold on the invoicing process for that customer, and do not send any more invoices until the issue is fixed. That would avoid any further damage.

- **Recovery of data**: While the team is fixing the issue for future occurrences, an analysis needs to be done to understand the scope/impact on the data and the way in which the data that has been damaged by the issue can be recovered/fixed.

- **Fix for the issue**: The issue needs to be analyzed, and the root cause needs to be fixed, tested thoroughly, and promoted to the production environment.

- **What we learned and how to avoid it in the future**: An analysis needs to be done to find out the cause for this issue to reach the production environment and the reason it was not caught in the previous rounds of testing. The analysis should help in finding a solution so that a similar instance can be avoided in the future.

- **RCA process:** Implementing the RCA process as part of bug fixes would help reduce the repeating bugs and improve the process.

One of my customers had a very thorough process for **RCA (Root Cause Analysis)**. Every time that a bug was introduced in production due to any release, you had to put together the complete RCA for the issue. It would include documenting the symptoms, impact to business, how and when the problem was reported, steps taken, short term, and long term resolution, and the changes made in the process due to the learnings. They made sure that they would not have any issue because of the same/similar mistake in the future. Moreover, it was so much work (and the team had to answer so many tough questions in a room full of people) to put together an RCA that the team made sure they did everything they could to avoid any issues in the future.

The deployment stage

It is important to have a formal release process and schedule. You need to reduce the number of deployments every week. Otherwise, it will be hard to provide a stable system to the business. The following are some components of a good deployment process:

- The deployment process should be well-documented and automated.

- The developers should not deploy into production. Make sure that your support team is up to speed on the deployment process prior to going live. The customer should own this process, and to enable ownership of the system and to save consulting dollars.

- Thorough testing and reducing deployments is important. While there may be some low-hanging fixes, they may backfire and create issues in production. Troubleshooting of issues becomes difficult with too many changes going into the production environment.

- Avoid deployments close to the month-end or on peak business days.

- Have a set of scripts created to verify the common business processes after the release. This is very important when you have multiple systems integrated with Dynamics AX. Changes in one system (or timing issues in deploying the related changes) may break integrations. Continue to improve the release validation process based on the issues that come up and which have a high business impact.

I was involved in a post-implementation review, and what triggered the review is as follows. The customer/partner had the development team working on the deployment. On the second day of going live, the developers made a mistake costing fifty-thousand dollars while doing a deployment. They forgot to take a backup of the database (they were tired due to long hours, and are human) and deployed the new code. Unfortunately, there was some object conflict as part of the database sync process, and Dynamics AX ended up dropping and recreating the table for credit cards and authorizations. Fifty-thousand dollars worth of credit cards and authorizations were lost; B2C customers could not be charged.

Troubleshooting tips and FAQs

Now that you have seen the trend of the support issues, start adding to the FAQs and troubleshooting techniques that can be used by the users prior to reaching out to support.

- **Clear the usage data**: There will be a high number of deployments required to stabilize the environment, and these deployments may cause conflicts with personalization on the forms. As a result, specific user(s) may see unexpected system behavior. Such issues may go away when the user resets their usage data. (**Tools | Options | Usage data | Reset**).

- **Shortcut keys**: Prepare documentation for the shortcut keys that can be used.

- **Execute in CIL**: If you have issues with CIL, some processes that run in IL may have issues as well. Try disabling the CIL operations as a temporary fix (**Tools | Options | Development | Execute Business logic in CIL**).

- Limit the number of windows.

- Limit the inactive session time.

- Uploading or downloading files from the local computer while using the remote desktop or a Citrix client for Dynamics AX.

- Printing from Dynamics AX to network printers.

Proactive preparation – what's coming

The following sections explain some areas that you need to think about as you begin the transition into system stabilization and optimization.

Preparing for the first month-end

The first month-end closing is a key milestone for the system. This is a good litmus test for measuring the success of the implementation.

Reporting requests

There will always be a need for reports that are critical for the executives and may have been missed during the previous phases. Watch out for such reports; some requests may be due to other system issues, such as a list of the invoices that had tax missing. Have a resource to respond to such requests. The guidelines given in *Chapter 6, Reporting and BI* will help in minimizing the need for these demands and will help you in responding to them.

Security and roles assignments

As mentioned in *Chapter 12, Go-live Planning*, you will need resources to respond to the security-related issues, and then lock down access to the system.

Form changes

It is common to see requests for adding more fields on the forms, or moving them from one from to another. Once the business has started using the system, and they have a better understanding of it, such requests will come up for improving efficiencies.

Performance reviews

Once you are live, it is important to review usage patterns for the data. The need for additional indexes, optimizing long-running queries, expensive queries in terms of resource utilization, and so on should be checked regularly. It is like a new car; you need to service it soon after using it a little bit and keep servicing it at regular intervals rather than waiting for it to break down.

The data growth

This is another item to pay attention to. You should undertake proactive maintenance rather than reacting to issues once they pop up. In high-volume environments, you can review the table-level data growth and pay more attention to the tables that are growing fast. You can also start reviewing the options for archiving or purging.

Training opportunities

Pay attention to the areas that are in pain and arrange for training to address the training issues. It may not be training on just Dynamics AX; there may also be some generic tools that are different. For example, the AP team did not use CSV files before and formatting for the leading zeroes was not known to them. They would not be able to effectively utilize the AP invoice upload functionality.

Engaging with Microsoft

Microsoft promotes the use of a partner network to engage with the customers. However, there are some plans that allow the customers to directly log incidents with Microsoft:

- **The Business Ready Advantage Plus (BRAP)** plan currently offers an unlimited number of incidents. I have seen this plan help customers in taking more ownership of their Dynamics AX environment and working directly with Microsoft on the issues. It also helps them save the consulting cost to work/coordinate on the product bugs.

- Engaging premier support is a good avenue to engage the experts from the premier support team to help with performance optimization, and retraining the internal resources for using the available tools.

A Microsoft support budget

Plan for annual support costs to be paid to Microsoft for staying up-to-date on the enhancement plan. Usually, it is 16 percent of your protected list price. The following are some of the points that you need to know about the enhancement plan:

- The customer is usually billed by the Microsoft Partner that is provided with the implementation services (unless you have an enterprise agreement with Microsoft). Ensure that you do not let it lapse.

- By paying the enhancement fees, you get access to the updates on the Customer Source, **Lifecycle Services (LCS)** portal, unlimited online trainings, access to product releases, service packs, hot fixes, and so on. It also protects your list price for future license upgrades.

- Prepare a process to periodically review and keep up with cumulative updates and hotfixes from Microsoft.

Business process optimization

Now that you are live, you need to take a holistic look at the business processes and identify the factors causing pain and the way in which it can be simplified. Break them into smaller projects. During implementation, you should stay away from any major business process improvements to avoid fighting any political battles and to keep the amount of changes manageable. However, now you can start focusing on the business process improvements. The first part is to fix the processes broken due to the new system. The next part would be to look at strategic projects (which may come as part of PIR, mentioned in the next section).

Once, I was given a $15 million challenge by a CFO. This was regarding their open AR. The open AR grew from ~$15 million to ~$35 million soon after going live. Of course, the CFO wanted to bring it back to ~$15 million, and he promised to stand reference for my organization if we helped in getting it back to $15 million within the next quarter. Many issues had contributed to the increased AR—invoice printing, delivery, user training in the collections team, low productivity of the collections team due to the manual processes, additional clicks, and the learning curve for the new system. Order entry, the returns process, and shipping issues made it even worse. Taking a holistic look at of all of these challenges, resolving the low-hanging fruit like training on the collection module, fixing a few invoicing bugs, statement printing, and form changes to reduce the number of clicks helped them get back to the $15 million mark.

The point is that reviewing specific issues/business processes in isolation can limit your ability to get to the root cause. You need to look at the big picture and take a holistic approach in defining the root cause of the factors contributing to the situation. For example, if the finance team has to make a lot of journal entries for corrections, they may want to automate the process. But the root cause of the issues really lies in the upstream business processes that can be handled by better training.

In addition to the processes that are reported as a challenge by business, efforts need to be put into finding the processes that are not working. Many times, several groups/resources in the organization will not proactively report the issues. They will simply accept them and put in more manual processes to work around those.

Open change requests

It is time to review the change requests that have been tracked during the implementation; most of the time, more than half are not needed any more, as the business learns more about the system or because things have changed.

- Work with the business to prioritize the tactical requests (low-effort changes) so that these can be taken up as the IT team gets a breather. Be careful in opening up the flood gates; you need to emphasize prioritizing the requests and planning the execution.

- Depending on the work load of the IT teams, it may be a good time to start looking at the low-hanging fruits (and these can be taken up while the team takes small breaks from the support issues) to help the business with their workload.

- Committing to deadlines on these change requests may be tough at this point, as you would have priorities changing day-to-day due to unknown production issues. Setting up a dedicated team for new efforts may be a good idea if these changes are needed to reduce the support issues or to improve business efficiency.

Post-implementation review

Once the system is stable enough, it is time to review the opportunities for taking the business to the next level. The initial implementation is phase one of the project and you may not see the direct ROI by just going live. Many times, the initial impetus of a new ERP system is risk avoidance of using a non-supported platform. Many business process improvement initiatives would have to be taken up once you have the foundation in place, and these would result in true ROI from the Dynamics AX project.

Why post-implementation review?

A PIR is useful for the following reasons:

- It identifies the unused potential of your Dynamics AX investments
- It helps in ascertaining what could be (or could have been) done better
- It helps in discover training opportunities
- PIR is important for the analysis of the business pain points, such as implementation issue, product gap, or process issues
- It provides opportunities for performance improvements

- PIR gets the business team re-engaged
- With PIR, you can build a backlog that would help redefine your roadmap: short term and long term
- You can prepare a long-term roadmap for what's coming (The next version that may have already been released or any structural/foundational changes that may need to be considered in the next upgrade)

Key factors to get the most out of PIR

The following is a list of some key factors that need to be considered for a successful PIR:

- Business involvement is crucial.
- Reviewing everything could be expensive; you need to clearly define the scope and stay laser-focused.
- An independent group to provide an unbiased opinion.
- Team of experts who can foresee the big picture and who have cross-functional knowledge.
- Experts who can understand/speak business and the technical language to get to the bottom of issues, analyze them, and make actionable recommendations. Some industry knowledge is extremely important.
- Keep the emotions, history, and personal attacks out of it. Getting into history and finger-pointing does not help. The goal should be to get to a better state.

Preparing for PIR

To ensure a successful PIR, make the following preparations:

- Collect the project documentation. The following is a list of a few key documents:
    - Business process flows
    - Functional and technical architecture, all other systems
    - Customizations list and specs
    - Requirements, Fit/Gap documents
    - Training documents
    - Issue list

- Engage all the business groups and IT, and have them come up with the top 5-10 pain points. Provide templates and gather information.
- Arrange for access to the environments (with a relatively recent production data).
- Install the required tools for tracing.
- Hold kickoff with business and IT. Define and clarify goals, expectations, and so on.

Pain points from experience

The following are some examples of pain points that you would see as part of the process:

- The inventory does not tie to the general ledger
  - Can't explain changes in the margin with inventory close
  - Our FIFO/weighted average is different from Dynamics AX
  - As-of-date inventory reports do not work
- The returns process is too cumbersome
- I am flying blind; I don't have reports to run the business
- Month-end closing takes a long time
  - Too many journal entries to post to classify the transactions that were not posted with the correct financial dimensions
  - Reconciliation of the sub ledger and the GL is time consuming
  - Need as-of-date AR reports
- The sales orders are too hard to unwind after a certain stage
- Can't understand the results of master planning
- Planning takes a long time to run
- Batch processes take too long to run; sometimes, nightly batches do not finish in time
- Performance of the sales order screen is poor
- Too many clicks in the collections module; need to see all the information in one view
- Developers often break production

Post-implementation review – an AX 2012 customer

The following diagram shows how the Business Pain points are centered with the combination of Unused Dynamics AX potential, Customizations and workarounds, and the noise created by the ISV add-on

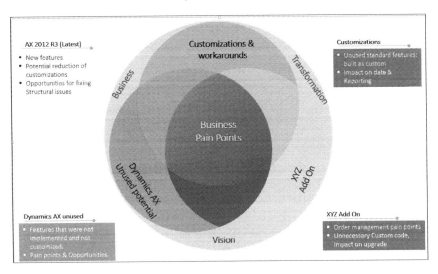

Current state – key challenges

The following diagram is a summary of the key challenges from the initial implementation, defined on the basis of the informati on gathered from the business teams:

	Add On	Product number	Month End	Trust in system	Production Type
Description	• Massive custom code (Mostly not used) • High cost vs low value	• Smart numbering for Product numbers	• Month end process takes much longer • Manual entries at month end	• Sales team does not have trust in the system • Issues in commissions	• Setup as discrete • While Business is process
Biz Impact	• Obstacles in use of Standard AX (& pain points) • Clean up work: Now vs upgrade	• Large number of Products • Duplicate info • Impact on Prod, logistics, sales	• Delays availability of P&L's • Additional work for Finance	• Sales floor is tracking every sale & margin (lost trust & Productivity)	• High customizations in Production • Impact on planning
Solution	• Remove add on iterative fashion • Cost and impact	• Use Product dimensions • Move current products new structure	• Fixing upstream processes that are causing errors /rework for Finance	• Inventory Costing and commission calc • Issues in Sales Reporting	• Use Process Manufacturing features • Batch Attributes
	NOW/PREUPGRADE	PRE/UPGRADE	NOW	NOW	PRE/UPGRADE

The unused potential of Dynamics AX

Dynamics AX has a rich functionality, but you may not have been exposed to all the features that can be helpful for your business. You would be overwhelmed to see how much more can be achieved on your current platform itself. The following image shows the low-hanging fruits, which can mostly be achieved through training:

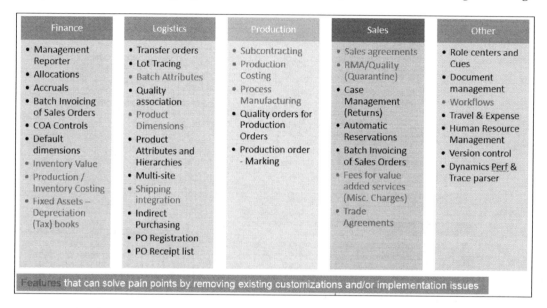

Improvement opportunities – processes and systems

There can be improvement opportunities in the business processes or the system processes. Dynamics AX is very flexible and provides multiple ways of configuring the system to meet the requirements. You can review whether there can be better ways to utilize the system to meet your business process requirements, as shown in the following table data:

Process	Recommendation	Saving	Effort
Invoice Review	Automate processes that have caused Sales NOT to TRUST the 'system', delays collection	HIGH	HIGH
Export documents	Tie them with Pick list (than Packing slip)	HIGH	MED
Upload for AP Invoices	Providing upload functionality to AP team can save many hours	HIGH	HIGH
Segment P&L reporting	Alignment of Financial dimensions per reporting needs, GL allocation processes, alignment of rest of the transactions to meet segment P&L reporting needs	HIGH	MED
Inventory Costing	Aligning setups for Costing method, frequency of close/recalc, and dimension settings. Issues with configurations that cause GL/Inventory to not tie	HIGH	HIGH
Role center & Cues	Help users manage exceptions; than reviewing every transaction. (Across all groups).	HIGH	LOW
Collection process	Ability to track follow up and processes for actively managing past due accounts. View of all the necessary information in single screen than having to navigate multiple places	HIGH	LOW

Items reported on Pain point list by business (remaining are identified by reviewers)

New features from the next release

It is very likely that by the time you go live and are ready for the post implementation review assessment, Microsoft may have already released the next major version of the product (like R2 and R3 of the same or the potential next version). It is good to know about the new features that are available in the product that can be utilized in the future (in some cases, Microsoft also releases backward portability options). This exercise is helpful in aligning your roadmap with the product roadmap to ensure that you don't build something (or buy another product) that Microsoft has already added, or is in the process of adding, to the next release:

AX 2012 R3 (New features)

Finance	Logistics	Production	Sales	Other
• Royalties • Budget planning process • Positive Pay • Auto Bank Recon • Prenotes (ACH Vendor pay) • Freight bill Reconciliation	• Product Management • Wireless warehouse • Demand planning • Freight bill reconciliation • Better Inventory Aging reports • Inventory hold • Improved inventory reservations	• Improvements in Process Manufacturing • Wireless warehouse • Several wins from Logistics and 'Other' enhancements	• Sales order holds • Automatic Order reservations • Customer Rebates • Several wins from Finance, Logistics and 'Other' enhancements	• Product Remodeling • Lot numbers remodeling • Remove Add-on • Human Resource Management

Features that would replace existing customizations, or not being utilized because of implementation issues

Summary

In this chapter, we went over the key areas of the post go-live phase, like managing the initial stabilization as you fly into the storm and proactively preparing for what's coming your way, leading from stabilization to business transformation.

This is the phase of the project when you learn the most about Dynamics AX implementation. How you overcome those challenges makes a successful implementation. While some learnings are expensive and could be painful for the business, ensuring that those are not repeated is important.

The real ROI from the Dynamics AX investments would usually start as part of the business transformation phase. Stopping the project after the initial go-live and stabilization would not give you the true ROI on your investments.

14
Upgrade

A Dynamics AX implementation is a big investment. Post implementation, organizations spend thousands of dollars on maintaining and extending the system on business process improvement projects to gain the real ROI of the new platform. At the same time, Microsoft invests millions of dollars on its research and development organization by using leading-edge technologies for platform and functionality improvements, which enable new features within their core product.

An upgrade enables the customers to get these functionality and technology improvements by moving to the latest versions. At the same time, upgrading to new versions can be overwhelming and can cost significantly high in terms of dollars, critical resource time, and potential business disruptions.

Dynamics AX or any ERP upgrade is not like a Windows upgrade where you start the upgrade and your system backs up on the new platform in a few hours. Upgrading of an ERP system requires extensive planning, preparation, and resources. It can take a few months to several years for this project, which largely depends on the number and type of customizations, changes in the core product (difference in the versions that you are upgrading), and the volume of data that you have.

The decision to upgrade is not easy. On one hand, you want to keep up with technological improvements and utilize the new features; on the other hand, Microsoft keeps releasing new versions (with major changes) of the product every 2-3 years. The change in operations and functionalities so often makes it hard for the business to adapt.

In this chapter, we will cover the following topics:

- When to upgrade
- The upgrade options
- The Dynamics AX upgrade process

When to upgrade

Upgrades aren't necessarily a good or bad idea in general, but it's important to carefully examine and evaluate the pros and cons before embarking on an upgrade project. The following sections mention a few considerations to keep in mind before an upgrade.

Benefit to the business operations

You should not just upgrade or implement a new technology platform. Instead, there should be a clear benefit to the business by upgrading to a new version. A thorough analysis of the new features that can be useful for the business needs to be done, and a vision scope for the upgrade should be put together. Some of these features may be new for the business while some could replace your existing customizations or third-party systems. The benefits could include new features and functionalities, increased efficiency and productivity, and transparency through better reporting. The benefits should also justify the time and cost required to execute the upgrade project. A proper roadmap to realize the benefits and returns on the investment should be established.

Are operations ready for the change?

Change is not easy. Upgrades often bring new user interfaces, functionalities, and processes with them and it's not easy for the business to tackle these changes. The following are some key considerations:

- Identify the competing business projects that would have to be reprioritized or delivered as part of the upgrade. Opportunity cost needs to be evaluated (as you would have to redeploy the IT/business resources and run into code freeze as part of the upgrade project).

- Upgrade is not a technology project and needs good involvement from the business. The business should be ready to commit resources for the upgrade project.

- Conduct an independent post-implementation review, and scope out what you would want to fix from the initial implementation as part of the upgrade like redoing specific customizations, redefining the product structure, redefining the legal entity structure based on business needs (like splitting sales and distribution companies), and so on. The lessons from the previous project should be defined to ensure that you are doing things differently this time for a better outcome. Changing only the VARs is not going to fix the fundamental issues.

Stabilization of the newer version

Our friends at Microsoft are not going to like this section. However, in reality, it takes a few months for any new release to stabilize. You wouldn't want to get burned with early-on product issues as part of the project, or let the business be affected due to the issues in production.

- If you choose to be early adaptors, ensure you have enough support and blessings from your partner and the Microsoft team, in case you run into issues.

- We would strongly recommend getting a BRAP support plan. This would allow you to open an unlimited number of tickets to resolve issues. These issues may be due to bugs in the product, undocumented settings, or features that are causing noise, learning curve for the consulting and implementation team, and so on). However, getting help from Microsoft would help reduce the implementation team's time on such issues, and ultimately, help deliver the project on schedule.

- For newly released modules, try to defer the implementation post upgrade until it is mature/stabilized enough. For example, when Dynamics AX 2012 R2 was released, the budgeting module was released as well. I would have planned to implement it post upgrade rather than along with the upgrade.

- You shouldn't wait too long either, and upgrade in the later part of the product lifecycle when Microsoft is about to release the next version.

Continued technical support

For many organizations, this is one of the key reasons for upgrade. It's important and critical for the customer to have continued vendor support and assistance if something goes wrong. For Dynamics AX, Microsoft provides mainstream support for five years or two years, whichever is longer, after the successor product is released. Microsoft also provides extended support following the mainstream support for five or two years, whichever is longer, after the second successor product (N+2) is released. The customer can go for extended support but you must know that upgrading to the latest version gets more and more complicated if you skip many major versions.

Upgrade versus reimplementation

Sometimes, it might be better to plan a fresh implementation of the latest version than upgrading from the old version. The following are the scenarios where reimplementation can be a better approach rather than upgrade:

- There is no direct upgrade path if you missed upgrading to several of the last version releases. For example, a customer using Dynamics AX 3.0 or 4.0 cannot directly upgrade to AX 2012 R3. They need to upgrade to AX 2009 first, and then they can upgrade to AX 2012.

- Structural changes between versions and lost opportunity due to upgrade: For example, AX 2012 had major structural changes in the Dynamics AX data models as compared to the previous versions; a lot of normalizations and improvements were made to support the scaling and performance improvements. The customers upgrading from the previous versions could not take full benefit of some of the features such as, the shared chart of accounts and dimension structure. Considerations need to be made for any potential limitations due to the current data and upgrade process.

- When you have heavy customizations, several of the customizations can be eliminated and replaced by the standard features.

- If the data quality of the current system is bad and it would require too much effort to clean the data to prepare for the upgrade.

- If there are changes in the fundamental master-data elements. For example, moving away from smart product numbers or implementing the product structure differently using product dimensions, changes in inventory costing, changes in the legal entity structures due to business reasons like splitting distribution, manufacturing, and sales companies.

Project strategy and planning

Just like an implementation project, an upgrade project needs proper project strategy and planning. To execute a successful upgrade project, you need a proper project plan, change management, test, training, and deployment planning.

Upgrading options

If you are planning to upgrade to the latest version of Dynamics AX (Dynamics AX 2012 R3 CU9) from one of the previous versions, take a look at the following table, which illustrates the upgrade options depending on the source Dynamics AX application version:

Source Version	Upgrade Options
AX 4.0 SP2	This is an indirect upgrade. You must upgrade to AX 2009 SP 1 first.
AX 2009 SP 1 (without retail)	This is a direct upgrade using the source-to-target model.
AX 2009 for Retail R1 AX 2009 for Retail R2	This is an indirect upgrade. You must first upgrade to AX 2009 for a Retail R2 Refresh.
AX 2009 for Retail R2 Refresh	Direct upgrade using the source-to-target model.
AX 2012 R2 Feature pack	In-place upgrade on a single system. No source-to-target workflow is used.
AX 2012 R2	In-place upgrade on a single system. No source-to-target workflow is used.

Source to target

The source to target model is an upgrade option available for upgrading to Dynamics AX 2012 from the previous major versions (From AX 4.0 or AX 2009). In this model, the final data upgrade activity will move the entire database (all data, transactions, and companies) into Microsoft Dynamics AX 2012 R3. In order to minimize the downtime window of the upgrade, Dynamics AX 2012 provides the ability to preprocess the data in the source system. The following diagram shows the source to target upgrade model:

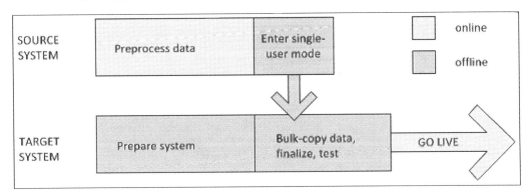

In-place upgrade

An in-place upgrade model is applicable when upgrading to Dynamics AX 2012 R3 from the previous Dynamics AX 2012 versions. In this model, the upgrade is performed directly on the target system.

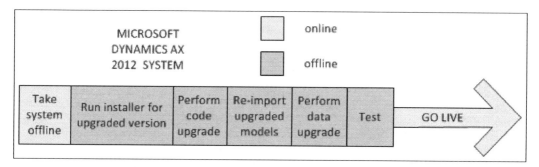

The Dynamics AX upgrade process

As described earlier, upgrades require detailed planning and consideration—it is just like executing an implementation project. The following diagram represents the typical upgrade project phases:

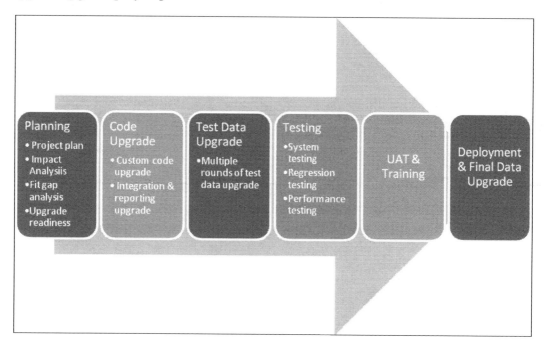

Planning the upgrade

Once you decide to upgrade, it's important to do detailed planning and analysis, just like what is done for the implementation phase before starting the project. An upgrade is like moving. You don't know how much stuff you have accumulated until you are moving. Similarly, an upgrade is when the people start realizing how many customizations they have made in Dynamics AX and in the external applications that are built around Dynamics AX, including reporting.

The following sections define the key areas to be considered when doing an upgrade project.

Managing customization (Fit/Gap)

Most of the upgrade projects that I have reviewed had a common theme. The new version was implemented in the old way, that is, all the customizations from the previous version were ported on to the new version—as is.

As part of the analysis/planning, you need to spend a good amount of time finding a match for the existing custom features, and deprecate the custom features. Most likely, Microsoft may have developed a feature that you had to customize years ago. This is your opportunity to unlock the power of a new version, and maximize your investment in the Dynamics AX platform by tearing off customizations. While it may sound like a no brainer, many projects fail to do so as it needs additional work to migrate the existing data from custom tables to the standard ones. A few minor customizations that are in place may be needed on top of a standard feature if the standard one does not completely replace what you have. Hence, shortcuts are taken and all of the old custom code is ported into the newer version.

For every customization you are porting to the new version, you need to think it through as if you were going to build that feature from scratch. Assess whether it is worth customization, or is there any feature in Dynamics AX that can be leveraged to meet your needs. Otherwise, you will end up bringing over all the customizations from the previous version to the new version and ultimately running the new version in the backward compatibility mode. The business will not get much value out of such an upgrade.

Also, there are customizations that may not be used anymore. Those need to be identified and removed/left behind as part of the upgrade project. Plan what customization can be replaced or reimplemented with new version. You should do a detailed Fit/Gap analysis for new features and see how these features can benefit the business, and if there are any gaps. Plan if they can be addressed during or after the upgrade. Fit/Gap analysis is also relevant for custom features in the old system—compare these features with any equivalent features in the new version. Identify the gaps and plan to address them as part of the upgrade. Sometimes, such a list of features can be overwhelming and may add significant scope to the upgrade project. Read the following section for ideas and experiences on managing the scope.

Managing the scope

What functionality is available in the version you are upgrading to versus what is in the scope for the upgrade project is the issue that needs to be decided.

In my experience, delivering the current functionality available to the business is the first step towards the new platform. No one would like to go backwards on the features they already had. However, you should negotiate for not implementing brand new features as part of the upgrade project itself. These new features can come as a next step after the upgrade, even if these features are available out of the box in the new version of Dynamics AX. You need to consider the time needed for the implementation of such features and the impact to the overall timeline of the upgrade. I would rather run parallel projects to implement several new features once I have moved to the latest version, than delaying the upgrade itself. This approach allows you to divide the scope into smaller projects for the new features and is easier to manage as well.

At the same time, you may consider enhancement to the existing features to be included as part of the upgrade project. To take an example, on one of the upgrade projects from AX 4.0 to AX 2009, the client wanted to add another financial dimension. This was a very complex Dynamics AX environment, where the sales orders were received from many sources, several applications were integrated with Dynamics AX, and very few people knew the end-to-end processes. Due to the overall complexity of the environment and lack of visibility to the impact, the team did not want to make that change as part of the upgrade project.

We were engaged by the finance team as this was a critical item for them. Upon 4-5 weeks of analysis of all the sales order transactions from several sources, we came up with a list of changes that had to be made in Dynamics AX and other applications/ integrations. It ended by taking up only 40 hours of development team's effort. Doing it with the upgrade was a big win for finance as they did not have to retest the entire application (the changes were tested along with rest of the upgrade testing). Another business challenge was addressed with the upgrade without much scope creep. It also helped in getting the finance team actively involved on the project (until then, they did not have much incentive to participate and looked at it as a technical upgrade). The bottom line is, you need to have a thorough analysis done for deciding on what to tackle with the upgrade, and it can help you address key strategic initiatives.

Many times, the users want everything that they are using currently to be included as-it-is. However, somebody needs to take stock of all the areas that are being utilized and put together the use cases of functionality that are being used. Otherwise, you would have a testing nightmare and also run the risk of porting over the old functionality, as noted earlier.

Managing the data

Evaluate the data in terms of quality and volume. Clean the data in the source system if possible. Dynamics AX 2012 provides an upgrade-readiness check tool that can evaluate your data and suggest clean-up activities that you should undertake before upgrading to the new version.

Consider purging or archiving the source data from the production dynamics AX environment to minimize the data upgrade time of the production environment. The Microsoft **IDMF (Intelligent Data Management Framework)** tool can be utilized to purge or archive data.

This would help reduce the time needed for each data upgrade iteration and the downtime needed for performing a production upgrade apart from improving the data quality in the next version.

Business engagement

Many times, upgrade projects are branded as a technology upgrade. For the very same reason, it's hard to get the business engaged in the upgrade projects. That might be true to some extent when you are doing a minor upgrade such as upgrading from AX 2012 R3 CU8 to AX 2012 R3 CU9. For major version upgrades like AX 2009 to AX 2012, business engagement is critical. You will need business agreement on various decisions, such as identifying unused features or customization, Fit/Gap analysis of custom features and the new features, defining the scope, data archival and purging, training, UAT, and so on.

Impact on integrations

You may have a lot of other applications in your ecosystem that are integrated with Microsoft Dynamics AX. An upgrade can impact those integrations for either the underlying technology changes or schema changes. For example, Microsoft has removed the business connector from AX 7. So if you are upgrading to AX 2012, you should redo your integration using services or other integration framework available. Any integrations built using AIF may also have to be changed if the underlying schema is changed.

> Microsoft Dynamics AX 7 is not yet available to customers. Information provided here is as per the information available in the public domain, and this may change.

Impact on reporting

How does the upgrade impact your reporting and BI solution? Do you have replicated data or data marts for ad hoc and external reporting? New versions may have significant schema change, which may require significant changes in all the reports and BI solution. Dynamics AX 2012 had huge changes in the data schema as compared to AX 2009; the tables were highly normalized, and several standard features were reimplemented from scratch.

Even small changes in the schema can significantly impact the reporting solutions. For example, one of the customers upgrading from AX 4.0 to AX 2009 had to update hundreds of reports written out of a replicated data source due to changes in the `CreatedDateTime` and `ModifiedDateTime` fields in AX 2009. Analyze all your reports and the ad hoc SQL queries that the business team uses to gather data, and plan to upgrade them. Another impact you may have to consider is the replicated data itself. If you are replicating tables from the Dynamics AX database, these tables may have been changed (new fields may have been added or deleted), or sometimes, the table itself may have been replaced with a new set of tables. These replicated data sources need to be rebuilt to support the new schema. One of my customers was feeding `LedgerTrans` data into their corporate data warehouse. Many processes and KPIs were dependent on this general ledger data. Removal of the `LedgerTrans` table in AX 2012 added a good amount of rework to the ETL process feeding the data warehouse.

Code freeze in the source system

Upgrade projects can take several months to year(s) for customers having many customizations and /or integrations. The customers also have continuous improvements projects and several business initiatives that require changes in their current Dynamics AX application. It is important to understand that these other projects may have to stop for a period of time for a smooth code upgrade, testing, data upgrade process, and avoiding rework in both the projects. It would also help in getting all the IT and business resources aligned for delivery of the upgrade project.

You may be able to make continuous improvements during the upgrade planning and analysis phase, but once the code upgrade activity is started, you should freeze the code of your current AX environment. Set the expectations with your business team for the code freeze start date and its impact on the existing projects that are in-flight, or have an approved budget. Prioritize the critical issues and fixes which need to be completed in the current AX implementation before starting the code upgrade project.

If any critical issues surface due to business priorities that cannot wait or for regulatory reasons, ensure that the coding changes are deployed in both environments (the current Dynamics AX Production and the code upgrade environment for the Dynamics AX upgrade project).

Infrastructure planning

You may not realize it, but upgrade projects will often also require new infrastructure, unless it is a small implementation with a fairly small database size or if you are planning for an in-place upgrade. You should be able repurpose some of your old infrastructure once the upgrade project is complete. You will need additional hardware for the following purposes:

- **The development environment**: You will need a new development environment for code upgrade and other development activities. Most of the time, it is possible to install and run different versions of Dynamics AX in a single box; but that can also create performance issues or other inefficiencies, and it is advisable to have a separate environment.

- **Test environments**: You must not disrupt your current test environment to test any critical production issues and hotfixes when the upgrade project is on. Hence, you will need a separate test environment to test the code upgrades.

- **Test data upgrade**: You will need a production-like environment to test your test data upgrade process. Many customers utilize their future production environment for the purpose of a test data upgrade.

- **The production environment**: In typical upgrade projects, your old system is used until the final cutover. It is similar to an implementation project where you are replacing your old legacy system. All the deployment activities will move to the new infrastructure without disrupting your old system. You may also want to keep your old system intact as part of the rollback plan, so that the business can continue using the old system if anything goes wrong with deployment. You will also need additional storage and horsepower requirement for upgrading the data during the upgrade period.

The upgrade analysis

Microsoft provides an upgrade analysis tool through Lifecycle Services to help the customers and vendors in planning an upgrade to Dynamics AX 2012. Upgrade analysis uses the **Rapid Data Collector** (**RDC**) tool to analyze information about the existing environment and helps in estimating the scale of the upgrade project. The following chart illustrates how the service works for both full-version upgrades and in-place upgrades:

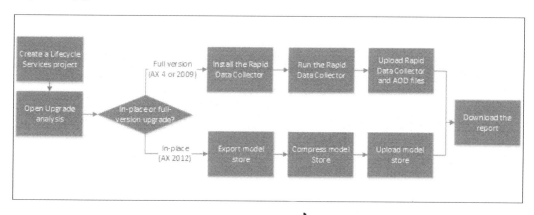

The upgrade analysis tool analyses the source version code artefacts (AOD files or model store files) and key metadata information, such as count of records in the tables to create reports to identify the scale of the code upgrade.

Upgrade analysis creates an overview report in HTML, and a detailed report as a Microsoft Excel file that you can download and review. The following are the tabs in the Excel reports:

Tabs	Description	Useful for
Upgrade summary	The summary list is a list of objects impacted in each module	

Tabs	Description	Useful for
Global tables	List of shared tables	Data upgrade, code upgrade
Customization statistics	List of all customizations	Code upgrade
Customization view	Number of customized tables and classes	Data upgrade
Modified objects	List of modified objects	Code upgrade
Modified object details	List of what is modified in each object	Code upgrade
Domain information	Lists companies, domains, and related users	Security upgrade
Table statistics	Lists table size, properties, and counts of rows and columns	Data upgrade, minimizing downtime
Parameters	Lists parameter values	Data upgrade, code upgrade
Tables without `DataAreaId`	List of tables that do not have a `DataAreaId`	Data upgrade
`SysUtilElementsLog` (AX Object Usage Summary)	Lists the usage patterns of MSDAX objects	Code upgrade

The code upgrade

The code upgrade in Dynamics AX is the process used to port customizations from the source environment to the target environment. The following are some key considerations to be kept in mind during the code upgrade process:

Planning for the code upgrade

Code upgrades are different in different projects and largely depend on the level of customization and the changes that Microsoft made between the source and target version. Depending on your project, you should consider the following when doing a code upgrade.

The code clean-up

Often, we find customizations in Dynamics AX which are not used. There can be various reasons for not using the customizations, such as change in the business process, development of a new advanced feature while the old version still existed, and so on. An upgrade project is a good time to clean up such customizations. Identify all such customizations and plan to remove them. Questions may be raised on the feasibility of investing time and money in removing the customization: what benefit do we gain by this clean up? Firstly, if you don't clean up old customizations, you might have to upgrade them as per the new version. This may introduce bugs and you will have to upgrade them again with the future upgrades; the obsolete code adds to the cost of each new upgrade. Having less code can also reduce your application-compile time and other application maintenance features.

New features that replace the existing ones

In some cases, you might have code which can be replaced partially or completely with the new version code or features. You should identify such features and utilize the new features or code instead of upgrading the old ones.

Standalone partner/customer code

Sometimes, a customer or partner might have added standalone code like creating new forms, classes, tables, and reports. Test these to make sure that the code compiles on the new version. It is also recommended to upgrade the UI and code patterns to utilize the latest features of the new version.

Changes in customization due to Microsoft refactoring in a new version

In some cases where Microsoft has changed the features, and the changes impact your customization, you will probably get compilation or runtime errors in your customization. You have to identify such areas and refactor your code to utilize the new code pattern.

The code upgrade process

The following diagram illustrates the typical code upgrade process:

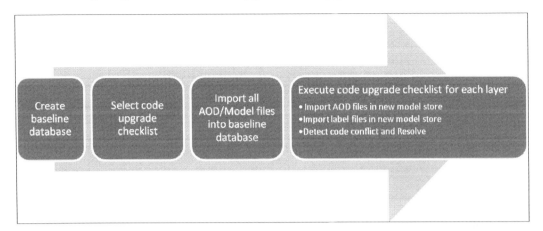

The baseline database

The very first step of the code upgrade process is to create a baseline database to store a read-only copy of the Microsoft Dynamics AX 4.0 or Microsoft Dynamics AX 2009 code. The baseline database is used for reference purposes during your code upgrade.

Selecting the upgrade checklist

The next step of the code upgrade process is selecting the appropriate code upgrade checklist. To get the code upgrade checklist, you must select **Register database for Upgrade Mode**, when you install Dynamics AX. When you open the Dynamics AX client the first time for the upgrade, you will be presented with some options, as shown in the following screenshot:

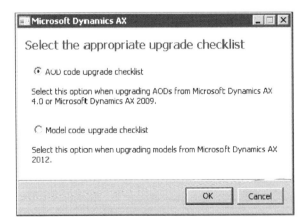

Importing AOD/model files into the baseline database

The next step is to import the license file and all the AOD or model files in the baseline database, as shown in the following screenshot:

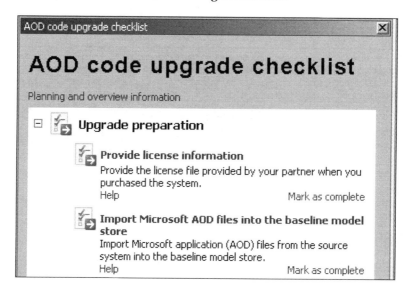

You should import layers from the lowest to the highest. For example, SYS first, then SYP, and so on, until you reach the last Microsoft AOD file.

Executing the code upgrade checklist

The final step of the code upgrade process is to complete a code upgrade checklist for each of the layers that you are upgrading. Dynamics AX provides you with multiple layers to build a custom code. For example, CUS, BUS, USR, and VAR are generally used for customizations and ISV solutions. For more information on layers, refer to *Chapter 9, Building Customizations*. It is important that you start at the lowest layer (for example, ISV). After the lowest layer is complete, start on the next layer up. Perform this task sequentially, until all the layers are upgraded.

The main goal of the code upgrade checklist is to detect code conflicts and to resolve those conflicts.

The following screenshot shows the code upgrade checklist for AOD files:

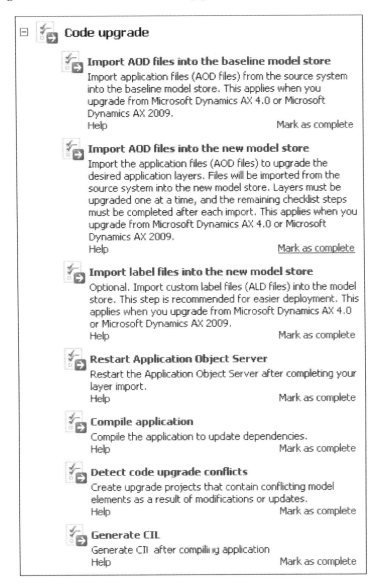

Code upgrade conflict tools

Microsoft Dynamics AX 2012 includes a tool to detect code conflicts. This tool analyses your customizations and creates a project (a project is a placeholder in AOT to group multiple objects, related to a specific functionality, together) that contains the application objects with conflicts. This tool is used when you upgrade from Microsoft Dynamics AX 4.0 or from Microsoft Dynamics AX 2009.

Conflict objects are code objects that have been both changed in the new release and customized in your application:

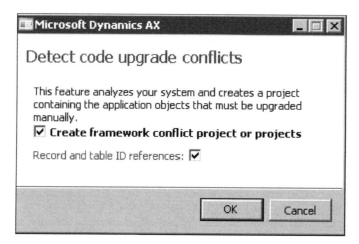

In some cases, especially on the forms, if the customizations are large, you may need to manually apply changes to the form to upgrade it.

The other alternatives for identifying code conflicts during the code upgrade project are the following:

- The project filter tool
- The code compare tool

The **project filter tool** can be used by a developer to create a project based on the criteria supplied in the query form. Such criteria could all be objects from a relevant layer or all objects that have a specific prefix, for example. Using the project filter, a developer can identify and group all the customized projects into a single project. The developer can later use the **code compare tool** to identify the code difference between the various layers and resolve them manually.

The upgrade script

In some cases where you are planning to replace the customization with standard AX features or refactoring a customization to work with a new version, you may have to write a data upgrade script to support the changes.

For more information, refer to the Microsoft Dynamics AX 2012 white paper—*How to Write Data Upgrade Scripts for Microsoft Dynamics AX 2012*—at http://www. microsoft.com/en-us/download/details.aspx?id=16375.

If you are upgrading from AX 2009 or older versions to Dynamics AX 2012, you may need the following type of upgrade script for your custom features:

- **Readiness checks**: It is very important to write a data-readiness check script for AX 2012 for the custom tables where ledger account/ financial dimensions, address, or inventory dimensions are used. The readiness-check validation script checks if all the related data exists in the source system.

- **Preprocessing and delta scripts**: The Dynamics AX 2012 upgrade provides the ability to preprocess the application data in the source system using preprocessing and delta scripts. Shadow tables are created to map any new fields and assign key relations to the standard tables.

- **Single-user steps and all target-side operations**: The target-side operation is the final step of the data upgrade process. Data upgrade scripts on the target side must include all the tables and field mapping information.

The security upgrade

The security framework in Dynamics AX 2012 has changed entirely since AX 4.0 and AX 2009. There is no automatic path to the upgrade of security configurations from the earlier versions to Dynamics AX 2012. However, Microsoft provides a security upgrade advisor tool, which can be used to help simplify the process of upgrading the security settings from the earlier versions to Microsoft Dynamics AX 2012.

The security upgrade advisor tool compares the user group access rights and roles in the current system to privilege mapping in AX 2012, and generates a list of matching privileges that can be used for a particular role. The following diagram shows the steps to upgrade security settings:

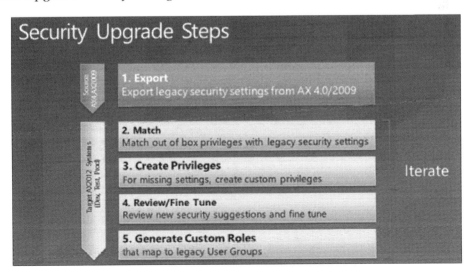

It is important to note that this tool is designed to help in upgrading security and developers are advised to review each suggestion carefully before making the final changes. For more details on the security upgrade tool, follow the Microsoft TechNet article at `https://technet.microsoft.com/en-us/library/hh394895.aspx`.

Testing the data upgrade

Data upgrade is the most important process of an upgrade project. As described earlier, the data upgrade process can differ, depending on the source version of Dynamics AX. Microsoft provides various upgrade checklists and scripts to convert table data from the source system to the target system. Data upgrade is, basically, executing the required checklists and the scripts necessary to transform and move data from the source system to the target system.

Testing the data upgrade is, basically, running the data upgrade processes on the copy of production data in a test environment. The key to having an optimal data upgrade experience is to plan well in advance, run multiple test cycles building on the lessons learned, and then plan the live data upgrade in complete detail, building in time for unexpected, last minute issues.

The following diagram shows a typical data test data upgrade process:

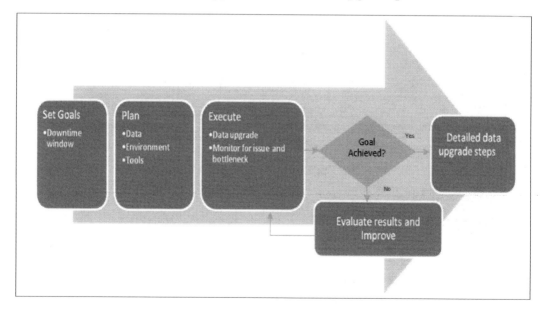

Objectives

The following are the key objectives of the test data upgrade:

- Testing of the data upgrade scripts
- Identifying potential issues/bottlenecks in the data upgrade scripts
- Ensuring data integrity and completeness of the upgraded data
- Identifying the time required for each activity, and calculating the final downtime
- Preparing the data for system and regression testing
- Planning for the final data upgrade in the production environment

Planning

The following are the key objectives to plan the test data upgrade:

- Make sure that the code upgrade and upgrade scripts are completed before you start your test data upgrade.
- Identify an acceptable downtime window of the production data upgrade. Talk to the business team and understand for how long the production system can be down, without impacting the operations significantly.
- Plan multiple rounds of the data upgrade cycle to test all the data upgrade steps consistently and to identify and tune the approximate downtime needed for the upgrade process in a live environment.
- Plan for an evaluation and optimization window with each test data upgrade. The objective is to reach an acceptable downtime window, agreed upon with the business team. More effort will be required to reduce the downtime window.
- Proper database sizing for the target database and the TempDB database is also extremely important to avoid any possibility of database resizing during the bulk-copy phase. Determine the correct sizing for the target Microsoft Dynamics AX 2012 database, and set it before you begin to upgrade. A rough estimate to use as a starting point is 30 percent larger than the expanded size of the source database. A rough estimate for sizing your TempDB database is 20–25 percent of the expanded Microsoft Dynamics AX 2012 database. Optimal performance may require splitting the TempDB database into separate files.
- Plan to use the production environment or hardware specification close to the production environment.

- Use a copy of production data for testing the data upgrade process. Try to use the latest copy of production with each round of the data upgrade testing.

Execution

The following are the key objectives to execute the test data upgrade:

- Follow the Microsoft recommendations for database and AOS configuration for the upgrade. There are many configurations which need to be set specifically during the data upgrade process. Follow the Microsoft white paper—*Data Upgrade Best Practices*—which can be found at `http://www.microsoft.com/en-us/download/confirmation.aspx?id=28701`.

- Take backups or database snapshots before each step of the upgrade process. Backups and snapshots can improve efficiency in case of failure during a particular step, so you don't have start the process from the beginning. It is also recommended to take a backup or snapshot during the final, live upgrade, in case of unexpected errors (out of disk space, network failures, and so on).

- Monitor the performance during the data upgrade process by using performance tools such as DynamicsPerf and the Windows Performance Monitor. Evaluate long-running queries and bad execution plans during batch processes and identify the areas where index tuning or code changes are needed. In some cases, an index created on the fly, within the test environment, can provide immediate benefit to a long-running process.

- Set the database recovery mode to simple during the data upgrade. At the conclusion of all upgrade activity, set the recovery mode to full.

- Increase the max degree of parallelism setting for the target upgrade processing (in the single-user mode, the bulk-copy process gains a significant performance benefit with parallel query processing). After target upgrade processing, return max degree of parallelism to the default setting.

- If the source database and target database are on separate servers, network latency and performance are also important factors that should be monitored. In some tests, multi-server environments with no network latency issues have shown a 30 percent slowdown over a single-server environment. Extreme slowdowns are possible if there are latency issues as well to deal with.

Outcome

The following is the outcome of the test data upgrade:

- Document the activities performed during the test upgrade process and record the execution time for each step.

- Identify and document the performance issues encountered and solutions for tuning.
- Validate the outcome of the data upgrade—validate completeness and data consistency after each data upgrade round. The upgraded data can be used for system and regression testing and training phases.

Upgrade testing

Like any other project, testing is important for an upgrade project. However, the nature of the testing will be different in an upgrade project. The following sections define the key areas to test in an upgrade project.

Data validation

When upgrading using the source-to-target upgrade model, it is very important to validate the upgraded data for completeness and data integrity. SQL scripts can be used to compare the number of rows between the source and target databases. Assemble a test team to plan high-level data validation for configuration as well as transaction data between the source and target systems.

System and regression testing

It's important to perform, system and regression testing after the code and data upgrade to identify the issues, if any. It is recommended to use the upgraded data during the test upgrade cycle for system and regression testing.

There may be features or customizations which are re-implemented or upgraded to the target version. Proper system and regression testing should be done to ensure that the features are working as expected.

Test that the security roles implemented in the target system are working correctly. Users in Microsoft Dynamics AX 2012 should have access to the data they had access to on the source system, and they should be able to perform all the functions which they were able to perform in the source system.

Test whether the upgraded and standard reports are working as expected in the new system.

Integration and end-to-end testing

As described in the earlier sections, your upgrade project may result in changes in integration, reporting, and so on. Testing of the upgrade must cover any such areas which are impacted. Depending on the impacted applications and changes, you may need to involve other departments in your organization or third-party application teams to test end-to-end scenarios.

End-user adoption

Dynamics AX 2012 has a significantly different user interface than the previous versions, Dynamics AX 4.0 and AX 2009. It is important to train the end users in the new system for the new user interface as well as the new and changed features. The following are the key considerations for end-user training.

- In the upgrade planning phase, make sure that training is provided often, both, early in the process and after the upgrade

- Provide early access to key business users after the code and data upgrade to familiarize them with new system

Deployment planning and execution

Just like an implementation project, it is very important to plan the final upgrade on the live system. All activities which need to be performed during the go-live should be well documented, including the test data upgrade steps.

Final deployment will include several activities such as stopping transaction processing in the old system, stopping any integration points to the old system, deploying the code, final data upgrade, data validation, and so on. The following table shows a sample plan for the final upgrade process:

Step	Description	Type	Owner	Estimated time	Actual start time	Actual end time
	Target system					
1	Build target system – create database, validate storage settings, and so on.	Pre-release	Steve			
2	Deploy the latest code build on the target system	Pre-release	Steve			

Step	Description	Type	Owner	Estimated time	Actual start time	Actual end time
	Source system					
3	Preprocessing start	Communication				
4	Run preprocessing jobs in the source system	Release	Steve			
5	Validate preprocessing	Validation	Steve			
6	Run final preprocessing	Release	Steve			
7	Send final communication for system downtime	Communication	James			
8	Shut down user access, stop all the batch processes, stop AOS	Release	George			
9	Take database backup	Release	Peter			
10	Set to single-user mode	Release	George			
	Target system					
11	Connect to the source database	Release	George			
12	Presynchronize	Release	George			
13	Create tables	Release	George			
14	Generate table mappings	Release	George			
15	Take database snapshot	Relcase	Peter			
16	Generate upgrade task prioritization	Release	George			

Step	Description	Type	Owner	Estimated time	Actual start time	Actual end time
17	Set batch threads to twice the number of cores. For example, with 8 cores, set the number of batch threads to 16.	Release	George			
18	Start the data upgrade	Release	George			
19	Communication – data upgrade completed	Communication	James			
20	Run data validation scripts	Validation	Peter			
21	Go/no go	Decision	Steering committee			
22	Deploy reports	Release	John			
23	Deploy integration solution	Release	John			
24	Restart all AOS	Release	George			
25	Run IT validation	Validation	Joe			
26	Run business validation	Validation	Tina			
27	Go/no go	Decision	Steering committee			
28	Set Database recovery mode to full	Post release	Peter			
29	Set max degree of parallelism to 1	Post release	Peter			
30	Communication- go live	Communication	James			

 This is an example deployment plan; the actual steps can be different on your project.

There may be many activities which need to be done after the upgrade. The following are a few activities which may be applicable:

- After the upgrade, the indexes in the Microsoft Dynamics AX 2012 database will be highly fragmented. Before you start with the normal processing activities, it is strongly recommended to rebuild the indexes.

- Validate and reset the database settings, such as the max degree of parallelism; set the database recovery mode to simple.

- Rebuild and process database replication and additional reporting and BI solutions.

- Plan and upgrade the DR application code and data, if applicable.

- Monitor applications for performance and take corrective actions.

Summary

In this chapter, you learned about upgrading your Dynamics AX application to a new version. A Dynamics AX or any ERP upgrade is not easy and requires lots of planning and analysis. We started the chapter with exploring the different considerations to evaluate if you are ready to take up an upgrade project. Then we looked at the different options available to upgrade to Dynamics AX 2012.

Major version upgrades can be as complex as an initial implementation project. We went through the various phases of the upgrade project. In the planning phase, you learned about the importance of managing customizations, managing scope, business engagement, and impact analysis. You learned about the best practices and recommendations in various other phases, such as code upgrade, test data upgrade, testing, and end-user training. In the end, we went through deployment planning and looked at activities that need to be done once the upgrade process is complete.

Index

Symbols

.NET Business Connector 63
.NET Framework 62

A

Agile methodology
  about 14
  recommendations 14
AIF
  about 29, 53, 177
  adapters 57
  architecture 54
  cloud-based integration 58, 59
  key concepts 55
  message processing 57, 58
  services 55
ALM
  about 196
  best practices 198
  build, creating 197
  defect, fixing 197
  development 196
  guidelines 198
  reference link 198
  testing 197
alternate key 174
American Productivity and Quality
    Center (APQC) 242
analysis phase
  key deliverables 26
AOS server
  planning 47
AOT objects
  naming conventions 162

Application Integration Framework. *See* **AIF**
Application Object Server (AOS) 29, 206
asynchronous integration 52, 53
Azure
  with Microsoft Dynamics AX 2012 R3 43-45

B

batch parallelism
  about 218
  batch bundling 218
  individual task modeling 218
  top picking 218
big picture diagrams
  about 128
  flow of data 130
  functional architecture 129
  integrations 130
breaking point 204
Budget Control Framework 179
business contingency planning 250-252
Business Intelligence (BI) 29
business logic
  about 175
  Application Integration Framework
    (AIF) 177
  code, customizing 181
  code, reusing 180
  custom code, adding 181
  customizing 180
  development frameworks 178, 179
  events, using 180
  FormLetter framework 176
  number sequence framework 176
  other application 178, 179
  RunBase framework 176

M

master data management (MDM)
about 61, 62
features 62
message processing 57, 58
Microsoft Dynamics AX 2012 R3
on Azure 43-45
Microsoft Dynamics ERP RapidStart
Services
about 146, 147
features 147
middle tier
about 29
Application Integration Framework
(AIF) 29
Application Object Server (AOS) 29
Enterprise Portal 29
services 29
workflow system 29
models 161

N

natural key 174
non-clustered index 172
non-production system topology 41, 42
number sequence framework
about 176
reference link 176

O

Optical Character Recognition (OCR) 124

P

performance, impacting factors
about 211
code and queries 216
environment setup 213
infrastructure 211
performance issues
about 220
analysis strategy, defining 220, 221
analysis strategy, planning 220
approaching 219

corrective actions, implementing 221, 222
root causes identification, investigation
strategies 222-225
root causes identification, scenarios 222-225
performance issues, in code and queries
about 216
batch parallelism 218
data caching 216
long-running queries 219
methods, displaying on form grid 219
RPC calls 217
set-based operations 217
performance monitor tool
about 206
advantages 206
performance testing 202
performance tuning
about 201, 202
datasets 203
environment, identifying 203
execution stage 203, 204
expectation, setting with executives 203
outcome 204
preparing 203
scope, defining 203
tools, identifying 203
personalization
training environment 243
Platform-as-a-Service (PaaS) 42
Policy framework 179
post implementation review (PIR)
about 268-271
Dynamics AX potential 272
improvement opportunities 272
key challenges 271
new release 273
obtaining, key factors 269
pain points, examples 270
preparing 269
uses 268
primary key 174
Product Data Management Framework 179
production system topology
about 39-41
applications layer 40
database and platform layer 40
perimeter network layer 40

Thank you for buying
Microsoft Dynamics AX
Implementation Guide

About Packt Publishing

Packt, pronounced 'packed', published its first book, *Mastering phpMyAdmin for Effective MySQL Management*, in April 2004, and subsequently continued to specialize in publishing highly focused books on specific technologies and solutions.

Our books and publications share the experiences of your fellow IT professionals in adapting and customizing today's systems, applications, and frameworks. Our solution-based books give you the knowledge and power to customize the software and technologies you're using to get the job done. Packt books are more specific and less general than the IT books you have seen in the past. Our unique business model allows us to bring you more focused information, giving you more of what you need to know, and less of what you don't.

Packt is a modern yet unique publishing company that focuses on producing quality, cutting-edge books for communities of developers, administrators, and newbies alike. For more information, please visit our website at www.packtpub.com.

About Packt Enterprise

In 2010, Packt launched two new brands, Packt Enterprise and Packt Open Source, in order to continue its focus on specialization. This book is part of the Packt Enterprise brand, home to books published on enterprise software – software created by major vendors, including (but not limited to) IBM, Microsoft, and Oracle, often for use in other corporations. Its titles will offer information relevant to a range of users of this software, including administrators, developers, architects, and end users.

Writing for Packt

We welcome all inquiries from people who are interested in authoring. Book proposals should be sent to author@packtpub.com. If your book idea is still at an early stage and you would like to discuss it first before writing a formal book proposal, then please contact us; one of our commissioning editors will get in touch with you.

We're not just looking for published authors; if you have strong technical skills but no writing experience, our experienced editors can help you develop a writing career, or simply get some additional reward for your expertise.

Microsoft Dynamics GP 2013 Cookbook

ISBN: 978-1-84968-938-0   Paperback: 348 pages

Over 110 immediately usable and effective recipes to solve real-world Dynamics GP problems

1. Understand the various tips and tricks to master Dynamics GP, and improve your system's stability in order to enable you to get work done faster.

2. Discover how to solve real world problems in Microsoft Dynamics GP 2013 with easy-to-understand and practical recipes.

3. Access proven and effective Dynamics GP techniques from authors with vast and rich experience in Dynamics GP.

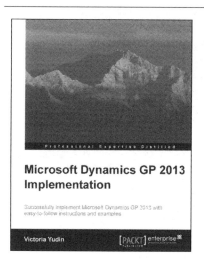

Microsoft Dynamics GP 2013 Implementation

ISBN: 978-1-78217-784-5   Paperback: 430 pages

Successfully implement Microsoft Dynamics GP 2013 with easy-to-follow instructions and examples

1. Plan, install, and implement Microsoft Dynamics GP 2013 with real-world advice from a Microsoft Dynamics GP MVP.

2. Learn how to set up the core modules in Microsoft Dynamics GP effectively following detailed, step-by-step instructions.

3. Discover additional tools and resources available for your Dynamics GP.

Please check **www.PacktPub.com** for information on our titles

Developing Microsoft Dynamics GP Business Applications

ISBN: 978-1-84968-026-4   Paperback: 590 pages

Build dynamic, mission-critical applications with this hands-on guide

1. Make your business more efficient with fully customizable applications.

2. Develop mission critical applications with Microsoft Dynamics GP.

3. Learn how to enhance your application with sanScript.

Microsoft Dynamics GP Techniques [Video]

ISBN: 978-1-84968-932-8   Duration: 02:08 hrs

Watch and learn techniques to master Microsoft Dynamics GP; improve know-how and maximize your performance

1. Learn how to keep data tidy while speeding up data entry and reducing entry errors.

2. Follow carefully organized sequences of instructions as they're performed in an easy to follow step-by-step video guide.

3. Learn advanced methods of enquiring, reporting, and system maintenance.

4. Clear, concise, self-contained videos each covering a technique, tip or feature.

Please check **www.PacktPub.com** for information on our titles

Made in the USA
Lexington, KY
25 September 2015